Too Much for Our Own Good

Too Much for Our Own Good

The Consumeritis Epidemic
and Good Movies

Harrison Sheppard
and
Alex Aris

ARISTOTLE & ALEXANDER PRESS
San Francisco

Cover photo by Kiyyah, courtesy of iStock International Inc.

ISBN-10: 0-9779914-0-7
ISBN-13: 978-09779914-0-2
LCCN: 2006925673

Publisher offers deep discounts to non-profit and corporate educational institutions for bulk orders.

Published by
Aristotle & Alexander Press
P.O. Box 170267
San Francisco, California 94117

AAPressLLC@yahoo.com
Visit our web site at www.AandAPress.com

Printed in the United States of America

To
Alexander & Aristotle and Christopher & Dillon
with the hope that they, and their generation,
will enjoy peace in a harmonized global
community and the secure right to their own
unique pursuits of happiness.

Contents

Illustrations

Tables

Movies Discussed or Quoted

(In order of reference, by chapter)

*Movies quoted in text

Note from the Publisher

THE WISDOM OF the ancient Greeks gave voice to reason and birth to philosophy, but it was also expressed in myth. The myth of King Midas, for example, vividly demonstrated how we may wrongly choose to have too much of a good thing. King Midas was offered a reward by the god Dionysius for having done the god a service; Midas asked for the power to turn everything he touched to gold. Midas's wish was granted, but he soon discovered that he could not live on gold alone, and that the great wealth his power allowed him to acquire was more than he really wanted. The myth reminds us that while there are some things we can never get enough of, wealth may not be one of them. We can never get enough happiness, for example. Or good health. Or love. An abundance of happiness, good health, or love is never likely to be "too much for our own good." Many other good things, however, can be experienced to such excess that they really do become *too much* for our own good. There are obvious examples more common than the Midas touch. We can drink too much of even a very fine wine, or eat too much of the very best food. Though a thing may be good in itself, if we become so addicted to its pleasures that it interferes with our enjoyment of things we value more, or if it prevents us from obtaining them, we may rightly say that it has become too much for our own good.

"Moderation in all things" is a maxim of ancient philosophy, most famously expounded by Aristotle. In the original Greek, *Pan metron ariston*, the saying is equally well translated as "Balance in all things is best." This ancient maxim retains the force of wisdom to this day. Some insights about the human condition and the problems we face as human beings do not alter with changing times. Some teachings of the ancient poets, sages, and philosophers point the way toward as much practical wisdom as we are ever likely to have.

While science may lead us to new knowledge and give us great power over nature, it is not knowledge of physics or biochemistry that chiefly helps us learn how to live happier lives, become fuller human beings, or get along better with others. Achieving such human goods requires practical wisdom, what the ancient Greeks called *phronesis*. This difference between the realm of scientific knowledge on the one hand and human wisdom on the other was the reason Socrates chose philosophy—the love of wisdom—as a way of life rather than seeking knowledge of the physical universe. After considering the question deeply, Socrates decided he could best occupy his time by learning more about his own humanity and how he could live as good a life as possible. He therefore devoted his life to following the advice of Apollo's oracle at Delphi: "Know thyself." There is no better advice anyone can give to help us find a true path to our own happiness. If we do not know ourselves well enough, we cannot possibly learn what it is that will make us happiest.

Too Much for Our Own Good is the inaugural publication of Aristotle and Alexander Press. It is the first in a planned series of nonfiction books addressing major issues posed by the conditions we live in now. The motto of Aristotle and Alexander Press, "Thought and Action," is partly inspired by recollecting that ancient Greece's greatest thinker, Aristotle, instructed antiquity's most successful man of action, Alexander the Great, whose military strategies and tactics continue to be studied at military academies throughout the world, including West Point.

The rest of the books in the series will, of course, also examine their subjects in light of what modern science and its techniques can help us learn. They will, however, be particularly informed by what ancient practical wisdom can teach us about the human condition through insights that have remained relevant for more than two millennia. In this connection, *Too Much for Our Own Good* recalls to its readers practical ancient wisdom relating to the need for moderation—not only in our individual material pursuits but in the uses we make of nature's resources. It is a special challenge of life in this century to harmonize the achievements of natural science with the social sciences by learning, for example, how to reconcile our economic aspirations with the ecological health of the environments in which we live. Harmonizing our physical and spiritual natures in the choices we make in the conduct of our lives, liberty, and pursuits of happiness requires a renewed respect for achieving a more balanced relationship between our individual needs and wants on the one hand, and the health of family, community, and society on the other.

The problems and public issues explored in *Too Much for Our Own Good* all relate in one way or another to excess: excessive materialism; excessive commercialism; excessive consumption; excessive personal and public debt; and excessive reliance on nonrenewable energy sources, to name some of the principal ones. It is necessary, however, to recognize that "too much" means, almost necessarily, that there is somewhere a correlative "too little." If something is "too much" for our own good, then there is also something too little going on—if only too little good judgment. There is one particular dimension of this "too little" that we feel especially obliged to address here. This book asserts (and seeks to demonstrate) that we Americans see ourselves too much as "consumers" and too little as a community of "citizens"; that many Americans, by trying to keep up with the Joneses, are consuming too much for their own good—that is, they are buying things they not only don't need but that actually divert them from finding their own happiness. But we also recognize that there are Americans whose problem is not too much but too little. As a democracy, the United States is committed to *equality*. Democratic equality in the United States means commitment to the principle of equality before the law, an equality of rights. This is not the same as a commitment to an economic equality of wants or needs. By asserting that America's materialistic consumerism is too much for our own good, we do not ignore the fact that a significant number of Americans do not have enough to live comfortably, let alone to indulge in material excess. There may be some respects in which the consumeritis that is too much for our own good contributes to the fact that there are some Americans with too little, but the issue of domestic economic inequality is not addressed in this book. Future books published by Aristotle and Alexander Press may explore this issue and its complexities. The present volume focuses instead on inviting readers to consider aspects of our American culture of buying and selling that have become too much for our own good, and what we may be able to do about *that* problem.

One of the coauthors of this book, Harrison Sheppard, has presented some personal anecdotes in the first person. Everything else is the opinion of both authors, although the pseudonymous Alex Aris wishes to remain anonymous.

Note from the Publisher

I hope readers will find the following pages engaging enough to hold their attention, and that they will find the authors' arguments persuasive enough to provoke their own further thought and action on a path of wisdom toward their pursuits of happiness.

Dimitri Magganas
San Francisco, California
May 1, 2006

Preface

It's a Wonderful Life*

ON APRIL 16, 1973, a young lawyer stood in front of the nine Justices of the United States Supreme Court in Washington, D.C., and was welcomed to practice before them by Chief Justice Warren J. Burger. The young lawyer—born in Philadelphia, educated for four happy years at St. John's College in Annapolis, Maryland, and having graduated from law school in California—was proud and happy to share this sublime moment with his young wife, whose labors had helped put him through law school and who sat in the audience watching the ceremony. Five years before, she had witnessed his taking the lawyer's oath of fidelity to the U.S. Constitution, following his admission to the State Bar of California. That oath was administered to her husband and to four of his law school classmates by Justice William O. Douglas in his Supreme Court chambers. The young lawyer's admission to the bar of the U.S. Supreme Court was moved by a member of the Federal Trade Commission for

---

It's a Wonderful Life, RKO Pictures (1946); produced and directed by Frank Capra; written by Philip Van Doren Stern, Frances Goodrich, Albert Hacker, and Frank Capra; starring James Stewart as George Bailey. See also *Mr. Smith Goes to Washington,* Columbia Pictures (1939); produced and directed by Frank Capra; written by Lewis R. Foster and Sidney Buchman; starring James Stewart as Jefferson Smith and Claude Rains as Senator Joseph Harrison Paine.

whom he worked at the time, the Honorable Philip Elman, an outstanding public servant who at the beginning of his own legal career had clerked for U.S. Supreme Court Justice Felix Frankfurter, and been appointed to the Federal Trade Commission by President Kennedy in 1963.

The young lawyer is Harrison Sheppard, now sixty-six years old, author of this preface, and the coauthor of this book who is speaking for himself whenever the personal pronoun "I" is used. I have never actually argued a case before the U.S. Supreme Court, but the moment still stands out to me as a glistening instant in a wonderful life. My grandparents and great-grandparents were immigrants to the United States of America, having fled from an oppressive Eastern European regime, and neither my father or mother, children of the Great Depression, had ever had the opportunity to go to college. Raised in very modest circumstances to say the least, I found myself at the age of thirty-three—now half a lifetime ago—married to a loving wife, proud father of a healthy young son, employed as a legal advisor to a presidential appointee, and being graciously accepted as a colleague before the highest court in the land.

My privileged position was an opportunity given to me through our secured rights to life, liberty, and the pursuit of happiness declared in the founding document of our country and established in its Constitution. And as I stood before the Justices of the U.S. Supreme Court, I was, indeed, secure in my pursuit of happiness—partly through my own steady labors, partly as a result of the education I was privileged to receive at St. John's College, partly as a result of the friendship and support of many others, and partly as the result of some good luck.

In pursuing my happiness, I had decided at an early age that great material wealth was not an essential part of it, so I chose government service as the first use of my legal education and admission to the State Bar of California. Later, upon early retirement after nearly twenty-three years of service with the U.S. Department of Justice and the Federal Trade Commission, I chose to continue my pursuit of happiness on the same terms—without money as my main object. My solo private law practice in San Francisco, firmly established after two perilous years, in fact has provided me with most of the happy moments of my pursuit, helping others to resolve difficult conflicts to their satisfaction, mainly without the costs, stresses, and delays of courtroom litigation.

It is partly gratitude for this wonderful life that led me to conceive this book. I wish for my son and grandchildren and their children the same opportunities and secure rights to life, liberty, and the pursuit of happiness that I have enjoyed. When I first arrived in Washington, D.C., in 1967 to serve as an attorney for the United States, I took enormous pride and satisfaction in that opportunity, because the governmental institutions of the United States then stood very high in my esteem and in that of most Americans. A great deal has changed since then. These changes have included the results of an unpopular war in Vietnam; the scandal of Watergate, giving the country the spectacle of a president, an attorney general, and a counsel to the president found guilty of violations of law that constituted betrayals of their oaths to uphold the laws and Constitution of the United States; the progressive transformation of the typical practice of law from that of a learned profession to an enterprising business; and a general decline in popular mores from a people highly mindful of the cherished political legacies of their citizenship to an overheated, commercialized, and largely politically apathetic consumer society manipulated by what was once referred to as Madison Avenue, but which now occupies many more august addresses.

These changes, among others, make this aging lawyer, who as a young man could be confident that his proud patriotism was shared by most Americans, fearful for the security of his grandchildren's future. They may yet have a wonderful life; it *is* still a wonderful life. But what is wonderful about it has nothing to do with a treadmill race to acquire more than enough. As the poet Wallace Stevens once wrote to his daughter, "Forget about earning a living; it has nothing to do with any of the great things in life." Stevens didn't mean that there was no need to earn enough money to get along. He meant that earning the money was not what made life worth living. What makes life worth living is enjoyment of our own freely chosen, unique pursuits of happiness, including their struggles. Does that banner still wave o'er the land of the free and the home of the brave? To the extent that it may not, perhaps *Too Much for Our Own Good* can help remind its readers how wonderful life can be—especially without hearing "a word from our sponsors," or too many of them.

Harrison Sheppard
San Francisco, California
February 12, 2006

Definition

CONSUMERITIS: A SPECIES of excessive materialism, now a pathological condition of epidemic proportions with which many Americans are actively or passively afflicted, and which is spreading to other countries. It is characterized by personal addiction to the purchase of consumer goods and services beyond what is needed to satisfy personal needs broadly understood, often beyond the victims' financial means, and commonly diverting victims' energies and resources from more fulfilling activities and pursuits of happiness. The term is substantively related to *oniomania,* a word of Greek origin (from Greek *xnios,* for sale, derivative of *onos,* price + *mania,* madness) signifying an excessive, uncontrollable desire to buy things.

Humphrey Bogart as Frank McCloud and Edward G. Robinson as the gangster Rocco in *Key Largo* (Warner Brothers Studios, 1948)

Introduction

What This Book Is About

I N A HUMPHREY Bogart movie, *Key Largo*, celebrated in a song of the same name, Bogart plays a war hero named Frank McCloud, who is held captive in a hotel by a paranoid gangster named Rocco, played by Edward G. Robinson. Rocco has taken over the hotel to complete a counterfeit money deal. McCloud asks Rocco what he wants out of life, and when Rocco hesitates, McCloud, who recognizes the mobster's greed as the key to his character, answers his own question for the benefit of his fellow captives: "He wants *more.*" The villain agrees. "Yeah," he says, "that's it. I want *more!*" McCloud then asks Rocco whether he will ever get enough, and Rocco says, "Well, I never have. No, I guess I won't."

I first saw *Key Largo* in a movie theater, and, as an avid movie lover, I might want to watch it again and again on TV. But commercial television today has so much advertising that I watch fewer and fewer broadcast movies. On most commercial TV channels, scenes from movies seem to occupy only slightly more time than the dozens of commercial messages broadcast during the films. In fact, in the broadcasting industry itself, the movie scenes are now referred to as filler, and the ads as the real broadcast content. Even going to the movies has recently brought new kinds of exposure to commercial advertising. Movies in theaters are now commonly preceded by slide-show ads before the

1

movie begins—a time once given over to music while the theater was filling—and filmed ads after the theater has darkened but before the previews of coming attractions. In addition, movies themselves are now often vehicles for product placement: advertisers pay a film's producers to have the actors use their products conspicuously in the film.

The American culture of buying and selling is now a culture of "more," fueled by ever more invasive advertising that interferes not only with our enjoyment of broadcast movies but with many other, more significant, aspects of our lives. A torrent of advertising invites—indeed, urges—us to spend money, often letting us know how we can borrow the money to buy what is being advertised. Americans have been responding to this advertising not only by getting ever deeper into credit-card debt but by changing the way they think about themselves. *Key Largo* was produced in 1948; it was not until more than a generation later that American citizens came to regard themselves, and to be regarded by their government, primarily as consumers rather than as citizens, so much so that federal agencies now refer to us as their customers in the option menus of their recorded messages. This shift to cultural consumerism constitutes a radical transformation of the idea of consumption from a negative to a positive one. As the author Jeremy Rifkin has pointed out:

> No one, and especially no American, would deny that we are the most voracious consumers in the world.... The term "consumption" dates back to the early fourteenth century and has both English and French roots. Originally, to "consume" meant to destroy, to pillage, to subdue, to exhaust. It is a word steeped in violence and until the twentieth century had only negative connotations. Remember that as late as the early 1900's, the medical community and the public referred to tuberculosis as

"consumption." Consumption only metamorphosed into a positive term at the hands of twentieth century advertisers who began to equate consumption with choice.

We all know that money can buy things and pleasures, but neither greed nor the common desire to have more money to increase our acquisition of things and enjoy material pleasures is the same as our yearning for genuine happiness. What makes life most worth living is, for the most part, neither material things nor transient pleasures but the intangible rewards of a good life: love, friendship, family, and community; physical and mental health; enough leisure time to enjoy the fruits of our labor and a job well done; the delights we can take in play and sport; music, song, and dance; art, learning, and philanthropy; and appreciation of the beauty we can find all around us in both nature and humanity, from the wondrous splendors of the earth, sea, and sky to the glowing aura of a happy child. For most of us, of course, having enough money to ensure some degree of financial security is necessary to avoid a miserable existence. But beyond securing the basic necessities, it becomes largely a matter of individual choice where we direct our energies and focus our attention to make our days as fulfilling as possible and our lives not only worth living but genuinely happy. As a 1992 periodical put it:

> Real choice for humans, both as consumers and as social beings, is a matter of quality, not quantity. Shelves filled with impersonal goods, like address books filled with reminders of shallow friendships, present us with meaningless choices. As the Earth's possible end comes into view... it could be that caring for what really matters to us is what will save us.

There are many miserable people among the rich, and many truly happy people of modest means. In fact, studies of both rich and poor countries throughout the world show that "above $20,000 per person, additional income is not associated with greater happiness." Since most people agree with the well-known saying that money can't buy happiness, why are so many Americans choosing to go into debt to buy things that are unessential to enjoying the best that life has to offer?

The choices that Americans are now being led to make, and the dominant focus of their energies, are symptoms of a pathological condition of addiction. They are not choices they would make if they were free of this addiction; addictions do not help people focus on getting where they most want to go. Americans have become consumer junkies, shopaholics, manipulated into addiction by a triumphant advertising culture of buying and selling that is making us and our children less healthy in mind, body, and spirit, and progressively reducing our capacity to pursue and enjoy the deeper happiness for which we all yearn. We are suffering from what we may call consumeritis, a cultural pathology of epidemic proportions that threatens to make us and our children sicker and sicker.

Advertising is accustoming Americans, especially our children, to lies—fundamental lies about the real goods of life and how to enjoy them. It is a long-recognized, insidious sociopsychological principle that repeating a lie often enough tends to make it believable and believed. This is the principle that has transformed commercial advertising—and much American political campaign advertising—into a competition to find the most believable lies and deceptions that will lead Americans to spend money beyond their means for products that do them little or no good. The American shopping mall has become increasingly hazardous to the public's health and well-being.

This book describes how consumeritis is leading us to take a tragically self-destructive path, and how we may rescue ourselves from its debilitating diversions. It explains the importance of arresting what we call the consumeritis epidemic to avoid the inevitable outcome of a critical disease that is seriously degrading our physical and mental health, driving millions of Americans into debt they cannot afford, fracturing our families, threatening to leave a legacy of insecurity and ill health to our children (already suffering from increasing obesity, diabetes, and depression), undermining our political freedoms, and preventing us from having or keeping control over our own lives. The book thus examines the adverse social effects consumeritis has on us as individuals and family members, and also on our community spirit. It explains the threats consumeritis poses to our long-term financial interests and the damage it causes to the environments in which we live. It also addresses the ill effects the advertising techniques that promote consumeritis have on American politics and our status as citizens. Finally, the book examines the destructive global effects of consumeritis: its damaging environmental effects, the increased hostility of other nations and peoples to American culture, and a consequent reduction in both our domestic and our international security.

After considering all of the major spheres of domestic and international civil life on which consumeritis is having a negative impact, we consider a range of possible remedies to mitigate the worst of its effects, and possibly even arrest the epidemic. Along the way, we entertain readers with stories drawn from life and from good movies, illustrating both the mistaken paths that those of us who are afflicted with consumeritis are taking, and the better routes we may take to secure our own happiness.

You Could Instantly Win • You Have Been Chosen • Save 75 Cents • Open Stock Sale • Below Cost • Introductory Offer • Only $2.00 • Special Savings • Fall Sale • Come on Down

The advertising culture of buying and selling has come to

dominate American society so thoroughly that it is progressively infecting the nature of our social and political relationships; so much so that it is now threatening the vitality of American democracy itself. As Richard Brodie, who created Microsoft Word and was a former assistant to Bill Gates, has pointed out, "Advertising runs hand-in-hand with politics in its calculating manipulation of the masses." A few simple examples will illustrate how pervasively the advertising culture of buying and selling has invaded our lives, just as advertising sound bites such as those scattered in the pages of this introduction are constantly being thrust on our consciousness.

And Now These Messages • Look Inside for Special Savings • No Waiting • Satisfaction or Your Money Back • Save 20% or More with These Coupons • Last Day Sale • No Interest Until 2008 • Order Now & Get These Savings • No Money Down • Grand Opening • 2000 Free Minutes • Special Offer • Pay Nothing for Ninety Days • Dream Prices

For many years, my day regularly began with classical music coming from my radio alarm clock. This seemed to me a mellow way to start my waking day. During the past decade or so, I have become much less fond of this habit. Nowadays, no matter what the hour at which I set my radio, the first sounds I hear are almost as likely to be those of a commercial message as the musical treats of Mozart, Bach, or Beethoven. Instead of my first daily experience being one that allows me to think my own thoughts, I regularly find myself being told during those first waking moments—sometimes in nerve-jangling tones and terms—to buy something I have little interest in or just don't care to consider as my first thought of the day. This is only one of the small signs by which I have become aware that the culture in which we now live is characteristically a culture of buying and selling. Radio and television broadcasting in general similarly illustrate this.

I regularly use my car radio when I drive, especially long distances. My dial is pre-set to a classical music station, an all-news station, a popular music station, and a country-and-western station. The instances when I can find nothing but a commercial on any of them are now far too frequent for my taste. It was not always so. (As we point out in chapter 8, we can be grateful for the fact that there are now a variety of ways available to us to reduce or eliminate the intrusion of commercial advertising into our enjoyment of broadcast entertainment and information.)

Buy Now • Limited Offer • Fifty Percent Off • Clearance Sale • Save Now • No Interest for Twelve Months • Super Low Prices • Bonus Rebate • Summer Sale • Instant Savings • Rollback Prices • Special Buy • Save 20% or More • New and Improved • Four for $4.00 • Free Gift • Our Lowest Prices • White Sale • Smoother Taste • Buy of the Year • You've Been Pre-Approved • Call Now • Free Trial • Visit Our Web Site • Money Back Guarantee

Another example of how pervasively the culture of buying and selling has come to dominate our cultural life is the rampant and extended commercialism that has become the hallmark of the present "Christmas spirit." As Charles Dickens's magic story *A Christmas Carol* shows, in Victorian times the holiday was anticipated only a day or two before it occurred; perhaps longer for those who took the time to make their own Christmas cards for their friends. Shortly after World War II, in the late 1940s, the Christmas season officially began in late November, on Thanksgiving Day, when Macy's held its annual Thanksgiving Day parade in New York, ending with the arrival of Santa Claus. By the 1970s, stores began Christmas merchandising after Halloween. Nowadays, we can expect Christmas sales to begin shortly after Labor Day, for a period of Christmas commercialism at least five times longer than our parents or grandparents had to suffer through.

Just $9•99 • You Have to See It To Believe It • Winter Sale • Buy One Get One Free • All Offers Considered • Garage Sale • Bargain Prices • Service with a Smile • Last Chance • On Approval • Seller Financing • Thanksgiving Day Sale • You've Been Pre-qualified • New Lower Rate • Fixed Introductory APR • Easy Payments • Important Please Open Immediately • You May Already Have Won Cash Back $100 • Just Arrived • Final Sale

And then there is the mail, both regular and Internet. Discarding the thousands of junk-mail advertisements we receive annually now ritually precedes reading mail at both home and office. During the first three months of writing this book, the volume of junk mail delivered to my office (a solo law practice) exceeded 530 pieces, commonly containing multiple separate ads; it weighed well over thirty-seven pounds. During that same time, a much greater volume, including more than two hundred mail-order catalogues, arrived at my home post office box. These advertisements are written in the words and music of the culture of buying and selling to which we have become far too accustomed. The words of plenty and the plentitude of words listed intermittently in this introduction have been taken from actual printed and electronic ads. They characteristically imply that we can save money by spending it, and secure greater happiness for ourselves if we just take advantage of the offered "deal."

Free Gift • Bonus Miles • No Annual Fee • Extraordinary Offer • Credit Line Up to $100,000 • Why Wait? • Christmas Sale • Are You Tired... ? • Easy Credit • First Time Offer • Buyers Wanted • President's Day Sale • Fly Now Don't Wait • Open 24 Hours • New and Used • So Hurry On Down! • Only $10•99 Plus Shipping & Tax

Commercial advertising was once largely limited to notices in newspapers. It extended to broadcasting in the 1930s, soon after broadcast licenses were allocated by the federal government, despite representations from early applicants for radio licenses that their privileges would not be used for commercial purposes. Billboards were likewise a twentieth-century innovation. Today, we can anticipate seeing ads everywhere we look: on the sides of buses; on TVs installed for that purpose in the back of taxicabs; on supermarket floors; in skywriting; in pouches in front of us when we travel on airplanes; on trees and telephone poles; on transmissions to us through our own cell phones; and, believe it or not, in sand writing at the beach. Proposals are now even being made to project moon-sized billboards of logos into outer space so they will be visible to practically everybody on earth.

What You've Been Waiting For • Unbelievably Fluffy • Weekend Sale • Santa Has Arrived • Instant Rebate • Bring the Kids • We Specialize in Bad Credit • Don't Look Any Further • Fire Sale • One Time Only • Free Delivery • Don't Miss This Bargain • The Biggest Sale Ever • Pick Up the Phone • Happy Hour • Buy Now • Lowest Price Ever

Commercial advertising has thus become a presence dominating our cultural life. We are now thoroughly immersed in the culture of buying and selling as a regular part of our daily lives. Most people over forty will remember that commercials were once a relatively incidental part of entertainment and public communication, clearly subordinate to the diverse cultural offerings of mass media. In quantitative terms, the average American is now exposed to upwards of forty thousand TV commercials a year. By the time they are twenty, average Americans have been exposed to as many as one million commercials from all advertising media. This torrent of commercialism has had, and is having, a destructive effect on many aspects of our lives. Not only does it sour many formerly sweet experiences of daily living but it also relates to many of the most critical social, political, and economic ills of America in the twenty-first century. It infects as well much of the rest of the world with a contagion that is threatening to grow even more pathological. Indeed, the techniques of commercial advertising have, as most of us now recognize, become so large a part of politics and political campaigning in America that they have virtually killed rational political discourse. They now threaten to replace the substance of our democratic institutions with empty shadows of democratic political freedoms.

The seriously damaging consequences of increased commercialism in broadcasting was foreseen in 1958 by the CBS newsman Edward R. Murrow, when he admonished broadcasters to pursue serious news stories and use the airwaves to educate and inform, in spite of corporate and advertising pressures to entertain. Murrow, easily America's most trusted pre-Cronkite anchorman, said television "is being used to distract, delude, amuse, and insulate us," when he ardently believed it "can teach, illuminate, even inspire. But it can do so only to the extent that humans are determined to use it to those ends."

Mail In Rebate • Coupon Price • Lifetime Guarantee • Why Pay More? • They Have to Go • Home Sale • Beat The Crowd • Forty-Two Flavors • Fast Relief • Extra Savings • Over $6,000,000 in Jackpots Paid Monthly • Act Now • No Down Payment • Buyer's Market • Don't Miss Out • Priced to Go • Unlimited Offer • Let Your Fingers Do the Walking • Low Payments • Sunday Sale • Special Offer & Invitation To Join • "E-Membership $40" • Free Installation • This Week Only • You have been pre-approved for a $300,000 Home Loan at a 3.45% Fixed Rate • Your Own Web Site, With Your Own Domain Name • Biggest Blowout Sale of 2005 • Free ready cell phones with 1 YEAR of FREE SERVICE! • To claim your free pocket PC, click on the link below • Better Performance • A Unique Opportunity • All New • Run Don't Walk • Everyone A Winner! • Low Low Prices • Take the Cruise You've Always Wanted • Going Out of Business • Sheriff's Sale • Bankruptcy Sale!

In sum, this book describes and documents an American

consumeritis epidemic, and the poisonous effects that the American culture of buying and selling has on the lives of most Americans and on America's influence on and standing in the world. It argues that American economic life makes victims of its supposed beneficiaries—we the people—by distracting us from understanding what it really means to be free, healthy, human beings capable of achieving authentic happiness. Even so, it takes the optimistic view that we Americans are resilient enough so that it is not too late to remedy the malady that is progressively injuring us and our republic; and it recommends adoption of specific personal and institutional measures to help remedy the consumeritis epidemic.

The people who founded the United States of America considered their project an experiment. It is an experiment that has grown and flourished for more than two hundred years. We hope this book will help alert you to the possibility of imminent failure of our experiment in democracy as a result of the materialist addictions suffered by many of us. We also hope that by documenting the destructive effects of consumeritis in so many spheres of our lives, this book may help rescue us and our children from continuing to mistake the ubiquitous cultural counterfeits of happiness for the real thing; help us better appreciate the fact that "more" may now commonly be *Too Much for Our Own Good*; and help us realize when, in other words, enough is enough.

～

For your ease and convenience, beginning with this introduction and throughout the book, cited references and comments that amplify the text appear at the end of each chapter instead of in footnotes. We recommend that you read the text first without referring to the notes; then, if you choose to, you may review any parts of the text that particularly interest you in conjunction with their notes.

Notes

1 *In a Humphrey Bogart movie,* Key Largo, *celebrated in a song of the same name*   The movie *Key Largo* was produced by Jerry Wald, directed by John Huston, and based on the play written by Maxwell Anderson, with screenplay by Richard Brooks and John Huston (Warner Brothers Studios, 1948). The song *Key Largo* was written by Bertie Higgins, and as of this writing may be heard in its original version at *www.ladyjayes.com/keylargo.html.*

Even going to the movies recently has brought new kinds of exposure to commercial advertising   For a detailed indictment of commercialism in movies, see "Movies and the Selling of Desire" by Molly Haskell in *Consumer Desires: Consumption, Culture, and the Pursuit of Happiness,* ed. by Roger Rosenblatt (Washington, D.C.: Island Press, 1999), 123-135.

2 *The American culture of buying and selling*   See Peter Whybrow, *American Mania: When More Is Not Enough* (New York: Norton, 2005); and Pamela N. Danziger, *Why People Buy Things They Don't Need* (Ithaca, NY: Paramount Market Publishing, 2002).

As the author Jeremy Rifkin   Jeremy Rifkin, *The European Dream* (New York: Jeremy Tarcher/Penguin, 2005), 379-80.

3 *Real choice for humans*   Anuradha Vittachi, "What Really Matters: A Possible Route—Beyond the Lies, Towards Global Survival," (hereafter "What Really Matters") *New Internationalist,* Issue 235 (September 1992), *www.newint.org/issue235/what.htm* (accessed September 22, 2005).

many truly happy people of modest means   See "What Really Matters," in which Vittachi writes, "To live simply and frugally according to the values one has chosen is not to be 'poor', as many people who have chosen the spiritual path of voluntary simplicity will attest. The key lies in that word 'voluntary'. If I have very little because that is all I have chosen to have, I am rich: for I have everything I want."

4 *above $20,000 per person, additional income is not associated with greater happiness*   Richard Layard, *Happiness: Lessons from a New Science* (hereafter *Happiness*) (London: The Penguin Press, 2005), 32-34.

pathological condition of addiction   Robert Manning, *Credit Card Nation: The Consequences of America's Addiction to Credit* (New York: Basic Books, 2000); Juliet Schor, *Do Americans Shop Too Much?* (Boston, MA: Beacon Press, 2000); Richard Brodie, *Virus of the Mind* (hereafter *Virus*), (Seattle, WA: Integral Press, 1996).

consumeritis, a cultural pathology of epidemic proportions   The pathological nature of American consumerism has also been termed "*Affluenza.*" See John de Graaf, David Wann, and Thomas H. Naylor, *Affluenza: The All-Consuming Epidemic* (hereafter *Affluenza*) (San Francisco: Barrett-Koehler Publishers, 2001). The term "consumeritis" has occasionally been used by other writers to describe the pathology of excess consumption. For example, see Bill Wiser, "That Hole in Your Soul," stating that "consumeritis is highly contagious," at *www.bruderhof. com/articles/Hole-in-Your Soul.htm* (accessed September 2005); and the following definition offered by Open Circle, exhibiting at the 2003 Havana Biennale, of "Neuro Terminal Hyper Regressive Consumeritis Syndrome" as "an infectious bacteria that invades the mind first and then the body… thriving… on radio, and television," and stating that the symptoms of this malady include "constant irritation which subsides only after making a purchase," *www.opencirclearts.org/03_nthrcs. htm* (accessed September 2005); and the September 1992 issue of *New Internationalist* cited above.

It is a long-recognized, insidious sociopsychological principle that repeating a lie often enough This propagandistic principle was especially relied on by Adolph Hitler; see August Kubizek, *Young Hitler I Knew* (Boston, 1955), quoting Hitler as follows: "The chief function [of propaganda] is to convince the masses, whose slowness of understanding needs to be given time in order that they may absorb information; and only constant repetition will finally succeed in imprinting an idea on their mind… The success of any advertisement, whether of a business or a political nature, depends upon the consistency and perseverance with which it is employed."

6   *Advertising runs hand-in-hand with politics*   See *Virus*, 162.

7   *As Charles Dickens's magic story* A Christmas Carol *shows*   Charles Dickens (1812–1870) wrote *A Christmas Carol* in 1843.

   Nowadays, we can expect Christmas sales to begin shortly after Labor Day   A survey conducted by BIGresearch, reported on the front page of the *San Francisco Chronicle* on November 25, 2005, showed that 15.3 percent of Christmas holiday shoppers began their shopping even before September; 6.3 percent began during September; 18.5 percent in October; 37.4 percent in November; and 25.5 percent in December.

9   *on transmissions to us through our own cell phones*   Aaron O. Patrick, "Commercials by Cell phone," *Wall Street Journal* (August 22, 2005), B1.

   visible to practically everybody on earth   See *Affluenza*, 152.

10   *pre-Cronkite anchorman*   Walter Cronkite is a former CBS Evening News anchorman whose commentary defined issues and events in America for almost two decades. A major poll once named Cronkite "the most trusted figure" in American public life.

   television "is being used to distract"   Edward R. Murrow (1908–1965), as quoted in "Edward R. Murrow at the movies—just when we need him most, some say," by Jessica Warner in the *San Francisco Chronicle* on October 8, 2005. The article chronicles the debut of a biographical film about Murrow, *Good Night, and Good Luck* (2005), produced and directed by George Clooney, and co-written by Clooney and the actor David Strathairn, who plays Murrow in the film.

Humphrey Bogart as Sam Spade, Peter Lorre as Joel Cairo, Mary Astor as Brigid O'Shaughnessy, and Sydney Greenstreet as Kasper Gutman (left to right) in *The Maltese Falcon* (Warner Brothers Studios, 1941)

1

Too Much of a Good Thing: An Overview of the Culture of Buying and Selling

The business of America is business.
—President Calvin Coolidge (1925)

But ya gotta know the territory!
—A Traveling Salesman in
The Music Man (1962)

T HE MOST PROSPEROUS economies of the developed nations of the world are beneficiaries of industrial and technological revolutions, free markets, and free enterprise systems. America's outstanding productivity is also a result of the fact that full-time American workers have been working more hours every year than workers in Europe for at least the past fifty years. This productivity has brought us a general level of material abundance unprecedented in human history.

American Affluence, Productivity, and Consumer Credit
In *The History of Consumer Credit,* Rosa-Maria Gelpi and François Julien-Labruyère write:

> The United States was the first country where a majority of the population disposed of an income well above

subsistence level. Consumer aspirations rose and goods which had previously been considered as luxury items progressively became part of everyday life. The household wish of owning a house and living in rich suburbs (greater travel, better cinema and the introduction of television) led to an increase in demand for consumer items and social pressures to "keep up with the Joneses." This was the America of which the rest of the world dreamt, the modern America as depicted by Hollywood.

The greatest emperors of ancient Rome and China would be amazed by the luxuries now available to Americans of even relatively modest means. From ice cream and the Internet to blue jeans and fine wines, DVDs, cosmetics, and cappuccinos, the goods and services readily available for purchase in the United States today outstrip any imaginings of antiquity. They constitute luxuries available to most Americans beyond the dreams of avarice in former ages:

> Could the Emperor Tiberius have eaten grapes in January? Could the Emperor Napoleon have crossed the Atlantic in a night, or gotten from London to Paris in two hours? Could Thomas Aquinas have written a two-thousand-word letter in two hours—and then dispatched it to one thousand recipients with the touch of a key, and begun to receive replies within the hour? Computers, automobiles, airplanes, VCRs, washing machines, vacuum cleaners, telephones, and other technologies—combined with mass production—give middle-class citizens of the United States today degrees of material wealth, control over commodities, and the ability to consume services that previous generations could barely imagine.

Commercial advertising has played a critical role in helping us achieve this unprecedented level of affluence and abundance, just as it has played an essential role in America's free enterprise system generally. When advertising provides us with accurate, nondeceptive information, it helps us make wise purchasing decisions and enjoy the benefits of products we might otherwise not even know existed; it also provides information we can use to improve or secure our physical health and general well-being. But in the opinion of many observers (as our bibliography attests), commercial advertising has now reached a point of volume, excess, and deception at which its costs to the American public exceed its benefits in a variety of critical ways, including diverting us from pursuits of greater happiness than can be provided by the material goods and pleasures the advertising promotes. To understand how we came to reach this point, it will be useful to examine some of the landmark moments in the history of American advertising and the indispensable adjunct responsible for its unprecedented success: consumer credit.

Consumer credit has had more than an economic function in American society. It has also had a revolutionary egalitarian social function. Consumer credit developed not only as a means of serving business in a highly commercialized society; it may also have constituted an ethical response to the unequal distribution of wealth between capital and labor. In the early twentieth century, consumer credit was condemned as an imprudent diversion of capital from its role in increasing the means of production to its role in the procuring of unproductive consumer luxuries. The lending of money to a spendthrift, a German professor wrote in 1911, "causes labor to be directed to producing truffles and champagne, not factories and machinery." This point of view was consistent with that of the oracle of capitalism, Adam Smith, who wrote in *The Wealth of Nations*:

> The man who borrows in order to spend will soon be ruined, and he who lends to him will generally have occasion to repent of his folly. To borrow or to lend for such purposes, therefore, is in all cases, where gross usury is out of the question, contrary to the interest of both parties.

This was, moreover, a view supported by the economic ethos of early American culture as exemplified by Benjamin Franklin's sayings in *Poor Richard's Almanac*, such sayings as:

> If you would know the value of money, go and try to borrow some; for he that goes a borrowing goes a sorrowing; and indeed so does he that lends to such people, when he goes to get it again.
>
> But what madness must it be to run in debt for superfluities. We are offered by the terms of this sale six months credit; and that, perhaps, has induced some of us to attend it, because we cannot spare the ready money, and hope now to be fine without it. But ah! Think what you do when you run in debt; you give to another power over your liberty.
>
> My son, I implore you, take heed! Never buy what you do not need. Watch the ones who rely upon credit, slowly sink down, down into debit. The greatest pains, the greatest frets, arise my son from unpaid debts.

From the point of view of classical economics, consumer credit was regarded as being largely targeted for extravagant expenditure, and condemned as social waste. (But a distinction was made between consumer durables such as home sewing machines and goods like silk stockings or lace curtains, with the former being preferable to the latter as adding to the stock of goods, and therefore to the wealth of the country.) Condemnation of consumer credit was a conventional economic dogma of the eighteenth century in England, on the European continent, and in America. But things began to change radically in the nineteenth century when consumer credit on a large scale first became common. The large scale was made possible by "hire purchase sales," in which ordinary people were able to buy household appliances on a lease-buy basis, with a down payment and payments over time sufficient to complete the purchase. As the French authors of *The History of Consumer Credit* put it:

Until the 19th century, consumer credit was seen only as the underside of society's operations... But in 1850, in the United States, it took on the truly revolutionary form of hire purchase sales in order to finance home equipment for new settlers.

From then on, it became the most obvious support for, first Americans', then Europeans' improving standards of living. As an indirect effect, it helped stabilize industry in those same countries. From the sewing machine to the automobile, from the refrigerator to the television, it is impossible to disassociate Western standards of living from hire purchase sales. *In this sense, consumer credit is the greatest single factor of social integration.* The American example, which some Europeans consider excessive, offers a salutary lesson to those who are willing to examine it closely. For centuries, the nearest thing to consumer credit, that is the moneylender, acted as a social lifebuoy for the poorest families. The United States transformed this calling into something positive. The idea of hire purchase was not to ease a difficult or even a dire present situation, but to project the consumer into the future with new domestic appliances. (emphasis added)

The great pioneer in this innovation was the Singer Sewing Machine Company. It started selling its machines on hire purchase in about 1850. The provision of household consumer durables of an industrial nature in return for monthly payments became an overnight success. "It is worth noting," the authors of *The History of Consumer Credit* point out, "that it was in relation to a machine aimed at women that our day-to-day lifestyle was changed." The success of this innovation was further augmented by the efforts of traveling salesmen of exactly the kind represented by Professor Harold C. Hill in Meredith Willson's *The Music Man*:

> The more the frontier extended westward, the more the traveling salesman became the lifeline linking the frontiers to Chicago, which became the center of this backup trading. A vital link was thus established between the crude homes of the young families going west and

business on the shores of Lake Michigan. Credit became a necessary part of the conquest of the West. To this very day, Chicago remains the largest national mail-order network as well as being home to the major specialist credit companies. The Windy City still has this role because of its history as a supplier for the settlement of the West. It is the symbolic capital of modern consumer credit, which first saw the light of day with the expanding railway and the opening of the West.

Despite its obvious contribution to American expansion, credit still had a poor image as late as the 1920s. In Europe, it continued to be condemned for ideological (essentially religious) reasons, and partly through the stigmatization of lenders as usurers. In contrast, its continuing poor reputation in the United States looked more to the borrower than to the lender. Borrowers were still considered economic failures, and class distinctions contributed to the opprobrium in which credit was held. Credit made it possible to separate current consumption from current income, and thus blurred social distinctions.

During the 1920's, the climate changed. Households saved less, and to be in debt became respectable. What made this evolution possible was the generalization of hire purchase for the acquisition of automobiles. To borrow ceased to be an indication of poverty, or credulity when it was generalized in order to buy a luxury item, a car. This was the era of the great credit societies… of which The General Motors Acceptance Corporation and the Ford Credit Company are the direct descendants… This gives us an idea of the impact of the 1920's on the history of consumer credit. With time, because of the items it brought within the reach of the poor, credit came to be seen as the greatest catalyst in the famous melting pot. This parallel [with "the melting pot" metaphor] holds one of the most fundamental keys to the American success story.

Moreover, once sale on credit has been generally established, its development leads to some positive

economic results. By creating the base for a large market
it facilitates mass production and therefore an enormous
reduction in unit costs. American economic vitality in
the 20th century stems from this correspondence. The
immediate availability of durable goods contributes also
to improve the well-being of the household....

In 1972 an official report of the [U.S.] National Commission on Consumer Finance "underlines the magnitude and importance of the *consumer credit industry ... as the vehicle largely responsible for creating
and maintaining in this country the highest standard of
living in the world.*" (emphasis added)

American prosperity is the envy of much of the world, which
is continually tantalized, as the preceding suggests, by the sometimes exaggerated images that American TV, movies, and advertising present of American lifestyles. A third of the world's population in 2000 lived in countries "with a level of material output
per capita less than that of the U.S. in 1900." Along with envy
comes, almost inevitably, some resentment. And among people
living in cultures that question materialism, such resentment has
escalated to actual hatred and may even form part of the twisted
rationale for international terrorism. Antipathy to American
culture is not, however, confined to anti-Western ideologues. It
extends to people living in many highly sophisticated nations and
cultures who wonder why, as it appears, Americans live simply to
work instead of working to live a fuller life. American productivity and hours worked have continually risen since 1975 compared
to the productivity and hours worked by Europeans. In contrast,
by statistical measures, happiness in the United States "has stag-
nated since 1975, while it has risen in Europe." It is no surprise
that the unprecedented level of affluence Americans enjoy, even
though attributable to our own industriousness, has not made us
a happier people. Studies of both rich and poor nations throughout the world show that "above $20,000 per person, additional

income is not associated with greater happiness." Even in the United States, the percentage of people (6 percent) earning more than $50,000 a year who say they have achieved the American dream is not much greater than the percentage of people earning less than $15,000 per year (5 percent) who say that.

We Americans may afford to sneer at the gripes of others about our consumerist culture of buying and selling; but we cannot afford to be content with how that culture has come to undermine and threaten not only our personal happiness but our physical health and that of our children, our national well-being, and our social and political institutions. As examination of its costs in the following sections of this chapter will demonstrate, the successful excess of commercial advertising has helped to transform "consumerism" into "consumeritis." It is thereby proving to be too much of a good thing —in fact, too much for our own good. The United States is no longer a pioneering society in which the availability of consumer credit to its citizens is virtually indispensable to their establishing a decent standard of living while meeting the challenges of new frontiers. Nor are novel commodities being offered to the general public beyond their financial reach, commodities that have the potential, as the automobile did in the early twentieth century, of expanding the range of critical life choices for individuals, families, and communities. During the last quarter century especially, the dynamic energy given to consumer credit by the seminal innovations of the Singer Sewing Machine Company and Henry Ford has translated into an acceleration of American consumer demand that is at least questionably proportionate to real human need, with dramatically counterproductive and damaging consequences. As late as the 1980s, we could be mostly entertained by imaginative commercial advertising. At this point, we are more easily disturbed than entertained by its ubiquitous, insistent call to buy more and more and more of what American enterprise offers. To understand the harm that is being done to us, we "gotta know the territory." The rest of this chapter will therefore detail how consumeritis is relentlessly fueled by the exaggerated, dream-weaving claims of commercial advertising (most notably television advertising); what the excesses of consumeritis are; and what they cost us. We begin by considering the costs.

What Consumeritis Costs Us

> *What's good for the country is good for*
> *General Motors, and vice-versa.*
> —Charles E. Wilson, President of General Motors,
> later U.S. Secretary of Defense (1953–1957)

In 1935, during the depths of the Great Depression, Warner Brothers released its film version of Charles Dickens's classic autobiographic novel, *David Copperfield*. The comic actor W. C. Fields made one of the most memorable characters in that novel, Mr. Wilkins Micawber, equally memorable in the film. Micawber, who was a kindly friend to the young David Copperfield when Copperfield was most in need of friends, is a jobless pauper, always in danger of debtor's prison, but always optimistic that "something will turn up." Toward the end of the story, Micawber and his family emigrate to Australia to begin a new, debt-free life. David accompanies the family to the dock from which they will board the ship for their voyage. Having nothing to give David as a farewell gift but advice, Micawber draws a moral from his own misfortunes and says to David, "Annual income, 20 pounds, annual expenditures 19, 19, 6, result, *happiness.*" Then, in his widely imitated drawl, W. C. Fields delivers Micawber's punch line: "Annual income 20 pounds, annual expenditures 20 pounds ought and 6, result, *misery.*" This was a message with special resonance during the 1930s, when unemployment was at an unprecedented high (over 20 percent), and many millions of Americans were struggling for bare subsistence.

Micawber's advice is also likely to resonate with millions of Americans today. Americans possess more than a billion credit cards, but less than a third of credit-card holders pay off their balances each month. In 2004, consumer credit-card debt totaled nearly $820 billion (out of more than $2 trillion in overall consumer debt) or more than $7,000 for every man, woman, and child in the United States. The number of personal bankruptcies filed in 2004 (1.6 million) was more than six times greater than the number of filings in 1980. In fact, since 1996, the number of bankruptcies filed every year in the United States has been greater than the number of students graduating from college. Unlike Micawber's England in the nineteenth century, the United States in the twenty-first century has no debtor's prison; but more than one and a half million personal bankruptcies no doubt represents a whole lot of personal misery.

In macroeconomic terms, since the film version of *David Copperfield* was released, the amount of American consumer debt as a percentage of the nation's gross domestic product (GDP) has increased more than six times, from less than 3 percent to more than 18 percent. Even more disturbing is the fact that, over the past twenty years, the annual increase in consumer debt has, on average, exceeded the amount of growth in the GDP by more than 1 per cent, so that American productivity has been continually shrinking relative to the growth of personal indebtedness. Though we may be working harder, we are progressively outspending our gains. And if the result is not yet "misery" for most people, it is clearly less happiness. Compared to 1957, Americans today own twice as many cars per person, eat out twice as often, and enjoy innumerable commodities that weren't around then: big screen and color TVs, microwave ovens, personal computers, SUVs, cell phones, and iPods, to name just a few. By 1992, people were, on average, four and a half times wealthier than their great-grandparents at the turn of the century, and occupied more than twice as much residential space per person than their parents did in 1950. But this acquisition of greater affluence has not added to the mental health of most Americans: "Compared with their grandparents, today's young adults have grown up with much more affluence ... and much greater risk of depression and assorted social pathology." We are now apparently a nation of debtors to no good end.

The sharp increase in credit-card debt during the past generation is largely the result of progressive increases in consumer spending. Examination of American personal spending during the past twenty-five years or so indicates that the malignant form of consumeritis began to strike Americans severely in the early 1980s. The amount of money Americans spend on consumer goods (technically termed "PCE," for "personal consumer expenditures") as a percentage of GDP remained constant around 62 percent from 1951 until 1981. By 2004, PCE had reached 70 percent of GDP, a 13 percent increase in growth rate over a twenty-three-year period above the growth rate of GDP. Since 1981, our PCE growth has thus, on average, outpaced GDP growth by more than half a percent a year, progressively shrinking our increased production in relation to what we are spending.

Even more significant as a measure of the debt pressure Americans experience from consumeritis is the fact that PCE has been sharply increasing as a percentage of *personal disposable income*, that is, the amount of money Americans have left to spend after providing for their necessities. In 1981, Americans spent, on average, more than 86 percent of their disposable income. By 2004, they were spending almost 95 percent, leaving very little for savings. The American personal savings rate averaged close to 10 percent from 1970 to 1984. By 2004, it had dropped to less than 2 percent; it now approaches zero. In contrast, the Japanese savings rate is about 14 percent, Indian and Pakistani workers save about 25 percent, and the Chinese save about 50 percent of their earnings.

The precipitous drop in Americans' savings rate is one of the most ominous symptoms of consumeritis. Lower savings means less investment, which in turn means lower future economic growth. Growth in consumer spending already exceeds growth in American production (GDP). Coupled with a concomitant anticipated *decrease* in economic growth, it is clear that continued consumeritis is unaffordable not only in terms of Americans' personal economic security, but in macroeconomic terms. What's good for General Motors, in other words, may no longer be so good for all of the country. And if the business of America remains business as usual in its encouragement of consumeritis, the country may be headed—as chapter 4 explains in detail—for economic disaster at both personal and national levels.

Civilizations grow, prosper, and decay. We know of no empire in recorded human history that has not fallen through excesses made possible by its own success. Imperial China and imperial Rome are the most spectacular examples, but virtually every civilization that has earned the name "empire" has been subjected to this fate. (Consider also, for example, the late Renaissance Spanish and the French empires of both Louis XIV and Napoleon.) During the twentieth century, following its crucial triumphs in World Wars I and II and the Cold War, the American empire, by political, economic, and military measures, became the greatest in history. Its fall may therefore be the most spectacular of all. It is presently the world's only superpower, and dominates the globe militarily as well as in the export of its commercial culture.

The signs of possible exhaustion of its power from both private overspending and the excesses of the military-industrial complex, of which President Eisenhower warned in his 1960 farewell address, are becoming increasingly evident, and multiplying. Just as Roman civilization and its grand republic were succeeded by the arrogance of empire, and then its people were diverted from their common sense by "bread and circuses," twenty-first century Americans, infected with consumeritis, are in danger of forgetting the principles that gave birth to their country and allowed it to grow. Two critical questions facing open-eyed Americans today are, therefore, (1) how imminent may the fall of America's empire be? and (2) if it is a relatively imminent possibility, how, if at all, may it be avoided?

Securing human rights to "life, liberty, and the pursuit of happiness," we should recall, was among the reasons the founders stated for forming the United States of America. Our prosperity is the legacy not only of a free economic market and American industriousness but also of political liberties and a civic community that define the political order of a democratic republic. American consumerism is drowning the *civic spirit* in which American liberties and community were born, choking our original, healthy American character to death in a glut of *stuff* and the techniques of its flacking. This possibility for the outcome of American acquisitiveness as part of the American pursuit of social and economic equality was foretold as early as 1840 by Alexis de Tocqueville in his prophetic study of American culture when he wrote:

> I seek to trace the novel features under which despotism may appear in the world. The first thing that strikes the observation is an innumerable multitude of men, all equal and alike, incessantly endeavoring to procure the petty and paltry pleasures with which they glut their lives. Each of them, living apart, is as a stranger to the fate of all the

rest; his children and his private friends constitute to him the whole of mankind. As for the rest of his fellow citizens, he is close to them, but does not see them; he touches them, but he does not feel them; he exists only in himself and for himself alone; and if his kindred still remain to him, he may be said at any rate to have lost his country. Above this race of men stands an immense and tutelary power, which takes upon itself alone to secure their gratifications, and to watch over their fate.... It covers the surface of society with a network of small complicated rules ... The will of man is not shattered, but softened, bent, and guided ... Such power does not tyrannize, but it compresses, enervates, extinguishes, and stupefies a people, till it is reduced to be nothing better than a flock of timid and industrious animals, of which the government is the shepherd.

In later chapters of this book we consider in detail how American "getting and spending" —a phrase the poet William Wordsworth coined in 1807— is now not only sinking Americans deeper and deeper into debt, emotional depression, and personal unhappiness but also degrading American social, political, and moral well-being. But the extent to which Tocqueville's prophesy accurately predicted twenty-first-century life in the United States should first be assessed by considering the actual patterns of contemporary American consumption and how they are promoted by advertising.

The Excesses of Consumeritis

In the same year (1935) that Warner Brothers released the film version of *David Copperfield*, MGM released its hilarious Marx Brothers movie, *A Night at the Opera*. In a famous scene, Groucho Marx, playing a character named Otis B. Driftwood, and Chico Marx, playing an Italian immigrant named Fiorello, are reviewing a proposed contract. Chico questions one of its first provisions, and Groucho tells him, "It's all right, that's in every contract. That's what they call a sanity clause." The wary Chico replies, "You can't fool me! There ain't no sanity clause." As the getting, spending, and wasting responses of Americans demonstrate, there is evidently no sanity clause in the contracts formed by what American advertising offers and American consumers accept.

Americans have become the most voracious consumers in the world. In 2002, per capita U.S. consumption expenditure was nearly one and one-half times greater than that of the European Union, nine times more than that of Mexico, fifty times more than that of China, and seventy times more than that of India. In other terms exhibiting excess consumption, Americans now throw away 7 million cars a year, 2 million plastic bottles every hour, and enough aluminum cans annually to make six thousand DC-10 airplanes. Total American waste would now annually fill a convoy of garbage trucks long enough to reach halfway to the moon.

As further evidence of the accuracy of Tocqueville's prediction that Americans might tend eventually to be "incessantly endeavoring to procure the petty and paltry pleasures with which they glut their lives," witness the fact that by 1987, there were more shopping malls in the United States than high schools; that, on average, Americans shop at least six hours a week but spend only forty minutes a week playing with their children; that more Americans (70 percent) visit shopping malls each week than attend churches or synagogues; and that, on average, Americans will spend one full year of their lives watching TV commercials. As a final, microcosmic illustration of the present dominance of getting and spending in the American hierarchy of values, also witness the fact that the greatest tourist attraction in Virginia may be the Potomac Mills shopping mall. It is such a popular tourist destination that airlines have offered excursion flights to it from distant cities.

The excesses of American consumeritis have become so great, they can no longer escape notice. Some observers—perhaps too optimistically by their own admission—believe that it may now have reached its peak. An article by the architect Arrol Gellner, in the *San Francisco Chronicle* on October 8, 2005, clearly reflects this point of view with its headline: "America may be at the peak of latest materialistic cycle." After describing ebbs and flows in materialism from Victorian times, the author acknowledges the present situation's excesses:

> Needless to say, America is once again at the peak—at least one hopes it's the peak—of one of these materialistic cycles. As we preside over the dawn of the 21st century, the typical new house has bloated to more than twice the size of an average home of 1950, even though families have gotten smaller.... Along the same lines, it's become routine to see feather-weight housewives wrestling gigantic 7-foot-high SUV's on half-mile grocery runs. Alas, it doesn't end there, either. Recently, in a shopping mall in a middle-class suburb of Portland, I came across three boutiques selling clothing, diet supplements, and confections—for dogs. Perhaps there is a point when too much is really too much. We've all seen that bumper sticker beloved by the terminally empty-headed: "He who Dies With the Most Toys Wins." Yet few intelligent Americans would argue that having a huge house ... much less a larder stocked with dog pastries, has actually made their lives any happier.

As Gellner's essay suggests, Americans may be waking up to the harm done by the plague of consumeritis that infects so many of us, and we may be feeling less comfortable with what it has been doing to us and to our children. The growing literature indicates increased awareness of the dangerous direction in which our fevered materialism has been driving us. Thoughtful observers of contemporary life in the United States echo

Tocqueville's predictions of a self-absorbed American preoccupation with "paltry pleasures glutting our lives" by pointing out "that we've become too materialistic, too greedy, too selfish, too self absorbed, and ... need to bring back into balance the enduring values that have guided this country over generations." They likewise associate consumeritis with a "rampant individualism [that] has become increasingly the norm," diminishing our sense of community with others and the vitality of civic concern about the fate of our country.

Sixty percent of Americans say that our children are not just materialistic but that they're "very materialistic." According to the child psychologist Allen D. Kanner, "The materialistic shift happening in our society is having an enormous impact and major influence on children's lives that is highly psychological in nature. It needs to be a focus of our profession right now." Juvenile materialism is a predictable result of commercial advertising. Advertisers have exponentially increased their marketing to young children and teenagers, who constitute the largest targeted commercial markets today. On average, American children are now exposed to more than forty thousand TV commercials a year. The present annual advertising budget to young "consumers" is now about $15 billion (about two and one-half times the spending in 1992). This advertising is competition for the $600 billion worth of annual spending children now influence.

The advertising engine of the American culture of buying and selling is doing serious damage to our young people beyond deepening their materialism and increasing their proneness to depression. As the next section of this chapter documents, the incidence of childhood obesity and diabetes, for example, has been growing at an alarming rate, attributable in substantial part to advertising directed at children. Public educational institutions, to which Americans evidently attach a lower priority than their consumeritis-infected participation in the culture of buying and selling, are permitting that culture to invade our public schools with pernicious effects. Some public schools permit commercial advertisers to expand their visibility on school campuses and in classrooms for the sake of the revenue this can add to under-funded school districts.

Nearly 80 per cent of undergraduate students in the United States hold at least one credit card; many of these cards have been procured through on-campus solicitations. Undergraduate credit-card debt is now leading some students to drop out of school to pay it off. The distress this breeds can easily be imagined. Emotional distress caused by consumeritis is not confined to those in such extreme circumstances. Indeed, distress from consumeritis may be felt most keenly by conscientious adults. The unhappiest people in our culture of buying and selling are evidently those who still respect values higher than materialistic pleasure, and thus feel some conflict between their consumerism and the higher order values they accept as valid. Consumeritis as a malady that allows our materialistic impulses to triumph over the better angels of our nature thus also adds to the psychological stresses felt in the daily grind of American industrial and technological society. (Chapter 2 explores the character and significance of the losing struggle Americans have been experiencing between the material and spiritual dimensions of their lives, and their growing awareness of the damage consumeritis is doing.) These dispiriting triumphs of consumeritis are, in large part, the signal accomplishment of American commercial advertising, on which we now focus our attention.

Commercial Advertising: The Stuff That Dreams Are Made Of

Dashiell Hammett's detective novel *The Maltese Falcon* was translated into an acclaimed 1941 movie written and directed by John Huston. The plot and characterizations of the novel, faithfully followed in the film, revolve about the ruthless efforts of a trio of unsavory characters to find a statuette supposed to have been encrusted with jewels by the Knights of Malta at a distant period, but lacquered over in black to disguise its true worth. As the story begins, Sam Spade, a San Francisco private detective played by Humphrey Bogart, is hired by a femme fatale (portrayed by Mary Astor) ostensibly to help find her missing sister or her boyfriend. Spade, justifiably suspicious of the lady's story, takes the job anyway, and assigns his detective partner (played by Jerome Cowan) the job of beginning the search. The partner is soon murdered in the course of his investigation; determined to find the murderer, Spade soon discovers that the murder is connected to a search for the Maltese falcon in which the Mary Astor character is involved, along with a Mr. Gutman (Sydney Greenstreet) and a man named Joel Cairo (Peter Lorre). Toward the end of the story, Gutman, who has been following the reputed trail of the statuette around the world for many years, finally gets it in his hands. He immediately cuts its lacquered surface to uncover the jewels he supposes lie beneath it, and finds it is a fake. Meanwhile, Spade has collected all the evidence he needs to enable the police to arrest the villains as conspirators in several murders. At the denouement, the police take the villains into custody in Sam's presence moments after Gutman has once again found himself frustrated in his search for the true falcon, and just as he and Cairo are about to leave to continue their search. The arresting detective picks up the fake falcon abandoned by Gutman and asks what it is. Spade's laconic reply is, "The stuff that dreams are made of."

"Sell them their dreams," a promoter told Philadelphia businessmen in 1923:

> Sell them what they longed for and hoped for and almost
> despaired of having. Sell clubs and proms and visions of
> what might happen if only. After all, people don't buy
> things to have things. They buy hope—hope of what your
> merchandise will do for them. Sell them this hope and
> you won't have to worry about selling them goods.

This is a point of view that continues to dominate the American commercial advertising industry. An Internet search in 2005 brought up the following as the leading message of a company that characterizes itself as "the ultimate source of information on advertising, promotion and other closely related subjects ... one of the most popular references available today":

> Advertisement that really works. Promoting dreams
> instead of just products and services. The secret of effec-
> tive advertising is in promoting hopes, dreams and emo-
> tions rather than just products and services ...

Counseling its readers about how to make their advertising most effective, the company message goes on to explain: "People rarely buy things as they are; rather they buy ideas, emotions, and hopes ... for the only sound reason for saving money is to purchase a dream with it." (But the text fails to note that Americans are no longer saving much of their money, so this rationale for advertising dream-making may itself now be a bit of the stuff that dreams are made of.) In fact, among the "proven, winning advertising headline phrases" in a survey of one thousand of them is the phrase "Realize your dream."

The amount of money American businesses spend to advertise their goods and services and identify them with "the stuff that dreams are made of"—the dreams of personal fulfillment that people "long for and hope for and almost despair of"—helps explain the increasing impact of the consumeritis epidemic during the past two decades (see table 1.1). Hang on to your hat: In the year 2000, commercial advertising expenditures in all media amounted to over $263 billion, or $934.81 for every man, woman, and child in the country. This represents a growth in advertising expenditures since the 1990 census ($169 billion) of more than 55 percent, or 37.8 percent per capita, taking into account population growth. The growth numbers for TV advertising are similarly impressive. TV advertising expenditures in 1990 were about $34.7 billion dollars; in 2000, they were $47.6 billion, a growth of more than 37 percent and an advertising bill of more than $169.00 for every American. Outdoor advertising expenditures in 2000 (for billboards, buses, trains, taxis and other transportation vehicles, bus shelters, telephone kiosks, and so forth) were very nearly $5.5 billion. In the same period, direct mail advertising expenditures grew at an even faster rate than advertising generally, from $30.4 billion to $47.4 billion, amounting to a 64 percent growth and about $168.00 for each person in the United States by the year 2000. Internet advertising was added to the mix beginning in 1997 with a reported $891 million in expenditures, ballooning to $6.9 billion in 2000 (an increase of over 700 percent), more than $20.00 per American. (All figures are in 2003 dollars; see table 1.1.) It has recently been estimated that this deluge of advertising from all media results in the average American being exposed to as many as three thousand commercial messages a day.

In quantitative terms, these figures demonstrate that American culture has become predominantly a culture of buying and selling; no other organized private segment of American activity of which we are aware annually spends per capita as much as the commercial advertising industry does. In any case, without doubt no other private segment spends as much as the commercial advertising industry spends to influence Americans.

Every modern technological advancement in communications has expanded the presence of advertising and the frequency with which Americans are exposed to commercial messages.

Development of the Internet is the most recent innovation. Total *daily* e-mail volume (31 billion) averages about 175 e-mails per person, although through various forms of blocking and for other reasons, most individuals evidently receive many fewer than this number. In addition to exposure to advertising in newspapers, magazines, radio, television, telephone solicitations, direct mailings, billboards, transportation vehicles, and all the rest of outdoor advertising, about 12.4 billion spam e-mails (40 percent of all e-mail messages) are now being sent to Americans every day, substantially adding to the daily volume of advertising messages to the public. More than five out of six (about 84 percent) spam e-mails are commercial advertising and marketing messages offering something for sale, so commercial spam is about one-third of all e-mails. On average, in 2005, Americans received about 2200 spam messages a year, and this figure is estimated to increase by 63 percent, to nearly 3600, by the year 2007. On a very conservative estimate, this addition to the volume of American advertising indicates that the consciousness of each American is being invaded by at least a thousand commercials a week, and perhaps many times more in urban areas.

There might be little or nothing wrong with the sea of commercial advertising in which Americans are now compelled to swim if it consisted only of useful information. But it does not consist only of useful information; it is "the stuff that dreams are made of," commonly deceptive appeals to our appetites calculated to get past the screen of our rationality and good judgment. It would be a serious enough problem if these insidious seductions were directed solely to adults, who are presumed to be sufficiently mature and responsible to make reasonable distinctions between fact and fantasy, and discern the difference between truth and likely falsehood. But the fact is that American commercial advertising is an increasingly massive onslaught on the immature and highly vulnerable judgment of our children, conditioning them to accept fantasy as reality and leading them to believe that the kinds of products that may in fact injure them are products that will be good for them. Young children "tend to accept ads as fair, accurate, balanced and truthful ... They don't see the exaggeration or the bias that underlies [advertising] claims. To young children, advertising is just as credible as [a trusted anchorman] reading the evening news is to an adult."

The emergence of the Internet as a child-friendly medium, as the following explains, thus further exacerbates an already serious problem that has deleterious psychological and physical dimensions. According to a 2004 market research report prepared by a consulting firm serving consumer products companies and allied businesses, "toddlers and older pre-schoolers in the under-6 age group are increasingly sophisticated in their media usage habits." The National Center for Education Statistics, in the study *Computer and Internet Use by Children and Adolescents in 2001*, reported that more than 16.5 million American children between the ages of five and fourteen regularly connect to the Internet. (See tables 1.2 and 1.3, which set out recent survey data for computer and Internet usage by five- to twelve-year-olds and five- to fourteen-year-olds, respectively). Of these 16.5 million children, 12 percent (1 out of 8), or over 2 million children, are already using computers to find product information on the Internet. It is no wonder, therefore, that the same 2004 marketing research report states that "industry research shows that kids are among the fastest growing online audiences," and that "the Internet is going to be the central media [sic] kids use. Advertisers are going to have to be there if they want to reach people" [the latter statement from the marketing research report quotes an article in the *Washington Post* on September 10, 2003]. A 2003 study conducted by Harris Interactive found that approximately half the Internet users in the eight- to twelve-year-old group had spent more than an hour online the previous day. These kids also said that they would rather be online than watching TV. The case of teenagers is different: Research shows that it is common for teens at home to watch television while surfing the Internet while e-mailing and instant messaging their friends while talking on the phone while doing their homework. Marketers take advantage of the multitasking propensities of today's teens by simultaneously using all communications technologies as platforms to reach teen consumers.

The dangerous effects of advertising on very young children and teenagers are not limited to the reality distortion and other adverse psychological effects we have already discussed. They extend as well to their physical and mental well-being. Chief among these damaging effects are those mentioned in the concerns expressed by public health officials about the relationship between commercial advertising and, first, a startling increase in the obesity of the young in the United States and, second, adolescent alcohol consumption.

> In recent years, health officials have become increasingly alarmed by the rapid increase in obesity among American children. According to the Centers for Disease Control and Prevention, since 1980 the proportion of overweight children ages 6–11 has more than doubled, and the rate for adolescents has tripled. Today about 10% of 2- to 5-year olds and 15% of 6- to 19-year olds are overweight ... Among children of color, the rates are even higher: 4 in 10 Mexican American and African American youth ages 6–19 are considered overweight or at risk of being overweight.

The American Academy of Pediatrics asserts that the increase in childhood obesity represents an "unprecedented burden" on children's health. Medical complications common in overweight children include hypertension, type 2 diabetes, respiratory ailments, orthopedic problems, sleep disturbances, and depression. The Surgeon General of the United States has predicted that preventable morbidity and mortality associated with obesity may exceed those associated with cigarette smoking. The implications of childhood obesity—which continues into adulthood at a rate of 80 percent—on the nation's health and health care costs are huge. Indeed, the American Academy of Pediatrics has called the potential costs associated with childhood obesity "staggering."

Experts have pointed to a range of important potential contributions to the rise in childhood obesity, some of which are unrelated to advertising and the media, such as reductions in physical education classes and after-school athletic programs, the trend toward supersizing food portions in fast food restaurants, and the increasing number of highly processed high-calorie and high-fat grocery products (which are, of course, highly advertised). But the evidence is clear and convincing, if not conclusive, that in light of children's use of media, one of the chief contributing factors to the increase in childhood obesity is commercial advertising. A survey of the evidence supporting this conclusion was published by the Henry J. Kaiser Family Foundation in its February 2004 *Issue Brief*, in an article titled "The Role of Media in Childhood Obesity," which pulls together the best available research on this subject. This entire *Issue Brief* will provide useful information on a range of issues of interest to parents relating to childhood obesity, especially including the relationship between childhood obesity and the time children spend watching TV. One study found, for example, that among twelve- to seventeen-year-olds, the prevalence of obesity increased by 2 percent for each additional hour of television viewed, and that "29% of the cases of obesity could be prevented by reducing television viewing to 0 to 1 hours per week."

The following conclusions implicating commercial advertising as a significant contributing cause of increasing childhood obesity were supported by research surveyed in Kaiser's *Issue Brief*:

> (1) Food advertisements children are exposed to on TV influence them to make unhealthy food choices. (Fast food outlets alone spend $3 billion in television ads targeted to children.)
>
> (2) The cross promotions between food products and popular TV and movie characters encourage children to buy and eat more high-calorie foods.

Indeed, the Kaiser *Issue Brief* research survey on the relationship between childhood obesity and children's media use reaches the following overall conclusion:

> It is likely that the main mechanism by which media use contributes to childhood obesity may well be through children's exposure to billions of dollars worth of food advertising and cross promotional marketing year after year, starting at the very youngest ages, with children's favorite characters often enlisted in the sales pitch.

As the *New York Times* has noted, the advertising industry's "courtship of children is no surprise, since increasingly that is where the money is," adding that marketing executives anticipated that children under twelve would "spend $35 billion of their own money and influence another $200 billion in household spending in 2004." For advertising executives and American commercial enterprise in general—the chief progenitors of consumeritis—the purchasing dollars spent or influenced by very young children have also evidently been found to be "the stuff that dreams are made of." But getting those "consumer" dollars through the kinds of advertisements aimed at the youth market may be causing nightmares (both literally and figuratively), not pleasant dreams, for our young children, and will continue to do so for all of us in the future unless some effective changes occur in the American culture of buying and selling.

Recent studies have also shown that the price we pay for our tolerance of insidious advertising extends to the damaging effects and costs of increased adolescent alcohol consumption attributable to the alcohol industry's commercial advertising practices.

> Public health advocates have expressed concern that alcohol advertising is a factor contributing to adolescent alcohol consumption. Both the level of alcohol consumption by adolescents and the level of alcohol advertising are considerable. Data from the 2001 *Monitoring the Future Surveys* show that 7.7% of 8th graders, 21.9% of 10th graders and 49.8 percent of 12th graders consumed alcohol within the past 30 days ... Competitive Media Reporting estimated that alcohol producers spent about $1.5 billion on measured media advertising in 2001. This was a 25 percent increase over spending in 1998. Alcohol industry reports to the FTC suggest that measured media advertising account for only one half to one third of total promotional expenditures. Other forms of alcohol promotion include sponsorships; internet advertising; point-of-purchase advertising; consumer novelties; product placements in movie and TV shows; direct mail ... expenditures [that] may enhance the effectiveness of measured media spending.

Despite alcohol industry codes that prohibit advertising content and placement which target underage individuals (prohibiting, for example, use of actors who appear underage, or the image of Santa Claus), the exposure of youth to alcohol advertising in magazines, on TV, and on radio is substantial. The use of cartoon characters is not among the alcohol industry's code restrictions, and beer advertisers have no restrictions on the use of sports celebrities. The Center on Alcohol Marketing and Youth found that in 2001, magazine advertisers delivered 45 percent more beer advertising to youth (defined as individuals under twenty-one) than to adults. For spirits, 27 percent more magazine advertising was delivered to youth than to adults. They also found that on TV, underage youth were exposed to two beer or ale ads for every three seen by an adult. Beer and ale ads on TV represent about half of all alcohol advertising in all media. On radio, youth heard 8 percent more beer and ale advertising, 12 percent more malt advertising, and 14 percent more advertising for distilled spirits than adults twenty-one and older. A 1995 review of research on the effect of alcohol advertising on attitudes and intention to drink by adolescents found that much of the imagery in alcohol advertising appeals to youth and that this advertising increases positive expectations about alcohol among adolescents.

While studies of advertising exposure have led some public health groups, such as the Robert Wood Johnson Foundation, to conclude that alcohol advertising and marketing are factors in our culture of buying and selling that help create problems of underage drinking, there was until recently almost no empirical evidence that alcohol advertising has any substantial effect on actual alcohol consumption by adolescents. Although both the level of alcohol consumption among adolescents and the level of alcohol advertising are substantial and well documented, the link between the two has been a controversial subject in the absence of that empirical evidence. A report by the National Bureau of Economic Research (NBER), *Alcohol Advertising and Alcohol Consumption by Adolescents*, expressly sought to fill this gap in 2003. Its conclusion was that "a complete ban on all alcohol advertising could reduce adolescent participation [in the consumption of alcoholic beverages] by about 24 percent and binge participation by about 42 percent." In related findings, the NBER report concluded:

> A 100 percent increase in alcohol prices would be needed
> to reduce adolescent monthly participation by 28 per-
> cent ... and binge participation by 51 percent. The effect
> of a complete elimination of alcohol advertising would
> be similar to a 100 percent increase in alcohol prices....
> As a result, both advertising and price policies are shown
> to have the potential to substantially reduce adolescent
> alcohol participation.

A 1999 Federal Trade Commission report documents that the damaging effects of underage drinking include reduced educational attainment, increased fatal motor vehicle crashes, increased suicide attempts, and increases in sexually transmitted diseases. (The probability of alcohol problems in adulthood also increases as the age of alcohol use decreases.) Such costly damage has been shown to be partly the result of "the stuff that dreams are made of," as such dreams are exploited by the American advertising industry's appeal to our children.

Conclusions

In sum, consideration of all the evidence presented in this chapter and in the introduction to this book supports the following conclusions:

(1) Beginning in the mid-nineteenth century, commercial advertising and salesmanship, in combination with the wider availability of consumer credit, largely contributed to the unprecedented prosperity of the United States. American consumerism in its early and middle stages also contributed to the dissolution of rigid class barriers based on access to consumer commodities, expansion of the American middle class and general public affluence, and development of a more egalitarian nation both socially and economically.

(2) As late as the early 1980s, commercial advertising continued to play a positive role in the economic well-being of the

United States. Its role in American society had not yet expanded to the point that it was souring many of the sweet experiences of daily life or was oppressively commercializing the most widely celebrated holiday season of the year or was substantially contributing to widespread personal financial insolvency or, through the volume, content, and intensity of advertising directed to children, was significantly contributing to increased impairment of their mental and physical health.

(3) By the end of the twentieth and beginning of the twenty-first century, however, American commercial advertisers had, through their relentless, ubiquitous fueling of consumeritis, helped transform American culture almost thoroughly into one of buying and selling, largely through its promotion of "dreams" of a kind that

> *... are the children of an idle brain*
> *Begot of nothing but vain fantasy*
> *Which is as thin of substance as the air*
> *And more inconsistent than the wind.*
> —Shakespeare, *Romeo and Juliet*

(4) The volume and accumulated force of these advertisers' appeals to our hopes and dreams substantially justifies the hypothesis that American commercial advertising has, to a great extent, brought about each of the injuries referred to in the second conclusion stated above, so that advertising has not only become *too much* of a good thing but the progenitor of a nightmare of threats to the quality of daily life in the United States, to the physical and mental well-being of Americans, and to their pursuits of happiness.

The precise ways in which consumeritis adversely affects our pursuits of happiness is the main subject of the next chapter.

Notes

15 *But ya gotta know the territory*   This line is from *The Music Man*, produced and directed by Morton Da Costa, written by Meredith Willson and Franklin Lacey, with Robert Preston as Professor Harold C. Hill (Warner Brothers, 1962).

The most prosperous economies of the developed nations   Adam Smith (1723–1790), in his classic work, *The Wealth of Nations* (1776), is the iconic eighteenth-century advocate of the economic benefits of a free enterprise system, guided by the "invisible hand" of individual self-interest: "It is not from the benevolence of the butcher, the brewer, or the baker that we expect our dinner, but from their regard to their own interest. We address ourselves not to their humanity, but to their self-love, and never talk to them of our own necessities, but of their advantage." *Wealth of Nations*, book 1, chapter 2. In the nineteenth century, Karl Marx (1818–1883), in his classic work, *Das Kapital* (1867), described the progress of the industrial revolution to his era, and accurately predicted many of the features of a market-driven capitalist system, such as the necessity for continual product innovation, for the long term of which he predicted great difficulties. As his editor, Frederick Engels (1820–1895) wrote in his preface to the first English translation of *Das Kapital*, "While the productive power increases in a geometric, the extension of markets proceeds at best in an arithmetic ratio." For an interesting early twentieth-century account of *The Rise of Modern Industry*, see the book by that name by J. L. Hammond and Barbara Hammond (New York: Harcourt, Brace, 1926). It traces the development of global commerce from its origins serving the aristocracy through its evolution in service to people in general, reminding us that commodities we now take for granted were once available for consumption only to a privileged few: "The discovery of the Atlantic routes [in the late fifteenth and early sixteenth centuries] caused ... a revolution that took some centuries to produce its full effect. Commerce began to assume not merely a new scale, but a new character... It shipped popular cargoes.... For commerce had begun to provide for the many; to depend on popular consumption; to enter into the daily life of the ordinary man ... Tea, when first imported by the East India Company, was a highly prized luxury, but by the middle of the 18th century it was a popular drink" (at p. 21).

American workers have been working more hours every year than workers in Europe   See *Happiness*, 50.

In The History of Consumer Credit, *Rosa-Maria Gelpi and François Julien-Labruyère*   Unless otherwise indicated, all quoted material in this section of chapter 1 comes from Gelpi and Labruyère, *The History of Consumer Credit* (New York: St. Martin's Press, 2000, translated from

the French by Mme. Liam Gavin; hereafter Gelpi and Julien-Labruyère);
more specifically, from chapter 7, the introduction to part II, and chapter 8. The first two quotations in this section from Benjamin Franklin's
Poor Richard's Almanac, and Adam Smith's *The Wealth of Nations* are as
quoted by Gelpi and Julien-Labruyère at pp. 85–86. (The third Franklin
quote is spurious.) The authors concentrate their study of modern consumer credit in the United States as "both the oldest and most highly
developed modern consumer credit market in the world," pointing out
that for this reason "the United States affords the best overview of [the
history of modern consumer] credit available. Gelpi emphasizes the
sharp difference between the American and European views of consumer credit persisting to the present day: "All the bad connotations
of America which can be summed up in two words, that is, 'too much,'
are to be found in the famous household debt rate (between 17 percent
and 20 percent of available income in recent years) which is cheerfully
blamed for a wealth of evils, a plethora of sins! Woe betide us the day
we reach the American level, seems to be the tacit refrain of European
consumer authorities and associations. As if it were a demon to be
avoided! At the same time, the same people do all in their power to
import the lessons of American consumerism.... What Europeans are
prone to consider as a fault in the economic system, is in fact the sign
of a modern day open society.... Whether we look at its social role or its
economic function, consumer credit constitutes one of the driving forces
in the American success story." Gelpi and Julien-Labruyère, 112–113.

16 *Could the Emperor Tiberius* J. Bradford DeLong, *Cornucopia: The
Pace of Economic Growth in the Twentieth Century, Working Paper
7602, National Bureau of Economic Research, Cambridge, MA 02138,
March 2000 (hereafter DeLong), fn. 2, p. 3. The abstract of this paper
reads as follows: "There is one central fact about the economic history
of the twentieth century: above all, the century just past has been the
century of increasing material wealth and economic productivity. No
previous era and no previous economy have seen material wealth and
productive potential grow at such a pace. The bulk of America's population today achieves standards of material comfort and capabilities that
were beyond the reach of even the richest of previous centuries. Even
lower middle-class households in relatively poor countries have today
material standards of living that would make them, in many respects,
the envy of the powerful and lordly of past centuries." In light of the
scope of European (and especially British) industry of the period, Adam
Smith, at the end of the first chapter of *The Wealth of Nations*, likewise
favorably compared the relatively high standard of living of Europeans
of even modest means at the end of the eighteenth century to potentates
in less developed parts of the world: "[W]e shall be sensible that without
the assistance and co-operation of many thousands, the very meanest
person in a civilized country could not be provided, even according
to, what we very falsely imagine, the easy and simple manner in which

he is commonly accommodated. Compared, indeed, with the more extravagant luxury of the great, his accommodation must no doubt appear extremely simple and easy; and yet it may be true, perhaps, that the accommodation of an European prince does not always so much exceed that of an industrious and frugal peasant, as the accommodation of the latter exceeds that of many an African king, the absolute master of the lives and liberties of ten thousand naked savages."

19 *traveling salesmen of exactly the kind represented by Professor Harold C. Hill in Meredith Willson's* The Music Man   *The Music Man* is a musical *comedy* about a traveling salesman. What some regard as the greatest American *tragedy* ever written is also about a traveling salesman, Willie Loman, the title character in Arthur Miller's 1949 play *Death of A Salesman* (New York: Penguin Books, 1998), which was made into a movie in 1951 directed by Laslo Benedek and starring Frederic March as Willie Loman. *Death of A Salesman* was also produced as a television movie in 1985 by CBS Television, in a version directed by Volker Schlondoff and starring Dustin Hoffman as Willie. The salesman's tragedy is his delusional American dream about the path to material success. The play ends at his graveside, where his wife, Linda, says "Attention must be paid to such a person."

21 *less than that of the U.S. in 1900*   The growth in U.S. GDP during the past century has also been remarkable. "U.S. GDP in 2000 … comes to an annual real GDP per worker (measured in dollars of the 2000's purchasing power) of $65,540. Back in 1890 … the GDP (at the year 2000's prices) was 300 billion dollars. With an 1890 labor force of 21.8 million that translates into an annual real GDP per worker in 1890 of $13,700." DeLong, 11. American GDP per capita has thus increased five times in the past century.

may even form part of the twisted rationale for international terrorism   See, for example, Trudy Govier, *A Delicate Balance: What Philosophy Can Tell Us About Terrorism* (Boulder, CO: Westview Press, 2002, 98): "Things such as foreign policies, repressive governments, deficiencies in educational institutions, resentments and humiliation, and religiously grounded hatred really are underlying causes of anti-American and anti-Western terrorism. These factors provide the contexts in which Islamist terrorists and terrorism grow. They have a genuine causal role, they are not irrelevant, and they provide part of the explanation of the events of September 11th and other anti-American and anti-Western attacks." For an express Islamic indictment and rejection of American consumerism, see Wael Nafee, "Cultural Imperialism: The Deadliest Export" (hereafter, "Cultural Imperialism"), Muslim Students for Universal Justice (July 18, 2005), *www.msuj.org/aritcle.php?id=29,* quoted at length in chapter 7 of this book. See also "Communication and Dakwah" by Andi Faisal Bakti, in Wayne Nelles, ed. *Terrorism and Human Security: From Critical Pedagogy to Peacebuilding?* (New York: Palgrave

Macmillan, 2003, 114–115): "Capitalism is seen [by some Muslims] as a possible road to materialism, leading Muslims to abandon spirituality (become nihilistic), and to accumulate wealth without limits. For Dewan Dakwah, rich people, following the Islamic teaching, should share their wealth with the needy. Moreover, there is a fear that capitalism would simply accelerate the exploitation of the natural resources of the Muslim world. Dewan Dakwah preaches caution to the Muslims in that respect. Capitalism, in addition to materialism and nihilism, is seen as 'basically tyrannical and corrupted,' and functions at the expense of people in the developing world, in particular in the Muslim world. Thus, a Muslim has the right to reject them...."

Americans live simply to work See, for example, *Happiness*, 50–51; and John Drake, *Downshifting: How to Work Less and Enjoy Life More* (San Francisco: Berrett-Koehler Publishers, 2000).

while it has risen in Europe See *Happiness*, 50–51.

22 *people (6 percent) earning more than $50,000 a year who say they have achieved the American dream* "Harper's Index," *Harper's Magazine* (October 1998), 15.

23 *Warner Brothers released its film version of Charles Dickens's classic David Copperfield* Produced by David O. Selznick, directed by George Cukor, screenplay by Hugh Walpole and Howard Esterbrook (Warner Brothers Studios, 1935).

autobiographic novel Charles Dickens, *David Copperfield* (1850).

24 *In 2004, consumer credit-card debt* Federal Reserve Board; Consumer Credit Outstanding (hereafter Federal Reserve Board) (G.19), *www.federalreserve.gov/releases/g19/hist/cc_hist_mt.html* (accessed August, 2005).

number of [bankruptcy] filings in 1980 On average, the debt load for people filing for personal bankruptcy equals twenty-two months of income. *Affluenza*, 20. U.S. Bankruptcy Filings 1980–2004 (Business, Non-Business, Total) (March 2005), *www.uscourts.gov/bnkrpctystats/statistics.htm#march* (accessed October 2005).

American consumer debt as a percentage of the nation's gross domestic product (GDP) Federal Reserve Board.

25 *wealthier than their great-grandparents at the turn of the century* As to relative wealth: Alan Durning, *How Much Is Enough? The Consumer Society and the Future of the Earth* (New York: Norton, 1992, 23); as to increase in residential space: Alan Durning, *Save the Forest: What Will It Take?* Worldwatch Paper #117 (Worldwatch Institute, 1993), 33.

Compared with their grandparents, today's young adults have grown up with much more affluence David G. Meyers, Ph.D., "Our Becoming

Much Better Off Over the Last Four Decades Has Not Been Accompanied by One Iota of Increased Subjective Well-Being," *American Psychologist* vol. 55, no. 1 (January, 2000), quoted in Tori DeAngelis, "Consumerism and its Discontents," *Monitor on Psychology*, vol. 35, no. 6 (June 2004).

Examination of American personal spending during the past twenty-five years or so indicates that the malignant form of consumeritis began to strike Americans severely in the early 1980s The PCE–GDP and disposable income data in this paragraph come from the Department of Commerce, Bureau of Economic Analysis, current as of September 2005. As to the hypothesis that consumeritis began its malignant phase in the early 1980s, see figs. 1.1–1.4 relating to personal consumer expenditures (PCE) and consumer credit. *The History of Consumer Credit* points out that "the financial innovations and reforms of the 1980's abolished constraints limiting credit offers.... Therefore, consumer credit continued to progress rapidly during the 1980's, apart from the period of economic recession from 1980 to 1982 ... It was favored not only by the intensification of financial competition and the development of the use of credit cards, but also by a decrease of lending rates from the temporary highs of the early 1980's. The growth of credit continued in the second half of the 1980's, thanks to home equity loans which, by doing away with the distinction between consumer and mortgage credit, allowed for longer repayment periods and enabled people to equip their homes with the mortgage guarantee." Gelpi and Julien-Labruyère, chapter 8, 107.

26   *the Japanese savings rate* In *Affluenza*, 21. In "[U.S. Treasury Secretary] Snow Urges Consumerism on China Trip," a story in the *New York Times* on October 13, 2005, Edmund L. Andrews writes that "China's savings rate is nearly 50 percent ... The savings rate in the U.S.... has sunk to less than zero in recent months and is one of the lowest rates in the world."

27   *Eisenhower warned in his 1960 farewell address* Dwight D. Eisenhower, *Military-Industrial Complex Speech* (Public Papers of the Presidents, 1960, 1035–1040), *coursesa.matrix.msu.edu/~hst306/documents/indust. html* (accessed October 2005). "This conjunction of an immense military establishment and a large arms industry is new in the American experience. The total influence—economic, political, even spiritual—is felt in every city, every State house, every office of the Federal government. We recognize the imperative need for this development. Yet we must not fail to comprehend its grave implications. Our toil, resources and livelihood are all involved; so is the very structure of our society. In the councils of government, we must guard against the acquisition of unwarranted influence, whether sought or unsought, by the military-industrial complex. The potential for the disastrous rise of misplaced power exists and will persist. *We must never let the weight of this combination endanger our liberties or democratic processes.* We should

take nothing for granted. Only an alert and knowledgeable citizenry can compel the proper meshing of the huge industrial and military machinery of defense with our peaceful methods and goals, so that security and liberty may prosper together" (emphasis added).

I seek to trace the novel features   Alexis de Tocqueville (1805–1859), *Democracy in America* (hereafter Tocqueville) vol. 2, 4ᵗʰ book, chapter 6, "What Sort of Despotism Democratic Nations Have to Fear" (1840), (New York: Alfred A. Knopf, 1972), 318.

28 *A Night at the Opera*   Produced and directed by Sam Wood; written by James Kevin McGuiness, George S. Kaufman, and Morrie Ryskind (MGM Studios, 1935); starring the Marx brothers.

29 *Americans have become the most voracious consumers*   The comparative consumption figures are per capita ratios in constant 1995 U.S. dollars taken from *World Development Indicators 2004* (from the World Bank data base), showing 2002 consumption expenditures in each country, and dividing these figures by each country's population. The U.S./EU ratio (actually 1.49) is based on figures that do not include four small EU nation economies, the addition of which would not appreciably affect the ratio given. Using the same database would show the U.S./Japan consumption ratio to be 0.8; taking into account, however, purchasing power parity equivalence, per capita U.S. consumption figures also would be greater than those of Japan at a ratio of 1.3 or 1.5, depending on whether constant or current currency units are used.

halfway to the moon   In *Affluenza*, a documentary film based on the book previouly cited (hereafter *Affluenza* film), 35:10–35:27.

spend only forty minutes a week playing with their children   Originally cited in Betsy Morris, "Big Spenders: As a Favored Pastime, Shopping Ranks High with Most Americans," *Wall Street Journal*, July 30, 1987, as referenced on page 6 of *The All-Consuming Passion* (1998 pamphlet produced by the New Road Map Foundation and Northwest Environmental Watch), which was cited in *Affluenza*, 14.

Potomac Mills shopping mall. It is such a popular tourist destination   In *Affluenza*, 14.

31 *we've become too materialistic, too greedy, too selfish*   Quoting Richard Harwood in *Affluenza* film, 2:19–34.

They likewise associate consumeritis with a "rampant individualism [that] has become increasingly the norm,"   In *Happiness*, 91.

our children are not just materialistic but that they're "very materialistic."   Quoting Richard Harwood in *Affluenza*, 3.

our profession right now   Allen D. Kanner quoted by Melissa Dittman in "Protecting Children from Advertising." *Monitor on Psychology*, vol. 35, no. 6 (June 2004), *www.apa.org/monitor/jun04/consumetoc.html* (accessed October 2005).

forty thousand TV commercials a year Melissa Dittman, "Protecting Children from Advertising. *Monitor on Psychology,* vol. 35, no. 6 (June 2004). This statistic is evidently based on the study reported by Kunkel, "Children and Television Advertising," in the *Handbook of Children and the Media,* D. Singer and J. Singer, eds. (Thousand Oaks, CA: Sage Publications, 2001), 375–393. The forty thousand figure has no doubt grown. Citing Kunkel, the Henry J. Kaiser Family Foundation's February 2004 *Issue Brief,* in the article "The Role of Media in Childhood Obesity," states (at p. 4): "In the late 1970's, researchers estimated that children viewed a average of about 20,000 TV commercials a year; in the late 1980's, that estimate grew to more than 30,000 a year. As the number of cable channels exploded in the 1990's, opportunities to advertise directly to children expanded as well. The most recent estimates are that children now see an average of more than 40,000 TV ads a year." *www.apa.org/monitor/jun04/consumetoc.html* (accessed October 2005).

The present annual advertising budget to young "consumers" is now about $15 billion Susan Lin, Harvard Medical School, in *Consuming Kids* (New Press, 2004), and references cited therein, as referenced by Karen Kersting, "Driving teen egos—and buying—through 'branding,'" *APA Online Monitor on Psychology,* vol. 35, 6, 2004, *www.apa.org/monitor/jun04/driving.html* (accessed October 2005). The Lin article that forms the authority for these figures is at *www.jbcc.harvard.edu/publications/05_youthmarketingsurvey.pdf* (accessed September 26, 2005).

incidence of childhood obesity and diabetes See *Affluenza,* 53: "Indeed 90% of food ads on Saturday morning children's programs still hawk high-calorie, sugary, or salt-laden items. Combine that with the time children spend in front of the tube and it's not surprising that children today are far more likely to be obese (obesity rates among American children doubled in the 1980s alone) than they were in the early days of television." As to the rate of childhood obesity, it is estimated that 30 percent of school children are overweight. A condition "that can mean future cardiovascular disease," according to a new study reported in the *San Francisco Chronicle* on September 22, 2005, under the headline "Teens' blood vessels show body fats' effects."

32 *Undergraduate credit-card debt* Jill Norvilitis quoted in Lea Winerman, "Maxed Out: Why Do Some Succumb and Others Steer Clear?" *Monitor on Psychology* vol. 35, no. 6 (June 2004), *www.apa.org/monitor/jun04/consumetoc.html* (accessed October 2005).

distress from consumeritis may be felt most keenly by conscientious adults James E. Burroughs and Aric Rindfleisch, "Materialism and Well-Being: A Conflicting Values Perspective," vol. 29, no. 3 (December 2002), quoted in Tori DeAngelis, "Consumerism and Its Discontents," vol. 35, no. 6 (June 2004) *www.apa.org/monitor/jun04/consumetoc.html* (accessed October 2005).

Dashiell Hammett's detective novel Dashiell Hammett. *The Maltese Falcon* (New York: Alfred A. Knopf, 1929). Hammett lived from 1894 to 1961. The novel was made into a Warner Brothers movie in 1941, written and directed by John Huston, and produced by Hal B. Wallace and Henry Blanke.

33 *the Knights of Malta* The Knights Hospitallers of the Order of St. John of Jerusalem, known as the Order of St. John, were founded in 1048; they were based in Malta from 1530 to 1798 and hence were also called the Knights of Malta. They were "hospitallers" to knights returning to Western Europe from the Crusades.

Sell them their dreams James Twitchell, "Two Cheers for Materialism," *Utne Reader* (November/December, 2000) as quoted in *Affluenza*, 138.

34 *the ultimate source of information* "Advertisement That Really Works. Promoting Dreams Instead of Just Products and Services," *AdMotor* (June 8, 2005), *hardware.admotor.com/advertisementthatreallyworks promotingdreamsinsteadofjustproductsandservices.html.*

Realize your dream "1000 Headlines," *Seven Design Avenue, www. 7designavenue.com/promote/1000.htm* (accessed October 2005).

The amount of money American businesses spend The economic data in this paragraph are derived from U.S. Statistical Abstracts 2005 (table no. 1274); see table 1.1 in this book.

35 *three thousand commercial messages a day* Carlin Flora, "Consumerism: One Choice Too Many," in *Psychology Today* online, citing and quoting Barry Schwartz, *The Paradox of Choice* (New York: HarperCollins, 2004), *cms.psychologytoday.com/articles/pto-20040116-000001.html* (accessed October 2005).

36 *Development of the Internet* The source for the e-mail statistics in this paragraph is *Spam Statistics*, 2004, downloaded September 17, 2005, from *spam-filter-review.toptenreviews.com.spam-statistics.html.* Spam e-mail is divided into nine categories: (1) products, 23 percent; (2) financial, 20 percent; (3) adult, 19 percent; (4) health, 7 percent; (5) internet, 7 percent; (6) leisure, 6 percent; (7) scams, 9 percent; (8) spiritual, 4 percent; and (9) other, 3 percent. For the sake of a conservative estimate, only the first seven of these categories were used as the basis in the text for calculating the percentage of spam e-mails that constitute commercial advertising and marketing messages, although category (9) might have been included, and some e-mails in all of the categories may be commercial offerings.

37 *To young children, advertising is just as credible* Melissa Dittman, "Protecting children from advertising," *APA Online Monitor on Psychology,* June 2004, quoting Kunkel, *www.apa.org/monitor/jun04/protecting. html* (accessed October 2005).

According to a 2004 market research report In *The U.S. Kids Market: Understanding the Trends and Lifestyles Affecting 3- to 12-Year-Olds*, Packaged Facts, A division of MarketResearch.com, 6th Edition, April 2004, *www.PackagedFacts.com* (accessed October 2005).

industry research shows that kids are among the fastest growing online audiences See the cover story in the March 27, 2006 edition of *Time* magazine, "Are Kids Too Wired for Their Own Good?"

38 *The case of teenagers is different* See *The U.S. Teens Market: Understanding the Changing Lifestyles and Trends of 12- to 19-Year Olds*, Packaged Facts, A division of MarketResearch.com, 5th ed., August 2002, *www.marketresearch.com*. A recent study, reported on September 28, 2005, in the *Christian Science Monitor* in a story titled "We swim in an ocean of media," shows that "this media multitasking, which the researchers call Concurrent Media Exposure" is not the province of only the young or the tech savvy. "All age groups multitask, though the pairings may be different." The reported research, a project of the Institute for the Future, a Palo Alto think tank, documents its assertion that "the world is seeing a 'Cambrian explosion' of media."

a startling increase in the obesity of the young The entire discussion that follows this phrase, including all quoted matter, from pages 38 through 40, on the increase in childhood obesity and its relationship to advertising directed at children and children's media use, comes from the article, "The Role of Media in Childhood Obesity" in the Kaiser Foundation *Issue Brief* of February 2004.

41 *the damaging effects and costs of increased adolescent alcohol consumption* The entire discussion that follows this phrase, including all quoted matter on pages 41 and 42 on the relationship of adolescent alcohol consumption and advertising, comes from the National Bureau of Economics Research paper, *Alcohol Advertising and Alcohol Consumption by Adolescents*.

42 *A report by the National Bureau of Economic Research* Working Paper 9676, by Henry Saffer and Dhaval Dave, May 2003, *www.nber.org/papers/w9676* (accessed October 2005). This report is also the source for the summary of the 1999 FTC report referred to in the following paragraph.

Charlie Sheen as Bud Fox (left) and Michael Douglas as Gordon Gekko in *Wall Street* (20th Century Fox, 1987)

2

Life, Liberty, and Our Pursuit of Happiness: The Struggle with Ourselves in a Culture of Buying and Selling

> *Materialism appears to work against people's*
> *attainment of well-being. A question then is how*
> *a modern nation can continue to experience the*
> *benefits of economic growth...and yet dampen*
> *the excessive materialism that seems toxic.*
> —Solberg, Diener, and Robinson, "Why
> Are Materialists Less Satisfied?"

> *In the West we have a society that is probably as*
> *happy as any there has ever been. But ... there*
> *is a danger that me-first may pollute our way of*
> *life ... The obvious aim is the greater happiness*
> *of all. If we all really pursued that, we should all*
> *be less selfish, and we should also be happier.*
> —Richard Layard, *Happiness*

FACTS ARE BETTER than dreams," Winston Churchill wrote at the very end of the first volume of his great history, *The Second World War.* A purer bred Englishman than Churchill (who was half American and an honorary U.S. citizen by the end of his life) poetically asserted, however, that we human beings are ourselves "such stuff as dreams are made on." It is a great part of our human imagination (and an expression of our higher nature) to find it even a noble thing "to dream the impossible dream," and to pursue goals that may be beyond our grasp. "A man's reach," the poet Robert Browning writes, "should exceed his grasp/Or what's a heaven for?" Even though commercial advertising may often exploit our dreams to the point of injury, most of us would not want to abandon the kinds of dreams that are the stuff of our legitimate human aspirations; dreams that help keep alive in us the possibility of a fulfilling, happy life. Among the questions most of us ask ourselves at one time or another, from youth to old age, are What kind of a life is most likely to bring happiness? Is it possible for me to have such a life?

Part of the miracle that has been the United States of America is the fact that its first founding document, our Declaration of Independence, explicitly asserted that it was among the purposes of government to secure our rights to "life, liberty, and the pursuit of happiness." If American materialism, aggravated by consumeritis, is not only failing to make many Americans happy, despite their affluence, but is even making many Americans unhappy, what can we do in our individual lives to rescue our right to be happy from the harmful excesses of materialism? This is a struggle that many Americans are having with themselves, and it is the purpose of this chapter to discuss this struggle on the way to considering possible remedies for the damage consumeritis has been doing to us.

The Errant Roots of Consumeritis

Auntie Mame is a 1958 movie based on a novel of the same name by the author Patrick Dennis, and is rooted in the author's experiences. It has much to say about the joys of life. It is the story of an orphaned boy, also named Patrick, whose care is entrusted to his Aunt Mame. Auntie Mame is a free spirit without racial, religious, ethnic, or class prejudices, who doesn't let misfortune get her down. (She is portrayed in the movie, exuberantly and magnificently, by Rosalind Russell.) When Patrick, a timid and frightened ten-year-old boy, first arrives from Chicago at his aunt's New York apartment, Mame takes him in with as much love as if he were her natural son. Her animated warmth dispels Patrick's fears and leads him to love his Auntie Mame as much as she loves him. The attitude Mame communicates to Patrick is that, in her words, "Life is a banquet, and most poor suckers are starving to death."

The story begins in the 1920s, when Auntie Mame is rich—until the Wall Street crash of 1929, when she is broke. Undaunted, she takes a series of jobs for which she is wholly unsuited to help keep herself and Patrick afloat. Her high spirits attract a wealthy man who falls in love with her, and they marry. When he is killed in a mountaineering accident, Mame is encouraged by her friends to write an autobiography, which she titles *Live, Live, Live*.

While Mame is writing her book, Patrick (who is by then in college) falls in love with a girl named Gloria Upson. After learning about Patrick's intention to marry Gloria—whom Mame later describes as "an Aryan from Darien with braces on her brain"—Mame arranges to visit Gloria's parents at their home in an "exclusive and restricted" Connecticut suburb. The Upsons are shallow bigots, self-impressed with their high-middle-class station in life. They assume Auntie Mame shares their snobbish attitudes, and accept Mame's invitation to a party celebrating the engagement. Mame's party arrangements are calculated to offend every prejudice of the Upsons, and expose their true character to Patrick. Gloria and her parents are thoroughly alienated from the idea of making a match with the ward of such a screwball aunt, and they leave the party in high dudgeon. Patrick needs little consoling. Before the party, he has met Pegeen, Auntie Mame's new secretary, who sees and sympathetically appreciates the comedy of Patrick's situation. They fall in love. Some years pass, and Auntie Mame invites Patrick and Pegeen's ten-year-old son, Michael, to come with her on an adventure to India. When his parents balk, young Michael reminds them that "life is a banquet, and most poor suckers are starving to death." The last scene of the movie shows Auntie Mame, in her usual exuberance, explaining to Michael what they have to look forward to together in India. If there is truth to Auntie Mame's view that life is in many ways a banquet, how is it that so many relatively affluent Americans are starving to death, apparently unable to dine at life's abundant table?

We have all been made suckers at one time or another by buying into the gimmicks of the advertising con game. As the statistics cited in chapter 1 demonstrate, we are being suckered into consumeritis at a greater and greater cost. In a culture of buying and selling, how can we fail to be ensnared on occasion by the seductive allure of the persistent glowing claims of advertising? As we have seen though, Americans are becoming increasingly wary of the insanities associated with consumeritis; some of the unhappiest people among us are those who still respect higher values, and feel some conflict between their materialistic strivings and the higher values they accept as valid. Many Americans nevertheless continue to be infected by consumeritis despite themselves, running a materialistic treadmill instead of enjoying the feast of life in more satisfying ways. Why is this so?

First of all, there is a strictly internal cause, one that has little or nothing to do with commercial advertising. Consumeritis—the habit of buying things we don't really need or can't afford—gives us something to do that we can think is worth doing. The seventeenth-century French mathematician and philosopher Blaise Pascal, in his soul-searching *Pensées,* pointed out:

> Nothing is so insufferable to man as to be completely at rest, without passions, without business, without diversion, without study. He then feels his nothingness, his forlornness, his insufficiency, his dependence, his weakness, his emptiness. [Without having something to do] there will immediately arise from the depth of his heart weariness, gloom, sadness, fretfulness, vexation, despair.

Getting and spending helps us to fill our time and avoid thinking too much. "If you want to assure your own misery," George Sand wrote to her daughter, "think about yourself." This is even more true if we've had a bad day or a bad week: shopping to give ourselves a gift, whether big or small, is a common way to give ourselves a lift as well, mitigating feelings of depression, boredom, or emptiness. (Some even call it retail therapy.) There is, of course, nothing intrinsically wrong or pathological about wanting to acquire things; the ability to do so is an ability to master part of our lives. The desire to acquire possessions is a natural, healthy aspect of our human being; it is not even foreign to the habits of other living creatures. But when occupying ourselves with the acquisition of things constitutes, in large part, an escapist habit, it assumes the dimensions of a pathology at least akin to consumeritis, and also diminishes the opportunity for us to enjoy more significant occupations.

The second, and the most dynamic, external cause of American consumeritis is the fact that American culture has become, more than anything else, a culture of buying and selling. "The business of America is business"—"busy-ness"?—fueled by commercial advertising. As the data summarized and annotated in chapter 1 demonstrate, the air that Americans breathe is virtually permeated by commercial advertising, compelling Americans to be constantly conscious of offers to buy goods and services, their availability, and ways to pay for them. Commercial advertising is visible almost everywhere, indoors and out, and the most popular American events and leisure activities—such as professional sports and television—have become the venue for the most intense advertising of all. Having been exposed to as many as one million advertisements by the age of twenty, it is hardly any wonder that urban Americans have consumeritis as an endemic characteristic of the their consciousness, and as an epidemic addiction. After being told so often (forty thousand times a year or more, and perhaps as much as three thousand times a day) that we ought to buy the things that our culture of buying and selling ubiquitously advertises, we are inevitably disposed to think that shopping is not only a natural but a good thing to do, at least if we can find the means to acquire what we (or those close to us) think or feel we (or they) would like to have.

The third reason is a mixture of the internal and external: we are social animals, and the quest for social "equality of condition," is, as Tocqueville carefully explained, the essence of the democratic spirit. "Keeping up with the Joneses" is almost a democratic imperative of principle. It is, moreover, an inherent characteristic of the social creatures we are: we like to be liked. What the economist Thorsten Veblen (1857–1929) called "conspicuous consumption" is a social habit. As Veblen observed, people living in a city or its environs are under considerable social pressure (even if they don't like to admit it) to keep up with the Joneses. It is also a natural human inclination to want to be respected by our peers and, as Veblen also pointed out:

> The consumption of luxuries ... is a consumption directed to the comfort of the consumer himself, and is, therefore, a mark of the master.... The basis on which good repute in any highly organized community ultimately rests is pecuniary strength; and the means of showing pecuniary strength, and so of gaining or retaining a good name, are leisure and a conspicuous consumption of goods.

Veblen further noted that, as the industrial (and now the technological) revolution progresses, the perceived value of conspicuous consumption as the basis for gaining social respect increasingly surpasses the value of leisure. This may help to explain why so many Americans (and younger people in particular, who tend not to worry too much about securing the leisure of their retirement years) have been increasing their consumer spending at the expense of their savings and at the risk of excessive debt. If we are young, we can easily be led to believe that a sexier car, more fashionable clothing, and owning the latest technological toy will increase our chances to make ourselves more appealing to others and achieve greater social acceptance. In its typical dream-selling, the bulk of commercial advertising—TV advertising most of all—at least strongly implies that higher social status and greater popularity, or even finding the kind of love we most crave will be the result of our conspicuous, trendy consumption of advertised products. If we are more mature, advertising appeals that lead to overspending may be similarly rationalized by persuading ourselves that our long hours and years of labor entitle us to enjoy as many luxuries as we can get, even though we have to increase our indebtedness to obtain them.

These emotionally triggered rationalizations have a further social dimension. American culture may retain a Puritan work ethic to some degree, but unlike the original Puritans, few

Americans today would say there is anything intrinsically wrong with seeking and finding our own material pleasures. Since we live in what is probably the most highly materialistic culture on earth, little, if any, social blame is associated with our enjoying ourselves in the acquisition of things to give ourselves pleasure; indeed, it is widely expected that we will do that whether or not we can really afford it. Those who have the least spend the little money they have to get whatever things they can; those of us who are more affluent generally feel no social guilt about giving a higher priority to our consumeritis than to the needs of the invisible poor, though we may feel some twinge of guilt or even shame when we are confronted directly by them at a moment of excessive spending. And, whatever the sacrifice of our financial security may be on the altar of consumeritis, and however tran-sient such pleasure is, we cannot deny that acquiring the things we'd like to have does indeed give us pleasure. The issue is not only whether such pleasures are costing us more than we can afford but whether they are in fact unnecessarily diverting us from pursuing the possibility of achieving greater satisfactions out of life than its "paltry pleasures" can ordinarily bring.

Fourth, although it may not be a *cause* of consumeritis, some socially conscious victims of consumeritis may justify their exces-sive spending by claiming (to themselves as well as to others) that their conspicuous consumption helps make the economy hum. "What's good for General Motors is good for the country." The more we spend, some may rationalize, the more we are helping to stimulate the economy and increase employment. We can there-fore believe that we may assuage any uneasiness we feel about our overspending by rationalizing our consumeritis addiction as a social good, something that is benefiting the community and helping others.

So, apart from the financial risks of the overspending that helps to drive more and more Americans into bankruptcy, what is it about consumeritis that should trouble us *personally*? Let's consider each of the four main considerations just offered as an explanation or rationalization for consumeritis despite ourselves.

The 1939 movie classic *The Wizard of Oz* was based on a much loved children's book by Frank Baum (1856–1919). It is about the dream of a girl named Dorothy, or so it would seem. Dorothy is played in the film by the young Judy Garland. At the beginning of the movie, we are introduced to Dorothy's life on a farm in Kansas, her family, and a mean-spirited neighbor (played by Margaret Hamilton) who threatens to kidnap Dorothy's dog, Toto. On her way home, in the midst of efforts to protect Toto, Dorothy is caught in a cyclone. She is whisked up and away from Kansas, and finds herself transported to the magical land of Oz, where she befriends a Cowardly Lion, a Tin Man without a heart, and a Scarecrow without a brain. Though spellbound by what she finds in the colorful land of Oz, Dorothy wants above all to get home to Kansas. She is told by the good witch Glenda that to get home, she must seek the advice of the Wonderful Wizard of Oz. Since the Cowardly Lion wants the Wizard to give him courage, and the Tin Man wants a heart, and the Scarecrow wants a brain, they all join Dorothy on her way "off to see the Wizard," the journey that is the main action of the story.

After many hardships, and after overcoming many perils put in her way by the Wicked Witch of the East (also played by Margaret Hamilton), Dorothy and her friends arrive at the Wizard's palace. When they are finally admitted into his magnificent hall, the Wizard (played by Frank Morgan) appears to them in a terrible gigantic form, and then callously refuses to grant the brave, heartfelt, intelligent requests of the quartet. Dorothy is indignant at the Wizard's meanness. She becomes suspicious, and begins to doubt whether the supposedly Wonderful Wizard of Oz actually has the power to grant their requests. She looks about the hall, sees a shaking curtain, and starts toward it. As she approaches it, the Wizard's voice loudly calls out to her, "Pay no attention to that man behind the curtain!" Pulling aside the curtain, Dorothy finds an ordinary man talking through a loud-speaker and manipulating the levers of a machine projecting his own image to produce that of the giant Wizard. Caught in his act, the "Wizard" tells each of the seekers that, in fact, they already have what they want.

As Dorothy sought the truth behind a sham appearance, let us examine the four major justifications for consumeritis to see what's behind the curtain; that is, what may be deceptive about them, and how we can recognize consumeritis as a pathology leading us to neglect what we may already have that can help us secure true pursuits of happiness.

The first, and most pervasive, internal cause of consumeritis can be found in our need and drive to keep busy. Our need to buy things—to engage in the *business* of buying—commonly reflects our need for busy-ness. As Pascal pointed out, busyness helps us to avoid thinking too much about the emptier aspects of our lives. Whatever emptiness either the young or the mature may feel in the quality of their lives may appear to be most easily filled up by acquiring the *things* that advertising tells us we can buy to make our lives more pleasurable and fun and thereby, supposedly, more fulfilling. This internal quest has been complicated by the effectiveness of commercial advertising. The cumulative pressure we feel from the deluge of advertising to which we are regularly exposed has tended to transform the express and implied dream-serving lies of advertising into practical truths, by insidiously submerging our awareness of our own needs and altering our perception of them. It is not easy always to remain conscious of the fact that the claims of advertising are not generally calculated to appeal to our rationality or deepest aspirations but, rather, are directed to our emotions. They are designed to appeal to our desire for transient pleasures—the counterfeits of happiness. To resist this appeal effectively requires us to be consistently—even stubbornly—conscious of the vagaries of life and true to ourselves. As con men know, one of the sharpest limitations of con games is the fact that "You can't cheat an honest man." But such consistent honesty, which amounts to unwavering self-respect, is difficult for anyone. Though we may be wise enough to understand that money can buy things but not happiness, we are constantly being seduced to forget that fact, and to veil our understanding with a conditioned ignoring of the limitations of materialistic pleasures. In reality, the equation by advertisers of materialistic and acquisitive pleasures with the achievement of a happy life is one emptiness appealing to another, and serious misfortune—sometimes to the point of tragedy—is often the result people suffer from being misled by this delusion.

Perhaps the earliest account in Western literature explaining the shortsightedness of equating acquisition of material abundance and pleasure with happiness is the story of Croseus and Solon told by the ancient Greek historian Herodotus (484–420 BC), in his *Histories*.

The ancient kingdom of Lydia was extended to an empire through the conquests of King Croesus, who succeeded his father to the throne in 560 BC. (This is the same person from whose name came the expression "rich as Croesus.") The Athenian lawgiver, Solon, reputed to be one of the wisest men in Greece, traveled to Sardis, the Lydian capital, to meet Croseus. According to Herodotus:

> Croesus entertained Solon hospitably in the palace, and
> three or four days after his arrival instructed some ser-
> vants to take him on a tour of the royal treasuries and
> point out the richness and magnificence of everything.
> When Solon had made as thorough an inspection as
> opportunity allowed, Croesus said: "Well, my Athenian
> friend, I have heard a great deal about your wisdom, and
> how widely you have traveled in the pursuit of knowledge.
> I cannot resist my desire to ask you a question: who is the
> happiest man you have ever seen?" The point of the ques-
> tion was that Croesus supposed himself to be the happiest
> of men. Solon, however, refused to flatter, and answered
> in strict accordance with his view of the truth.

Solon named as the happiest man he had ever seen an Athenian "who had wealth enough by Athenian standards," but who
was honored by his countrymen because he died a glorious death
in battle, bravely fighting for Athens. Croesus was, of course, taken
aback by Solon's reply, and, "thinking that he would at least be
awarded second place," asked who was the next happiest person
Solon had ever seen. In reply, Solon described the lives of two
young men who "had enough to live on comfortably," but who
died as a result of extraordinary physical exertions they had made
on their mother's behalf, and who were honored by their fellow
citizens because of that.

The story of Croesus may help us to understand why it is that
the unhappiest people in our culture of buying and selling are
those who still respect higher values, and thus feel some conflict between their materialistic strivings and the higher values
they accept. They know that mere acquisition and ownership of
things cannot adequately substitute for the gratifications of such
nonmaterial goods as love, friendship, community with others, doing well by doing what is right, and being honored and
respected not for their wealth or possessions but for the things

they do and the kind of people they are. They probably also sense that the energy spent acquiring more things than they really need (and the money or credit to buy them) may not only be a diversion from pursuit of the happiness for which they most long but can also be a snare, exposing them unnecessarily to the risk of losing what they already have. (As Herodotus tells us, Croesus did in fact lose all of his wealth.) To the extent, therefore, that our consumeritis is the result of a desire to avoid boredom or the discomfort of confronting our true condition in life, we can combat its insidious temptations by listening more honestly to the better angels of our own nature; that is, by finding better ways to occupy our time, ways that may bring us closer to others for reasons apart from our conspicuous consumption. Such redirection of spare energies directly toward ultimate desires is in fact more likely to increase the chances that we will find the kind of happiness that love, friendship, and a deeper experience of community with others may bring. (This proposed antidote to the Pascalian roots of consumeritis relates to our further consideration below of the third most important reason many of us are willing victims of consumeritis, namely, the desire for greater social acceptance, popularity, and respectability.)

The second and most dynamic cause of the American addiction to getting and spending—the tidal wave of commercial advertising in which we drown day and night—is the most insidious one, because it constitutes an external invasion of our psyches. The ubiquity of American advertising psychologically conditions us to be, and to think of ourselves primarily as, consumers, more constantly than we are conditioned to think of ourselves in any other social role. (One of the most depressing statistics in this respect may be the fact that Americans, on average, *spend* nearly ten times as many minutes shopping than the minutes they *give* playing with their children.) The process of conditioning members of the American public to think of themselves as consumers has been actively abetted by the U.S. government, not only by its benevolent (though often ineffective) "consumer protection" agencies and their widely publicized efforts but also, as stated earlier, by such things as government agencies referring to U.S. citizens as "customers" in the recorded option menus citizens are compelled to listen to when they seek information from those agencies, including, for example, the U.S. Immigration Service.

This conditioning of Americans to think of themselves as consumers is the direct result of the ubiquitous deceptions of American advertising that led to the need for creation and strengthening of government consumer protection agencies, whose public role began to be significantly expanded in the 1960s. The progressive acceptance by Americans of their status as consumers beginning in that decade has effectively diverted us from consciousness of our primary existential human status, and what our most important concerns and dominant preoccupations should be as *persons*, that is, healthy human beings. Even in the early 1960s, most Americans would have felt more comfortable being identified and identifying themselves as citizens, a much broader human status than that of consumers or customers. At least until that period, many and perhaps even most Americans would have been offended at being relegated to mere consumer status.

Americans' conditioning to think of themselves as consumers before they think of themselves as citizens and even parents, or—perhaps most importantly—as persons, brings with it epochally significant and deeply disturbing implications. It indicates far more destructive and important consequences to our well-being and sense of humanity than the potentially adverse economic consequences of consumeritis; indeed, they are what justify coining the term "consumeritis," and identifying it as a pathology, a disease of the soul.

What does it signify to think of ourselves as consumers, before we think of ourselves as citizens or persons? At the least, it suggests that we have become conditioned to seeing our social role as willing participants in the culture of buying and selling more than we value, or remain conscious of, our political role and rights as citizens of a democratic republic. Shouldn't we be habituated to consciously identifying ourselves more with our political rights as citizens of a republic than with our status as consumers, especially in a culture of buying and selling? It is, in fact, our rights as citizens that form the basis for any protections we may claim as consumers: our right to privacy, for example, or our right to be protected by the law at all in a democratic process. (This subject is considered in detail in chapter 6, "The Political Costs of Consumeritis.") More fundamentally, if we are conditioned to think of ourselves as consumers before we think of ourselves as persons, have we not, to that extent, been conditioned to subordinate our humanity to the economic function to which we have been reduced by advertising agencies and advertisers? One of the main purposes of this book, as further articulated below, is to help you, the reader, remain more aware of your full humanity, your personhood, in resistance to the pathology of consumeritis that advertising intrinsically promotes—to our increasing economic detriment and human loss.

The insidious transformation many Americans have undergone from thinking of themselves chiefly and primarily as persons and citizens, and accustoming themselves to be regarded as consumers, has resulted, among other things, in increasing public acceptance of the consumer role, even to the extent of rationalizing that role as a social obligation. This transformation is primarily the achievement of commercial advertising. The prescription for reversing this transformation is as simple to state as it may be difficult to achieve. Rather than allowing the tidal wave of commercial advertising simply to sweep over us, pretending to ourselves that we can ignore what it is doing or that we can screen it out by only half hearing or seeing the commercials affecting our consciousness, we need to resensitize ourselves to the manipulations of advertising. If, as soon as we are conscious of any commercial advertising assaulting us, we are able to keep in the front of our minds the fact that we are individual persons and citizens, not objects to be enlisted in a culture of buying and selling, we are far more likely to begin to recover from the addictions of consumeritis and, to that extent, combat its infection. Try this for only a day or two, and see what difference it may make in the extent you are able to perceive the true stature of your own humanity, and thereby resist manipulation by the culture of buying and selling. To this extent, at least, you may find that "facts are better than dreams."

The third important cause of consumeritis is the social support we find for it, and an ingrained conventional impulse, whether admitted or not, to "keep up with the Joneses." The fact that most of us resist admitting to ourselves that keeping up with the Joneses may be a significant part of the motivation for spending money on things for which we have no essential need is a revealing indication of our own deep disapproval of this impulse, and our inner rejection of it as a meritorious guide to the conduct of our own individual lives. (To put it somewhat harshly, as the French cynic La Rochefoucauld [1613–1680] did, "Hypocrisy is the homage which vice pays to virtue.")

Our Declaration of Independence acknowledges a common

human duty to have "a decent respect for the opinions of mankind." But the impulse or habit of keeping up with the Joneses is not really a decent respect for the Joneses' humanity or their opinions. Rather, as most of us implicitly recognize, it usually amounts to subservience to the tastes and buying habits of others stimulated by advertising, and—perhaps even more significantly—a lack of sufficient self-respect to make our purchasing judgments solely on the basis of our own individual needs, to satisfy our habits, perspectives, and even subjective tastes. Veblen astutely observes that conspicuous consumption is a social habit to which we have become accustomed in order to earn the respect of others. We can learn a lot from Veblen's perceptions of human nature in society, particularly from his observation that visibly enjoying our leisure also promotes the respect of our peers.

There is nothing intrinsically wrong in wanting to have the respect of our neighbors and of our community. Indeed, it is an important characteristic of our humanity. You will remember that according to Herodotus, Solon told Croesus that the three people he considered the happiest were people who were respected and honored by their communities. As old Aristotle also observed, human beings are social animals, and "who would live alone is either a beast or a god." We may therefore find an agreeable and constructive remedy to the harmful effects of the social conventions and pressures that contribute to consumeritis by valuing our own leisure at least as much as we value our neighbors' acquisition of possessions. Enjoying our own leisure time as we ourselves choose is a demonstration of social status that is likely to earn us as much if not more respect than matching the material acquisitions of others. The next time you notice someone buying something about which you may feel a bit of envy or lust of acquisition (presuming you can confess this to yourself) but for which you have no real need, try this: Ask yourself what greater leisure you may be able to take by foregoing the temptation and permitting yourself to enjoy, in your own chosen way, a little more of what life's banquet has to offer other than things to buy.

The fourth element that may lend some support to consumeritis—though not actually causing it, in most cases—is the rationalization that spending our money on things helps the economy as a contribution to the employment of Americans and to American prosperity. This gratifying rationalization is defective as a matter of economics in light of the present relationship between American and foreign economies. In today's economy, as we have seen, while we spend even beyond what we can really afford, foreigners are still saving their money at a healthy rate. The current level of consumption in the United States therefore largely relies on foreign savings and investment in the American economy. This is a trade-off that must, sooner or later, be traded back. At some point, Americans will be compelled to trade their excess consumption for greater savings, while foreigners, especially in Asian economies, do the opposite. Whether this transition will be smooth or rocky depends on many factors. (The most important ones will be discussed in chapter 4.) What is almost certain, however, is that American advertisers will continue to encourage consumers to sail the *consumeritis* ship, even though it is in consumers' best, longer-term interest to ground themselves and walk on the solid shores of greater savings before markets begin to punish unsustainable consumption in increasingly severe ways.

To sum up, consideration of the major causes of consumeritis and its claimed justifications leads us to this conclusion: The shallow and misleading character of the roots of consumeritis have helped create a pathology that may not only adversely affect our own lives and our country's economic well-being but also—

most important to us as unique, individual persons—tragically divert us from fully pursuing and enjoying our own lives, liberties, and greater happiness. We owe it to ourselves, therefore, to look continually behind the curtain of advertising's persistent dream-making lures to protect ourselves against their often damaging influence.

Several times in this and the preceding chapter we have referred to a kind of happiness we "most" want, or most "deeply" crave or yearn for. In the preceding summary of what is demonstrably wrong about the major causes of, and rationales for, consumeritis, we have also referred to our "greater" happiness. It is fair to ask, What exactly is meant by this "greater happiness" for which we supposedly yearn most deeply? The final section of this chapter explores that question; but before examining it, we need first to consider an intermediate question, one that goes beyond and also lies beneath the question of what is really wrong with consumeritis other than the economic risks it may pose to us as individuals. That intermediate question is, What is wrong with the materialism that consumeritis serves? May not complete satisfaction of our material wants be enough to make us as happy as can be? If complete satisfaction of our material wants is what will make us most happy, how can we condemn consumeritis to the extent that it represents pursuit of complete satisfaction of our material wants, and thus pursuit of our greatest happiness, even if that pursuit can be financially imprudent? In other words, is a purely materialistic basis for our pursuit of happiness good enough to secure as much happiness as most human beings are able to attain?

The Problem with Materialism

> *Greed, for lack of a better word, is good.*
> —Michael Douglas as Gordon
> Gekko in *Wall Street* (1987)

> *A lie keeps growing and growing*
> *until it's as clear as the nose on your face.*
> —Evelyn Venable, voice of the Blue
> Fairy, in *Pinocchio* (1940)

Those who think of themselves as complete, unqualified materialists will not agree with the proposition that materialism alone is not enough to help us achieve the greatest happiness possible. Materialists will not be swayed by any arguments that experience, psychological research, sociology, or logic may provide to support the view that nonmaterial goods are necessary for the most complete happiness. Many people accept the idea that values such as goodness, justice, and a duty to be kind and helpful to fellow human beings can be soundly and logically based on a wholly secular, nonreligious foundation. Even some atheists accept that proposition; but other atheists, of the pure materialist or even nihilistic variety, don't accept the validity of such values at all. David Hume and Jeremy Bentham are among the philosophers whose writings develop a wholly secular basis for ethical social behavior, moral imperatives, and nonmaterialistic values. On the other hand, complete materialists do not accept any such values as imperative. They hold that values regarded as higher than materialism or expressive of an asserted spiritual dimension of human life are vacuous. They hold that such values—for example, those following from belief in the existence of a duty to love one's neighbor or, for that matter, any duty to others at all, or a belief that human nature includes inherent ethical inclinations and a native intuition that there is a "right and wrong" in certain actions—are all essentially meaningless. Orthodox materialists generally maintain that the only reality is material reality; that the very idea of "spirit" is a merely conventional fiction, as are all conceptions of morality and qualities of human character most people would classify as human virtues. The basic elements of the materialist point of view were expounded in antiquity, most notably in *De Rerum Natura*, a poetic account of the material origins and atomistic nature of the universe written by the Roman poet Lucretius (96–55 BC), in which he declares, "Nothing exists that is distinct from both body and vacuity."

On the ground that nonmaterialist conceptions are essentially meaningless, the convinced philosophic materialist asserts that only materialist, hedonistic pleasures and satisfactions can produce any real happiness, and that the pursuit of happiness followed with nonmaterialist values in mind is a path of ignorant delusion. (This materialist conviction may be reflected in the title of Sigmund Freud's book on the status of religion in human life, *The Future of an Illusion*.) The consistent materialist will likewise assert that all human ideation and conceptions are merely the outcomes of mechanical, physical operation of the human brain, which has no more spiritual function or operation than an electronic computer. (This proposition is much debated in contemporary philosophy and microbiology. Efforts to support it with a consistently logical proof have so far failed, to the frustration and consternation of its advocates.)

In sharp contrast to the materialist outlook is the view of some modern psychologists and existential philosophers that the greatest evils in the world mostly, if not entirely, follow from the materialist conviction that not only human existence but all existence is meaningless. A belief that existence is meaningless, which may be called nihilism, can, of course, justify the kinds of actions, such as genocide, that most of us would call inhuman and barbaric. Such actions are generally taken only to promote the nihilist's will to power, or even his capricious choices. It is for this and related reasons that Alexis deTocqueville asserted that "liberty cannot be established without morality, nor morality without faith," by which he chiefly meant faith in the validity and reality of principles higher than the materialism animating our individual, narrow self-interest.

Ask a pure materialist, "Is materialism good enough?" and the reply would be a resounding "Yes!" to which he or she might add, echoing the Vanderbilt University football coach Red Sanders, "Materialism isn't everything, it's the *only* thing." Or maybe, "He who dies with the most toys wins." If we were engaged only in logical argument, we might reply to the materialist that his or her position has an inherent logical flaw. In choosing to pursue a wholly materialist philosophy as a guide to action, isn't the materialist accepting truth (as the materialist sees it) as a value preferable to fiction as the basis for the conduct of his or her life? And isn't this the adoption of a nonmaterialist value as among the most important of all to the materialist, as it is to most of us? The pure materialist is thus accepting as a criterion for his or her choices something materialism, in effect, asserts not to exist or, if it does somehow exist, has no necessary reason for being chosen in preference to any other nonmaterialist value.

Even pointing out the logical paradox of materialism, however, is not likely to interest pure materialists in the possibility of more than one answer to our question. Nothing short of a transforming epiphany—something like a religious experience—is likely to open their minds to the possibility that appreciation of nonmaterialist values may be required for us to achieve the greatest possible degree of happiness.

Most Americans, even those who are severely bitten consumerists, are not materialists of this kind; and we are not, in any case, engaged here in a merely abstract, philosophical argument of the kind that a pure materialist might paradoxically assert. The materialists with whom we are concerned by posing our question were defined more practically, in a way that directly relates to consumeritis, by the psychologist Mihaly Csikszentmihalyi in a paper titled "Materialism and the Evolution of Consciousness." The author first presents his definition of materialism itself:

> Materialism is the tendency to allocate excessive attention to goals that involve material objects: wanting to own them, consume them, or flaunt possession of them. What is "excessive" is relative to the total amount of attention at the disposal of the person.

The author also gives a practical working definition of the kind of materialists with whom we are most concerned and who are more likely than the logically pure variety to have an open mind about possible answers to our question:

> A materialist is a person whose psychic energy is disproportionately invested in things and their symbolic derivatives—wealth, status, and power based on possessions—and therefore whose life consists mainly of experiences with the material dimension of life.

These empirical psychological definitions of "materialism" and "materialist" are highly consistent with Thorsten Veblen's view of conspicuous consumption, formulated from a socio-economic perspective and summarized in the first section of this chapter. As we have suggested, materialists within this definition may have an open mind about possible answers to our question; and those of us who are already troubled or unhappy about the conflict between our materialistic consumerism and the higher, nonmaterialistic values we accept (at least in principle) may be most interested in them. Other readers of this book may not have thought of themselves as materialists until they read, comprehend, and consider these definitions, and conclude that they may relate to the conduct of their own lives in the amount of energy (and money) they are investing in material things, to the relative neglect of their experiences with the nonmaterial dimensions of life. We hope that such readers will also find themselves at least intellectually curious about the possible answers to our question. So let's begin a practical inquiry into whether materialism is good enough to secure as much happiness as human beings are able to achieve. We will begin our examination without any moral or nonmaterialist presuppositions to prejudice our conclusion, by scrutinizing the available scientific, psychological, and sociological evidence.

The most basic empirical data that can inform our inquiry are well-supported findings in the relevant scientific research literature, findings stating that materialists themselves generally tend not to be happy with their lives. A substantial body of research indicates that there is a consistent negative correlation between the degree of people's materialism and their own sense of subjective well-being; that is, the more materialist people's lives are, the less happy they tend to believe themselves to be.

People's perceptions of their own happiness are referred to in the relevant psychological literature as SWB, an abbreviation for "subjective well-being." Scientific research into the reasons for the inverse relationship between materialism and SWB is still in its infancy, and psychologists have called for more research to be done. But a number of scientific studies of this question do exist, based on six different hypotheses. In 2003, thirteen of these studies were summarized and closely analyzed by Emily G. Solberg, Edward Diener, and Michael D. Robinson; their article "Why Are Materialists Less Satisfied?" discusses their investigation and its results. Three of the six hypotheses were confirmed by testing and study. Two were given some support from the studies, but not enough to be considered conclusively established. One hypothesis—that research findings of an inverse relationship between materialism and SWB were based on inadequate scales of measurement—was found to be without support. Let's examine each of the five surviving hypotheses to see how they fared under study and testing, and the conclusions experts in the field have so far reached.

The two hypotheses whose testing was found inconclusive were (1) *unhappy people become materialists* (rather than the other way round); and (2) *thinking about materialist concerns leads to unhappiness*. As to the first of these hypotheses, the researchers concluded that "there may be something to the idea that distress makes people materialistic." This hypothesis is consistent with the view we stated at the beginning of this chapter (eloquently expressed by Pascal in his *Pensees*), namely, that a common human need to keep busy to divert attention from unhappy conditions of our lives provides fertile ground for consumeritis. Confirmation of this hypothesis would establish materialism as a kind of psychological defense mechanism. But even if this hypothesis were to be confirmed, it would not shed much light on the best answer to our question about the adequacy of materialism to secure our greatest happiness. The researchers found even less support for the hypothesis that thinking about materialist concerns leads to unhappiness.

Three Confirmed Hypotheses Explaining Why Materialists Are Unhappy

Now we'll look at the three hypotheses for which the researchers found support in the six studies testing them:

(1) *Materialists are unhappy because they tend to be further from achievement of their materialistic goals than the other goals they have in life.*

This hypothesis has been tested in at least three scientific studies. The researchers' conclusions are worth quoting in full:

> The results of these three studies indicate support for the gap hypothesis. In each sample, the largest gap between current and ideal status pertained to the financial domain. To the extent that participants valued this domain, they tended to have lower SWB. The results suggest that it is possible to be a happy materialist, but only if one is happy with what one has (rather than preoccupied with what one aspires to have). The problem with materialism, however, may be that this is rarely the case. It is always possible to have newer, better, and more goods, rendering material pursuits ultimately unsatisfying.

Confirmation of this hypothesis leaves open the question whether materialists who actually achieve their materialistic goals, whatever their other goals might be, may enjoy the greatest happiness possible as a result of completely satisfying only their materialism. The hypothesis itself acknowledges, however, that most materialists in fact also have nonmaterial goals. Although they may be less interested in such goals, the fact that they have a variety of life goals (as most people do) indicates that satisfaction of material goals alone is not likely to secure the greatest happiness of which materialists are capable. This conclusion is strongly fortified by the results of the second hypothesis confirmed by study and testing.

(2) *Materialists are unhappy because their focus on material goals conflicts with their other goals, especially their personal relationship goals.*

This hypothesis has been tested in at least two scientific studies. Here, too, the researchers' conclusions deserve quotation in full:

The results confirm that the effects of materialism on SWB are at least partly mediated by relationship quality. Materialists tended to have relationships of lower quality (as assessed by their family and friends). Furthermore, with relationship quality controlled, the relations between materialism and SWB decline. These results suggest that a materialist can be happy if he or she is able to preserve the quality of his or her relationships. However, the inverse relationship between materialism and relationship quality suggests that there are built-in trade-offs that tend to undermine the quality of materialists' relationships.

The successful testing of this hypothesis clearly indicates that materialism alone is not enough to secure achievement of the greatest happiness we may be able to enjoy. In the words of a song made popular by Barbra Streisand, "People need people" and "People who need people are the luckiest people in the world." Or, to repeat Aristotle's ancient teaching about the social nature of human beings, "Who would live alone is either a beast or a god." Without satisfying human relationships, even ostensibly successful materialists are not as happy as they would be with them, or as happy as they would like to be. Confirmation of this second hypothesis demonstrates that, at least for most materialists, materialism alone is not good enough to secure the greatest happiness of which we are capable.

(3) *Materialists are unhappy because material goals are less enjoyable to work toward than other goals.*

In addition to the fact that the data produced by the test of this hypothesis largely confirmed it, they also suggested, in the words of the researchers, that "something inherent to the pursuit of financial goals is detrimental to happiness." But this inference from confirmation of the hypothesis tells us only about the lesser satisfaction to be obtained from the *process* of working toward a materialist goal than from working to achieve other goals on the road to happiness. It does not tell us whether actual achievement of the goal is, by itself, good enough to secure the materialist's greatest happiness.

The thirteen studies that formed the basis for the preceding conclusions, and the researchers' assessment of them, offer what is probably the best scientific research and study available at the time of this writing, providing direct empirical evidence that can help us to decide the most likely answer to our question. The following statements from the researchers' overall conclusions after considering all thirteen of the research studies are the most relevant to answering our question and considering the implications of our answer:

> In summary, materialism appears to work against people's attainment of a sense of well-being.... It is not sufficient to criticize the material lifestyle; alternative value systems must be developed. Perhaps if people knew the costs of materialism, particularly with respect to personal relationships and SWB, they would be more likely to balance their materialistic and non-materialistic goals ... It may be possible to have one's cake and enjoy it too, although there appear to be forces ... that render the pursuit of one's [materialistic] cake less enjoyable.

The costs and likely consequences of consumeritis noted in chapter 1 may provide the kind of information needed to help discontented materialists achieve a better balance between their materialistic and nonmaterialistic goals. With respect to the question whether materialism is good enough to secure as much happiness as human beings are able to, the thirteen scientific studies and the general conclusions reached by the psychologists examining them lend strong support to our conclusion that the most likely correct answer to our question is, "No, materialism alone is not enough to enable us to achieve the greatest happiness of which we are capable."

If our answer is the probable truth, then an informed assertion that materialism is good enough to enable us to secure the
greatest happiness of which we are capable is probably false,
and a lie. In our opinion, the increased incidence, major causes,
demonstrable costs, and likely foreseeable consequences of consumeritis indicate that the sufficiency of materialism to secure
happiness is a widely advertised lie supported, for example, by a
notion made popular in the 1990s that "greed is good." Quoted
earlier in an epigraph, this statement from the movie *Wall Street*
is from a speech made to a corporate meeting by a character
named Gordon Gekko (played by Michael Douglas). It equates
self-seeking greed with the passions that motivate us to care for
others. Here is the conclusion of that speech:

> The point is, ladies and gentleman, that greed—for lack
> of a better word—is good. Greed is right. Greed works.
> Greed clarifies, cuts through, and captures the essence of
> the evolutionary spirit. Greed, in all of its forms—greed
> for life, for money, for love, knowledge—has marked the
> upward surge of mankind. And greed—you mark my
> words—will not only save [this corporation], but that
> other malfunctioning corporation called the USA.

The better word Gekko might have found is "love." To equate
greed with love and the desire for knowledge, solely because each
of these may be a passion, is a kind of humanistic blasphemy. It
is to say, for example, that love is no better than hate; that taking
pleasure in the success of others is no better than envy; and that
compassion is no better than anger. The statement that "greed is
good," especially in the context in which Gekko frames it, is a lie.
Indeed, it is a lie that has been growing and growing until it is
now as clear as the noses on our faces. And to say that it is greed
(rather than prudence, for example, or greater respect, regard,
and fellow feeling for the people of other nations) that will "save"
the United States from its political and economic mistakes is

an even bigger lie, one that could help lead us to disaster in our relationship to other nations.

The answer we have just given to the question of whether materialism is good enough still leaves open the more difficult question: What sort of happiness greater than satisfaction of our materialism might each of us human beings be capable of achieving? Those of us who value the pursuit of happiness as a right secured by the Declaration of Independence have more than one reason to seek an answer to this question. It is to this critical issue that we now turn.

Our Pursuit of Happiness

> *When I was a child, I spake as a child, I understood as a child, I thought as a child, But when I became a man, I put away childish things.*
> —I Corinthians 13:11

The villain Rocco in *Key Largo* wants *more*. In *Wall Street*, Gordon Gekko encourages us to take pride in our greed, confusing it with the kind of passion that is love, not lust. The scoundrels in *The Maltese Falcon* turn out to have murderously pursued the theft of a fake treasure, "the stuff that dreams are made of." In Charles Dickens's novel *Oliver Twist* (and in the filmed version of it), we are touched when Oliver tells his warders he wants more food and is punished for it. We are touched because Oliver is not being greedy; he just doesn't want himself or his fellow orphans to go to bed hungry. Likewise, Oliver's dream is precisely to escape from a life of theft with Fagin's boys to recover a life consistent with his own honest, decent character. Oliver knows himself; there was nothing fake about his dream.

The most serious problem in most commercial dream-making may be that rather than encouraging us to use our imaginations actively to recover the best that is in us, it allures and stimulates and corrupts our imaginations toward satisfaction of superficial material pleasures. It invites us to want "more" as Rocco did and to be happy with material greed as Gekko was, not to want "more" as Oliver did: to satisfy unmet physical and spiritual needs, braving the wrath of his warders for the love of his friends. Understanding this difference may be essential to understanding the greatest happiness of which most of us are capable.

This is one reason why we love good movies. Good movies, especially when uninterrupted by commercial advertising, can elevate us beyond the dimensions of our mundane strivings and help us see the possibility of achieving greater fullness in our own lives. They may help us recognize the best that is in us, and remind us, by way of contrast, what baseness really looks like. Indeed, this is the specific delight of the movie *Auntie Mame.* Good movies appeal not only to childhood fantasy but also to the legitimate dreams and aspirations of mature adults.

Finding Neverland is a film produced in 2004; *Peter Pan* is a play written exactly a century earlier, in 1904, by J. M. Barrie. (*Peter Pan* was also made into a movie, more than once.) The relationship between these two works of art helps illuminate the relationship between fake dreams and real ones, reality and fantasy, the dreams of maturity, and the fantasies of childhood. *Finding Neverland* is based on a play (inspired by true events) by Alan Kree, *The Man Who Was Peter Pan.* It tells of Barrie's friendship with a family that led him to create the tale of Peter Pan, a boy who, wishing never to grow up, magically remains eternally a boy. *Finding Neverland* depicts Barrie's life as one of creative artistic achievement in early twentieth-century London, achievement born from Barrie's love of children, childhood, and innocence. Johnny Depp plays Barrie in *Finding Neverland*, and the child actor Freddie Highmore plays Peter Llewellyn Davies, the young boy whose first name helped inspire the name of Barrie's greatest creation.

Peter Davies is depressed by the recent death of his father. In an early scene in the movie, Barrie entertains Peter and his brothers with an improvised play (Barrie was a playwright before writing *Peter Pan*) in which Barrie pretends that the family's dog, named Porthos, is a bear. Peter, in an aside to his mother, says, "But it's just a dog." Barrie, overhearing Peter's remark, interrupts his play with Porthos and gently approaches Peter.

> Barrie: *Just* a dog? Porthos, don't listen to him. Porthos dreams of being a bear, and you want to dash those dreams by saying "He's just a dog." What a horrible, candle-snuffing word. That's like saying he can't climb that mountain, he's just a man, or that's not a diamond, it's just a rock—*just!*"
>
> Peter: Fine then, turn him into a bear, if you can.
>
> Barrie: With those eyes, my bonnie lad, I'm afraid you'd never see it. However, with just a wee bit of imagination, I can turn around and see the great bear, Porthos.

And Barrie turns around and does exactly that, in a way that makes Peter's brothers and his mother at least see him too. By the end of the film, Peter has come to love J. M. Barrie's storytelling fantasies, and also to enjoy his own imagination, something we all must find out how to do on our way to maturity.

Finding Neverland and *Peter Pan* are both about the playful imaginations of children. We immediately recognize that a child is not in good health if he or she is unable to use his or her imagination in play. That is what draws Barrie particularly to young Peter Llewellyn Davies: the boy cannot use his imagination to play. The character Peter Pan is always a child because he is always and only playing, and that is all he wants to do. But Peter Llewellyn Davies will not always be a child; if he lives long enough, he will someday become a man. Barrie was a man who not only made his living but found his happiness by knowing what he most loved: imagination and the innocence of children. *Peter Pan*, a work of love, was the happiest of all his creations. By helping Peter give free rein to his childish imagination, the playwright Barrie gave Peter Davies not only a chance to grow and thrive as a child but also as a model for the adult use of his dreams when he found himself free to have them.

Each of us is a perfectly unique individual, which makes us all, at least in that respect, perfectly alike. In the most fertile fields, no one flower is born or blossoms or perishes precisely the way any other does. If we could look and measure closely enough, we would find that each blooming petal differs somewhat in shape and volume and even in scent from every other. And when the universe is fourteen trillion years old, instead of the fourteen billion years scientists now estimate; if it were to endure a *thousand trillion, trillion* years, as the Hindus say it has already done; still there would be no mortal being—such as you, dear reader—whose breath of life would be exactly the same as another's. There is little mystery in this. The real mystery is that, according to both the most informed modern science and many theologies, each and every one of us eternally unique beings had our origins in one primordial burst of light, which was then somehow formed into the stardust from which each different spark of life has descended. There thus glows in each of us an infinite beauty of finite being, possessing the radiance of truly unique works of art: eternally different, yet eternally one. It is from this paradox that both our potential happiness and our discontent are born.

In one way or another, the fact that we are distinct individuals is the most fundamental origin of our distresses. (The next chapter discusses the harmful social effects of consumeritis on us as individuals.) The way in which we can most fully realize our unique individuality, while at the same time harmonizing our being with others as completely as our distinct humanity allows, would therefore provide a sure—in fact, a necessary—path to follow in our pursuit of happiness. For virtually all of us, our pursuit of happiness requires us to come to some practical understanding of how we may reconcile ourselves to the necessity of simultaneously attending to our own needs and wants, and paying attention to the needs, wants, and demands of other individuals (and the institutions they have created) to a degree sufficient to avoid destructive conflicts with, and intrusions on, what we require for our own greatest happiness. This is something that can be accomplished, more or less, by most ordinary mortals. As Alan Ryan, reviewing a book titled *The Ethics of Identity*, writes:

> Ever since Aristotle, philosophers have observed that we move from childhood to adulthood by acquiring habitual allegiances to people, places, and values, and that only when that process is accomplished do we have the ability to pause and reflect on which of these allegiances to retain or reject ... To have a stable sense of who you are, what you think, hope, admire, and detest is a substantial part of what it is to have an identity.... We acquire both our individuality and our sense of who we are by learning how to fill the social roles available to us.

This suggests an important clue to finding our greatest happiness: Which allegiances do we really want to retain; which do we most want to reject? It also suggests that happiness itself may be elusive until we know ourselves well. "I know what time is," writes St. Augustine, "until you ask me." Happiness is like that. Most of us think we know what will make us most happy; but if we try to be thoughtful in our answer to ourselves, it becomes a more difficult matter to say what really makes us most happy.

Down through the ages, philosophers and poets, politicians and theologians, friends and strangers have argued about the nature of happiness. They haven't been able to settle on what happiness is exactly, but that hasn't kept them from chasing it down. In the end, and in the beginning, too, happiness may be a lot easier to experience than to define.

Acquiring a great deal of wealth? That may relieve us of anxiety about making a living and liberate us to buy as many things as we may want to buy for ourselves or others, but it is certainly not guaranteed to assure our greatest happiness. It may not even relieve us of anxiety, because people of great wealth not infrequently venture their capital beyond even their great means. Many multimillionaire entrepreneurs have gone bankrupt. Very many millionaires have. Moreover, as Ted Turner once said in a television interview, there are times when a man he knows, who may be the richest man in the world, feels that he does not have enough. Ask any very wealthy person if wealth is the source of his or her greatest happiness, and many of them will probably tell you, to the contrary, that it tends to be the source of their greatest *dis*pleasures, even if it may increase or has increased their ability to find out what their own greatest happiness might be. Even more generally, as pointed out earlier, having more money beyond a relatively modest amount brings little or no added happiness. What is the course, then, what are the objectives that are most likely to bring us a greater or even the greatest degree of happiness?

Our Declaration of Independence says it is one of the basic functions of government to secure our natural rights "to life, liberty and the pursuit of happiness." The founders had modified this from John Locke's formulation of natural rights to "life, liberty, and property," placing "the pursuit of happiness" above

and beyond mere material possession. As the following paragraphs explain, we may best understand the phrase "the pursuit
of happiness" as signifying that what is being secured to us is
our right to enjoy the special pursuits of our own which in fact
compose our happiness.

Webster's New Twentieth Century Dictionary defines "pursuit"
as "the thing pursued; occupation or the like ordinarily followed;
as mercantile *pursuit,* literary *pursuit.*" This definition suggests
that the "pursuit of happiness" may refer, most significantly, to
things we choose to do that will themselves constitute our particular happiness; in other words, that great happiness is usually
experienced as doing something rather than as an external reward.
This is a conception and understanding of happiness recognized
by most thoughtful people. As Victor Frankl, a psychologist who
survived the Auschwitz death camp, writes:

> Again and again I therefore admonish my students both
> in Europe and America: "Don't aim at success—the more
> you aim at it and make it a target, the more you are going
> to miss it. For success, like happiness, cannot be pursued;
> it must ensue, and it only does so as the unintended side-
> effect of one's personal dedication to a cause greater than
> oneself or as the by-product of one's surrender to a person
> other than oneself."

Despite Frankl's implicit expression of the conventional idea
of the pursuit of happiness as a seeking rather than a finding and
doing, he is confirming the fact that in his experience, we are
making a mistake when we consider the pursuit of happiness to
be something we aim for rather than something that occupies
us. His observation is also consistent with the strict philosophic
definition of happiness given to us in ancient times by Aristotle: "Happiness is an activity in accordance with human excellence." Happiness, in other words, is what we enjoy when we are
doing good things; those particular pursuits we find to be the

best things we as unique individuals are able to do, and which constitute things that only human beings do in relation to, for, or with the help of other human beings and their communities. Picasso, for example, was most happy when he was creating his art. He continued to paint to the end of his very long life, long after he had made enough money to retire. He once said that he did not care what influenced his painting "as long as it was not himself." What he meant was that if he thought of himself instead of his painting (whether or not he used techniques or ideas borrowed from others), he would not be happy with the painting that resulted, and it would not be a very good painting either, even if—perhaps especially if—it was "a Picasso."

To experience such happiness, though, we do not have to be a great painter like Picasso or a "great" anything other than ourselves. When I lived in New York City, I regularly saw a sandwich maker at a very busy deli who had an exceptional ability to make extraordinarily delicious sandwiches in great numbers in little time. Watching him was watching a *great* sandwich maker at work. I have little doubt, from the pride and joy he took in his ability to do what he did every day, that he was a very happy man while he was making *his* sandwiches. Achieving happiness, even the greatest happiness, is possible; seeking it outside of the pursuits we can most enjoy, using our own cultivated abilities, is generally a mistake. It would not be *Finding Neverland*; that is, it would not be leading us to use our imaginations and insights as adults—as J. M. Barrie did—to discover within ourselves what we may do with our own capacities, whatever they may be, in a way that will enable us to achieve authentic happiness rather than seeking happiness as something outside ourselves that is distinct from what we are doing with our lives.

Like all artists, we each must work with the material we are given to create the best work of art possible *with those materials;*

in this case, the work of art is ourselves at our best, the product of our unique, individual human excellences. This practical view of what brings us the greatest happiness is consistent with the way Americans in general think about achievement. Most Americans tend to equate well-being with individual personal achievement; in contrast, most Asian people, for example, tend to equate their personal well-being with a sense of group interconnectedness. (This difference suggests that people from each of these cultures may learn a lot from the other.) There is, moreover, evidence supporting the view that Americans are generally optimistic about themselves but tend to worry about the condition and well-being of the United States as a country. Consumeritis and the things that help to make it possible have evidently been undermining American optimism and self-confidence, while giving Americans good reason to worry about the state of their country.

Seventy-one studies from nine developed countries have shown that people in those countries believe that life in the past was life in the "good old days"—that life was better in the past than it is now, even though they also believe that they themselves are better off than in the past. These attitudes appear to be inconsistent. Examination of contemporary American conditions helps, however, to illuminate reasons for this apparent inconsistency—and helps to demonstrate the inadequacy of materialism to assure our happiness. An abstract of a recent sociological study, *The Paradox of Choice: Why More is Less*, by Barry Schwartz, professor of social theory and social action at Swarthmore College in Pennsylvania, says that the book explains:

> why many Americans are feeling less satisfied even as
> their freedom of choice expands ... and how the range
> of choices people face every day has increased in recent
> years. [The book] illustrates how difficult and demand-
> ing it can be to make wise choices; and highlights the

special difficulties faced by those "maximizers" who seek and accept only the best. [It] considers whether increased opportunities for choice actually make people happier and concludes that often they do not; identifies several psychological processes that explain why added options do not make people better off … [including] feelings of inadequacy in comparison to others [and] suggests that increased choice may actually contribute to the recent epidemic of clinical depression affecting much of the Western world.

It is, as this study and the studies reviewed earlier in this chapter indicate, precisely too many choices—too many for our own good—that simultaneously stimulate consumeritis and detract from both our daily sense of well-being and our chance to achieve greater happiness. Not only too many choices in the variety of breads, cereals, shoes, detergents, shampoos, and models of almost every other consumer product on the market, but too many choices about how and where we procure the petty and paltry pleasures with which we can glut our lives in a culture of buying and selling. Shouldn't those who are most empowered to shape American culture help us to maintain a greater emphasis on promoting our rights to life, liberty, and enjoyment of our pursuits of happiness?

I was privileged to enjoy a friendship with an eminent American named Kimon Friar, who had lived most of his life in Greece. He had earned his eminence by his translations of the greatest works of modern Greek poetry, including the works of a Nobel Prize winner who attributed his own celebrity in large part to the American's translation of his greatest work into English. A philanthropist invited Friar to return to live in the United States for as long as he liked, entirely at the philanthropist's expense. After two years, this accomplished American decided to return to Greece, where he remained until his death some years later.

After he had made his decision to leave the United States, I asked him why he had chosen to reject a generously subsidized, highly commodious life in the United States. He told me that he found the choices available to him in this country simply wearying; that he did not wish to be put to the trouble any longer of having to decide, for example, which of twenty or more different kinds of bread to choose when he went to the supermarket. He would rather have only two or three kinds of bread to choose from, as he did in the bakery in Greece where he did his shopping, where he also had the time to have a friendly talk with the baker. I have similarly been told by people from other countries visiting the United States for extended periods that after first being over-whelmed and positively impressed by the multitude of choices American consumers have, they found that those impressions gave way to discontent with the shallowness of our American preoccupation with getting and spending, to the neglect of more humanly interesting pursuits.

That American culture has become *predominantly* one of buy-ing and selling is more evident when we consider such observa-tions by people from other cultures and countries and, for those of us fortunate enough to have enjoyed foreign travel, when we consider our own experiences abroad. In a culture of buying and selling, *efficiency* is the dominant ethos: sellers must reduce costs to increase profits, and shoppers are encouraged to move along quickly in the checkout line. As in Kimon Friar's experience, shopping in Europe and in third world countries is commonly a social occasion, an opportunity to visit with the butcher, the baker, and the shoemaker. The efficiencies of corporate Amer-ica have largely deprived us of these experiences. As popular and ubiquitous as Starbucks and Tully's coffee shops are in this country, for example, we do not generally have or take the time to enjoy the leisurely social experience that people of many other countries still regularly enjoy in their café life, which remains an emblematic custom of cultures not yet entirely dominated by the imperatives of commercial efficiency. (Whether this will continue to be the case may depend on whether *Americans* can recover from consumeritis; we discuss this further in chapter 7.) The American efficiency frenzy is one of the reasons Europeans perceive Americans as people who live to work rather than working to enjoy more of life's leisurely pursuits.

American productivity has indeed made the United States a land of plenty. By relentlessly offering us such an extraordinary abundance of materialistic choices, however, advertisers have conditioned us to focus our attention passively on *those* choices. The effects of our living in a culture of buying and selling have thus increasingly deflected our energies from the more important choices we are at liberty to make: active, not passive, choices about pursuits that can bring us the greatest happiness of which we are capable. Consumeritis and the forces that create and perpetuate it habituate us to give relatively scant attention to these more important choices, such as giving more time to our own children or getting to know our friends and neighbors better. They also divert us from considering what it really is in our lives that create the holes we try to fill—almost inevitably unsuccessfully—with material satisfactions. Recall the definition of materialism offered earlier in this chapter:

> Materialism is the tendency to allocate excessive attention to goals that involve material objects: wanting to own them, consume them, or flaunt possession of them. What is "excessive" is relative to the total amount of attention at the disposal of the person.

The greater the amount of money we feel we need beyond enough for necessities, the more likely we will reduce our own sense of well-being. A significant number of recent psychological, sociological, and economic studies have demonstrated this to be the fact. Those of us who are suffering from a gap between our financial aspirations and what we already have, when we have enough to get along, don't need to be told that this is so by scientific research; we know for ourselves it is true. Getting and spending are processes. So is "finding neverland." It is the process we are free to undergo—as mature, healthy adults, young and old—of using our own imaginations actively to find, as only we ourselves can find, our pursuits of greatest happiness. We all need encouragement in that challenging task. Not discouragement and diversion. The fact is that our consumeritis and the collective consumeritis of others, mutually reinforcing excess consumption, undermines and threatens to worsen the condition of nearly every major dimension of our lives—personal and institutional—as these are now being experienced in the United States and other highly developed countries. The following chapters investigate the ways this is so; how consumeritis may adversely affect our social, economic, environmental, and political present and future, and the future of human life on the planet.

Our final chapter examines what each of us can and should do about the destructive effects of consumeritis, and what our government can do to help each of us increase the possibility of our enjoying the pursuits of greater happiness of which we are capable as individuals living in human communities.

Notes

55 *Life, Liberty, and Our Pursuit of Happiness* For further consideration of this topic, readers are particularly referred to the relevant articles in *Psychology and Consumer Culture: The Struggle for a Good Life in a Materialistic World*, edited by Tim Kasser and Allen D. Kanner (Washington, D.C.: American Psychological Association, 2003), referenced hereafter as Kasser and Kanner.

Materialism appears to work against people's attainment Emily G. Solberg, Edward Diener, and Michael D. Robinson, "Why Are Materialists Less Satisfied?" In Kasser and Kanner, 46.

In the West we have a society In *Happiness*, 125.

Facts are better than dreams Winston Churchill, *The Second World War*, vol. 1: *The Gathering Storm* (Boston: Houghton Mifflin, 1948), 667. Churchill (1874–1965) was prime minister of Great Britain twice, from 1940 to 1945 and from 1951 to 1955. This quotation is from the first of his six-volume history of the war.

we human beings are ourselves In *The Tempest*, Shakespeare writes, "We are such stuff as dreams are made on, and our little life is rounded with a sleep." *Tempest, IV, 1*.

56 *"A man's reach," the poet Robert Browning writes* Robert Browning, "Andrea del Sarto," *Men and Women* (1855). In lines 97 and 98 of his poetic portrait of the artist del Sarto, Browning (1812–1889) writes, "Ah, but a man's reach should exceed his grasp. Or what's a heaven for?"

Auntie Mame is a 1958 movie The movie was produced and directed by Morton DaCosta, and written by Mike Myers (Warner Brothers Studios, 1958).

59 *Nothing is so insufferable* Blaise Pascal, *Pensées* (New York: Random House, 1941), 47. Pascal (1623–1662) published *Pensees* in 1663.

If you want to assure your own misery Curtis Cate, *George Sand: A Biography* (New York: Houghton Mifflin, 1975), 445–517. George Sand (1804–1876), the French writer, was Frederick Chopin's lover; née Dupin, she married Casimir Dudevant in 1821.

60 *Keeping up with the Joneses* This phrase is attributed originally as a reference to Elizabeth Schemerhorn Jones who, in the 1890s, built a twenty-four-room turreted villa in Rhinecliff, New York, the most expensive house ever before built there; see Shari Bernstock, *No Gifts from Chance: A Biography of Edith Wharton* (New York: Scribner, 1994), citing as her authority for this attribution a New York State Conservation Association pamphlet about the house written by D. Campbell and dated August 20, 1899. Coining of the phrase

is also attributed to the cartoonist Arthur R. Momand in his titling of a 1913 series of cartoons in the *New York Globe.*

61 *The consumption of luxuries* Thorsten Veblen, *The Theory of the Leisure Class* (New York: Dover Publications, 1994), 43, first published in 1899.

the kind of love we most crave From an early period of twentieth-century advertising, this approach to consumers was recognized as being among the most effective. See James Twitchell, "Two Cheers for Materialism," *Utne Reader* (November/December 2000), as quoted in *Affluenza*, 138.

63 *The Wizard of Oz* The movie was directed by Victor Fleming; produced by Mervyn LeRoy; and written by Noel Langley, Florence Ryerson, and Edgar Allan Woolf (MGM Studios, 1939).

children's book by Frank Baum Frank Baum, *The Wonderful Wizard of Oz* (New York: Tor Classics, 1993). The book was originally published in 1900.

65 *You can't cheat an honest man* Attributed to David W. Maurer, *The Big Con: The Story of the Confidence Man* (New York: Bobs-Merrill, 1940), and quoted as a saying of confidence men in H. L. Mencken, *A New Dictionary of Quotations* (New York: Knopf, 1966), 161.

sometimes to the point of tragedy For example, Alan Gathright's article "Suicide Note Says Family Deep in Debt," in the *San Francisco Chronicle*, August 20, 2005, sec. B1, reports that a San Mateo, California, father "cracked" under the mounting pressure of accumulating debt, killing his wife and two daughters before committing suicide. For further examples of homicidal and suicidal violence attributable to the pressures of consumeritis, see the note to page 257 on page 299 that begins *stories of people—including some highly educated people—who have exploded into murderous violence.*

Perhaps the earliest account in Western literature Herodotus, *The Histories* (London: Penguin Books, 1954). According to *Webster's Biographical Dictionary* (Springfield, MA: Merriam, 1971), 702, "His systematic treatment and mastery of style have gained for him the title 'Father of History.'"

67 *Such redirection of spare energies directly toward ultimate desires* As Thomas Nixon Carver writes: "There is no reason for believing that more leisure would ever increase the desire for goods. It is quite possible that the leisure would be spent in the cultivation of the arts and graces of life; in visiting museums, libraries and art galleries, or hikes, games and inexpensive amusements [and] would decrease the desire for material goods. If it should result in more gardening, more work around the home in making or repairing furniture, painting and repairing the house and other useful innovations, it would cut down the demand for

the products of our wage paying industries." That statement by Carver is quoted by Benjamin Hunnicutt in *Work Without End* (Philadelphia, PA: Temple, 1988), 82, as quoted in *Affluenza*, 138.

68 *Even in the early 1960s, most Americans would have felt more comfortable*   See *Affluenza*, 60, quoting James Kunstler: "We've mutated from citizens to consumers in the last sixty years." Other scholars have also noted that the American public's self-identification as consumers began in the late 1960s. For example, Gelpi and Julien-Labruyère, 102, says: "The Russell Sage Foundation, founded in 1908 and initially concerned with the problems of borrowers victimized by lenders, undertook significant studies of consumer credit. It was the first indication of consumerism centered around credit (although the word was not coined and vulgarized until the end of the 1960s)."

70 *Hypocrisy is the homage*   François de La Rochefoucauld, *Maxims* (1665).

72 *This is a trade-off that must, sooner or later, be traded back*   See, for example, "The Great Thrift Shift," *The Economist*, September 22, 2005: "At the same time Americans are spending over $700 billion a year more than their economy produces, the equivalent of more than 6% of annual output ... These imbalances are weakening America's economy." In the same issue of *The Economist*, see "Anatomy of Thrift": "According to the economics textbooks, saving and investment are always equal. People cannot save without investing their money somewhere, and they cannot invest without using somebody's savings. Savings and investment are two sides of the same coin.... If a country has a savings deficit, its currency will fall to the point where its assets are cheap enough to lure foreign savings."

74 *David Hume and Jeremy Bentham are among the philosophers*   David Hume (1711–1776) is a Scottish philosopher and historian. Jeremy Bentham (1748–1832), an English jurist and philosopher, is one of the chief expounders of utilitarianism and the author of *Introduction to the Principles of Morals and Legislation*, expounding the ethical doctrine that morality of actions is determined by utility, that is, the capacity for rendering pleasure or preventing pain, according to which the object of all conduct and legislation is "the greatest happiness of the greatest number."

75 *most notably in De Rerum Natura, a poetic account*   Titus Lucretius Caros, *De Rerum Natura*. The line quoted comes from Book I of *De Rerum Natura*, "Matter and Space," as translated by R. E. Latham in the Penguin Classics edition (Baltimore, MD: Penguin Books, 1951). As to contemporary materialism, an address by the professed atheist Madalyn Murray O'Hair in 1962 illustrates some of its enduring tenets, which include the following: "Atheism is based upon a materialist philosophy, which holds that nothing exists but *natural* phenomena. There are no

supernatural forces or entities, nor can there be any. Nature simply exists. But there are those who deny this, who assert that only mind or idea or spirit is primary. This question of the relation of the human mind to material being is one of the fundamental questions dealt with by all philosophers, however satisfactorily. The Atheist must slice through all obfuscation to bedrock, to the basic idea that those who regard nature as primary and thought as a property (or function) of matter belong to the camp of materialism, and that those who maintain that spirit or idea or mind existed before nature or created nature or uphold nature belong to the camp of idealism. All conventional religions are based on idealism." *The American Rationalist*, vol. 17, no. 3, September/October 1962.

Sigmund Freud's book on the status of religion in human life Sigmund Freud, "The Future of an Illusion" (1927), vol. 21 in *The Standard Edition of the Complete Psychological Works of Sigmund Freud* (London: Hogarth Press, 1968).

This proposition is much debated in contemporary philosophy See, for example, "Our Brains Don't Work Like Computers," at *www.primidi. com/2005/06/28.html* (accessed September 29, 2005); and Darek Barefoot, *A Response to Nicholas Tattersall's "A Critique of Miracles by C. S. Lewis,"* arguing the question in some depth, with reference to Rudolf Carnap's work, *Philosophy and Logical Syntax* (1935), and the writings of the British philosopher A. J. Ayer, referred to as "the widely read expositor of the 'logical positivism' of Carnap and Viennese Circle," and containing (to illustrate the assertion annotated here) the following statements excerpted from Barefoot's argument on pp. 5–6: "Clearly, on one level the human brain is a kind of biological computer driven by electromechanical interactions between neurons. But is it nothing more than that? Are the brain and its thought processes strictly 'phenomenal'? ... And here is where the problem arises, because conclusions about reality occur in the form of thoughts during the reasoning process. If the conclusions we reach are actually configurations of objects in the brain, in other words, phenomena, then they can no more be put into the categories of 'true' or 'false' than can any other arrangement of objects, events or circumstances." This article was found at *www.secweb.org/asset.asp?AssetID=89* (accessed September 29, 2005). Some opponents of those who maintain that "the brain is just a computer" have argued that there is no way of proving this proposition without implicitly presuming its truth in one or more of the premises of the arguments. For the broader dimension of this discussion see, for example, John R. Searle, "Consciousness: What We Still Don't Know," *The New York Review of Books*, January 13, 2005, reviewing Christian Koch, *The Quest for Consciousness* (Roberts and Company, 2005), at p. 39: "The idea that all of our consciousness is sensory is wrong as a matter of experience. Often when I think about problems in logic and philosophy I have no sensory experience. Why should I? [It is a mistake] to argue that if consciousness does exist and is manifested in behavior it must be nothing more than a computer program running in the brain. [Such] mistakes leave out the real existence and the subjective character of qualitative conscious states. We are now in a position to investigate these states ..."

In sharp contrast to the materialist outlook See, for example, Rollo May, *Psychology and the Human Dilemma* (Princeton, NJ: Van Nostrand, 1967) and *The Discovery of Being: Writings in Existential Psychology* (New York: Norton, 1983).

76 *liberty cannot be established without morality, nor morality without faith* Tocqueville, *Democracy in America*, vol. 1.

77 *Materialism is the tendency to allocate excessive attention* Mihaly Csikszentmihaly, "Materialism and the Evolution of Consciousness," 92, in Kasser and Kanner, 91–106.

A materialist is a person whose psychic energy Ibid.

78 *People's perceptions of their own happiness* Kasser and Kanner, 29.

In 2003, thirteen of these studies were summarized and closely analyzed See Emily G. Solberg, Edward Diener, and Michael D. Robinson, "Why Are Materialists Less Satisfied?" In Kasser and Kanner, 29–48. Unless otherwise noted, material quoted in the rest of this section comes from this same source.

81 *Who would live alone* The complete statement referred to appears in Book I of Aristotle's *Politics* (c. 320 BC): "He who is unable to live in society, or who has no need because he is sufficient for himself, must be either a beast or a god ... A social instinct is implanted in all men by nature."

83 *"greed is good." Quoted earlier in an epigraph* The movie *Wall Street* was directed by Oliver Stone and Gordon Lonsdale, and produced by Edward Pressman, A. Kitman Ho, and Michael Flynn. The screenplay was written by Stanley Weiser and Oliver Stone (20th Century Fox, 1987).

84 *In Charles Dickens's novel* Oliver Twist *(and in the filmed version of it)* Charles Dickens, *Oliver Twist* (1837–39); film version, Sony Pictures (2005), produced and directed by Roman Polanski, with Barney Clark as Oliver; screenplay written by Ronald Harwood.

85 Finding Neverland *is a film produced in 2004* *Finding Neverland*, Miramax Films (2004), directed by Marc Forster, produced by Richard Gladstein and Nellie Bellflower, with a screenplay by David Magee.

Peter Pan *is a play written exactly a century earlier* James M. Barrie, *Peter Pan* (1904). Barrie (1860–1937) was a Scottish novelist and dramatist. The most recent film version of *Peter Pan* is a 2003 Universal Studios production directed by P. J. Hogan, produced by Lucy Fisher and Patrick McCormick, written by P. J. Hogan and Michael Goldenberg, and starring Jeremy Sumpter as Peter Pan. The animated Disney version was a 1953 Disney Studios production directed by Clyde Geronimi and Wilfred Jackson, with the actor Bobby Driscoll as the voice of Peter Pan.

86 *We immediately recognize that a child is not in good health*   Johan Huizinga's classic work, *Homo Ludens* (Boston: Beacon Press, 1955) explores the importance of play in human life. "Here then, we have the first characteristic of play: that it is free, is in fact freedom ... Every child knows perfectly well that he is 'only pretending,' or that it was 'only for fun.'"

88 *As Alan Ryan, reviewing a book titled* The Ethics of Identity, *writes*   The review of Kwame Anthony Appiah's book *The Ethics of Identity* (Princeton, NJ: Princeton University Press, 2005) by Alan Ryan quoted in the text appeared in *The New York Review of Books*, April 28, 2005, under the title "The Magic of 'I.'" Ryan says Appiah's book explores the demands of individuality and, rejecting extreme understandings of what autonomy requires, "considers the relation of personal and group identity to morals and ethics."

I know what time is   St. Augustine, *Confessions* (c. 425).

89 *Down through the ages, philosophers and poets*   Darrin M. McMahon, "The Quest for Happiness," *Wilson Quarterly*, Winter 2005, Washington, D.C. The nature of happiness and the need to understand it from psychological, economic, social, and political perspectives are subjects of wide current interest and inquiry. In addition to Richard Layard's book, *Happiness: Lessons from a New Science*, previously cited and quoted, see, e.g., Jonathan Haidt, *The Happiness Hypotheses* (New York: Basic Books, 2005) and Darrin McMahon, *Happiness: A History* (New York: Atlantic Monthly Press, 2006), both of which are reviewed in the February 27, 2006 issue of *The New Yorker* magazine in an article by John Lanchester titled "Pursuing Happiness"; and M. J. Ryan, *The Happiness Makeover: How to Teach Yourself to be Happy and Enjoy Every Day* (New York: Broadway Books, 2005).

The founders had modified this from John Locke's formulation   John Locke, *Second Essay on Civil Government* (1690), chapter 9: "It is not without reason that [man] seeks out and is willing to join in society with others ... for the mutual preservation of their lives, liberties, and estates, which I call by the general name, property." Jefferson himself, author of a Resolution for the University of Virginia adopted in 1825, confirmed that "as to the general principles of liberty and the rights of man, in nature and society, the doctrines of Locke, in his Essay Concerning ... Civil Government ... may be considered as those generally approved by our fellow citizens of the United States." Thomas Jefferson, *Writings* (New York: Library Classics of the United States, The Library of America, 1984), 479.

90 *Again and again I therefore admonish my students*   Victor Frankl, *Man's Search For Meaning* (Boston: Beacon Press, 1959), 16–17.

strict philosophic definition of happiness given to us in ancient times by Aristotle   Aristotle, *Nichomachean Ethics*, book I, chapter 7.

91 *He once said that he did not care what influenced his painting "as long as it was not himself."*   Gertrude Stein (1874–1946) attributed the statement to Pablo Picasso (1881–1973), the Spanish painter known especially as a post-impressionist and founder of cubism, in *What Are Masterpieces?* (New York: Pitman Publishing, 1970), 85.

92 *Most Americans tend to equate well-being with individual personal achievement*   See the review of cross-cultural evidence on happiness and well-being in "Cultural Constructions of Happiness: Theory and Empirical Evidence," by Y. Uchida, V. Norasakkunkit, and S. Kitayama, in *Journal of Happiness Studies*, vol. 5, no. 3, Special Issue (2004), 223–39.

Americans are generally optimistic about themselves   See Blendon and Benson, Working Paper, "How Americans View Their Lives: An Annual Survey," *Challenge*, vol. 47, no. 3 (Cambridge, MA: Harvard University, May–June 2004), 6–26.

Seventy-one studies from nine developed countries   Michael Hagerty, "Was Life Better in the 'Good Old Days'?" *Journal of Happiness Studies*, vol. 4, no. 2 (2003), 115–139.

why many Americans are feeling less satisfied   Barry Schwartz, *The Paradox of Choice: Why More Is Less* (New York: Harper Collins, 2004). The quotation is from an abstract of Schwartz's book in the Econlit Database, *www.econlit.org/*.

95 *A significant number of recent psychological, sociological, and economic studies*   In addition to the studies referred to in the preceding section of this chapter and cited in the notes, see, for example, Alois Stutzer, "The Role of Income Aspirations in Individual Happiness," *Journal of Economic Behavior and Organization*, vol. 54, no. 1, May 2004, 89–109.

Alicia Silverstone as Cher Horowitz in *Clueless* (Paramount Pictures, 1995)

3

The Social Costs of Consumeritis: Damage to Individuals, Families, and American Society

We were born to unite with our fellow-men,
and to join in community with the human race.
—Cicero, *De Finibus* (c. 50 BC)

CLUELESS, A FILM released by Paramount in 1995, is an entertaining teenage romantic comedy. Its plot is partly based on Jane Austen's novel, *Emma*, whose first sentence is, "Emma Woodhouse, handsome, clever, and rich, with a comfortable home and happy disposition, seemed to unite some of the best blessings of existence; and had lived nearly twenty-one years in the world with very little to distress or vex her."

The novel and the film both tell stories of beautiful, intelligent young women who, to their surprise, find love for themselves in the course of matchmaking for their girlfriends. The film is set in Beverly Hills, and parodies life on the fast track among upper-middle-class Southern California teens. The heroine, Cher Horowitz (played by Alicia Silverstone), is the daughter of a successful and somewhat obsessive litigating lawyer (Dan Hedaya). Mr. Horowitz loves his daughter but is concerned about her frivolous, trendy pursuits. We learn from the style of Cher's matchmaking that she has a narrow idea of what it is to be "cool." She leads her girlfriends to ignore their attraction to uncool guys Cher believes to be, like, really, definitely unawesome. Cher's deceased mother was Mr. Horowitz's third wife. The film turns on the relationship between Cher and Josh (Paul Rudd), who is Horowitz's stepson from his second marriage. Josh is a good-looking, intellectually serious young man who wants to be a lawyer. He is vacationing at the Horowitz house on spring break from college. In Cher's eyes, Josh is definitely a nerd, totally uncool. She and Josh are constantly at each other about their different lifestyles. During a dinner at home, the following trialogue takes place:

> Mr. Horowitz (addressing Cher): I'd like to see you have
> a little direction.
> Cher: I have direction!
> Josh: Yeah, towards the mall.

Josh's witty barb is accurate. Cher's main preoccupations are shopping for the most fashionable clothing of the moment (her fabulous wardrobe is enormous), matchmaking, and pot-smoking partying. To her chagrin, Cher discovers that her girlfriend Tai (Brittany Murphy), whom Cher has helped "make over" so Tai can become more popular at their high school, has become more popular than Cher herself. This depresses her, and she begins to think about the shallowness of her pursuits. Her meditations lead her to appreciate the individual merits not only of some of the guys she has led her girlfriends to reject but, to her astonishment, of Josh as well. In her anguish, she comes to realize that different people have talents and qualities that exhibit their different human excellences. Her new awareness awakens her to the fact that she is in love with Josh, and the movie ends happily with Cher's discovery that Josh also loves her.

Though *Clueless* is set in a highly affluent community, it tells us a lot—in a spoofing way—about social life in the United

States in the 1990s and to the present day. Society is composed of individuals, families, and communities, the latter defined either as people living in the same neighborhood or geographic political division, or as groups of people sharing interests who belong to one or more private voluntary associations. Such associations are even often referred to as societies (for example, the American Cancer Society, the Humane Society). In this chapter we examine the harmful effects of consumeritis on each of these fundamental constituents of American society. (We do not include corporations as fundamental constituents because they are artificial persons.)

Effects on the Individual Person

> *We are unutterably alone, essentially,*
> *especially in the things most intimate*
> *and most important to us....*
> *Reflect on the world that you carry within*
> *yourself, and name this thinking what you will ...*
> *Your innermost happening is worth all your love.*
> —Rainer Maria Rilke, *Letters to a Young Poet* (1908)

What does it signify for a man, woman, or child to be considered as an "individual" and as a "person"?

To be an individual means to be "one of a kind," an indivisible, singular consciousness who can be seen to be separate from others. The word "person" comes from the Latin word *persona*, a face mask for an actor on the stage. As persons, we each wear the visible mask of our individuality in a shape peculiar to each of us—we develop and assume our own personality. Our individuality and our capacity to develop a personality are each natural gifts of being human. (In contrast, our status as "citizens" is humanly constructed, although the founders of the United States of America believed that our citizenship should be constructed in recognition of our individual, equal, natural rights to life, liberty, and the pursuit of happiness.) We are not able to recognize ourselves as individuals at birth. As infants, we are undifferentiated consciousnesses, unaware that our existence as separate selves is something other than our sensations and experiences. If we perceive our being at all at that stage of life it is, for all practical purposes, a being at one with the world. I can specifically recall a moment when, at two or three years of age on a wintry day in Philadelphia, I became conscious of myself as a separate person. My mother, needing a break from mothering, bundled me up against the cold and sent me out the door to the sidewalk in front of our house. Shocked by the separation, out in the cold, I came to self-consciousness in the instant I recognized (and wondered at) my distinctly separate body and being. It was only then that I was able to begin to become a person conscious of wearing my own visible "mask."

The process of becoming a person is one of our greatest and potentially most satisfying human challenges, but it can also be a prolonged, arduous anguish. It is the pain teenagers keenly feel as they begin their adolescent struggle to decide, and to become, who they really are. This struggle continues well into adulthood. It is commonly not until as late as our fifties that we feel we know who we are with sure confidence. (Perhaps that is one of the reasons Plato says in the *Republic* that a person is not truly prepared for philosophy until he or she is fifty.)

The challenge of adulthood is in fact the challenge of personality laid down in some of the most memorable sayings of human culture. It is, for example, the challenge expressed in the command of the ancient Greek oracle at Delphi: "Know thyself." It is also the challenge of which Rainer Maria Rilke (1875–1926) spoke when he wrote in a letter to a young poet in 1904:

We must embrace struggle. Every living thing conforms
to it. Everything in nature grows and struggles in its own
way, establishing its own identity, insisting on it at all cost,
against all resistance.

It is, for a more contemporary example, the challenge reflected
in the anguished cry of boxer Terry Malloy in the movie *On the
Waterfront*, when he realizes that he will never have a crack at a
boxing championship: "You don't understand! I could've been a
contender. I could've been somebody, instead of a bum, which is
what I am." Terry Malloy thought and felt deeply that if he was
anything at all as a person, he was a champion boxer, and that
his brother, through his unsavory activities, had denied him the
fulfillment of his personality.

Whoever we may be, or struggle to become, as conscious
human beings we have the capacity to be someone (a "somebody") other than and much more than a "consumer." This is
the lesson Cher painfully learned about herself and others in her
adolescent struggle to become more aware, and no longer *Clueless*. What we have been calling *consumeritis* is an assault on our
individual personalities, masquerading as an aid to our growth.
"Be yourself by what you buy" is the misleading dream-making
message of much commercial advertising. Whoever we may be
or become as individual persons, we are not chiefly our clothing or the kind of food we choose to eat or where we choose to
eat it or our automobiles or our houses or any of our material
possessions. Each of these may do no more than help or hinder
potential perfection of our individual personalities. It is one of
the tragedies of our age that the American culture of buying and
selling has evolved to the point that it encourages us constantly,
almost everywhere we look, listen, and go, to confuse fidelity to
our individual personalities with habitual acquisition of things
offered for sale, whether or not we really need them to secure

our pursuit of happiness. If we are to realize the best in us as individual persons, it is self-respecting thought and feeling that should be the pivotal guides to the formation of our habits, not the trumpeting calls to consume more and more of the overly abundant goods and services American industry and labor have produced. To an excessive degree, victims of consumeritis tend to lose sight of this fact, and are persistently encouraged to do so, to their very great personal loss.

We have previously discussed some of the adverse personal effects that excessive or inappropriate consumption, amounting to consumeritis, has on us in our private individual capacities and as individual citizens of the United States. These include an increased risk of incurring excessive debt, often to the point of bankruptcy; diversion of our energies from more significant and fulfilling pursuits than addictive participation in the culture of buying and selling; the corruption of political campaigning by commercial advertising techniques that may mislead us from making rational political decisions (a subject discussed more fully in chapter 6); and the rising incidence of depression and stress associated with gaps between heightened materialistic goals and their fulfillment.

For a child or young person especially, not as a member of a class of consumers or statistically significant group but as a living, breathing, individual with his or her own developing personality and circumstances, consumeritis may have its most disturbing harmful effects. We have already seen that most Americans spend more hours a week shopping than playing with their children. The impact of consumeritis on family life is discussed in detail in the next section of this chapter, but we cannot help remarking here on the manifold ways consumeritis hurts our individual sons and daughters, our youngest family members, pupils, and friends. The commercial frenzy for product innovation that helps fuel consumeritis includes marketing new fast food offerings, sweets, and sweetened cereals to children. These consumerist stimulations are implicated in the increased incidence of obesity and diabetes in young children. Diabetes may have awful effects on the quality of life of a child who suffers from it. The daily life of an obese child is also often much less pleasant than it might be; in the most severe cases of obesity, it can be a source of daily humiliation and anguish resulting from the immature and often cruel attitudes, teasing, and name-calling of other children.

Emotional distress related to unhealthy physical conditions is probably not, however, the kind children most widely suffer as a result of consumeritis and its stimulants. Commercial advertising has become so powerful a cultural influence that many young people—and older people as well—have come to identify themselves with product "brands," a word that has its origins in the term meaning "to burn or impress a mark upon," as with cattle. Are you an Apple or a PC person? Nike or Reebok? Ford or Chevy? For a child living with a family that is not fashion conscious or that cannot afford to buy the latest and swiftly changing fashion in things (to which Cher was addicted), brand identification can continually create discomfiting peer pressure and embarrassment. To a ten-year-old boy, not being able to own an "in" brand of sneaker may cause keen pain; in the case of teenagers, the desire to own the most currently popular athletic shoe has actually led to homicide more than once. For a fifteen- or sixteen-year-old girl, not being able to afford the most fashionable new outfits can cause depression severe enough to lead her to seriously consider suicide. (As a former volunteer for the crisis line at the San Francisco Suicide Prevention Center, I can personally attest to this.)

The individual lives of both children and adults are being harmed in other ways by the agencies fueling and serving consumeritis. Most conspicuous among the latter is, as discussed earlier, commercial advertising. In the introduction to this book, we described how the omnipresence of commercial advertising routinely sours many of the sweet little pleasures of daily life; pleasures we would otherwise enjoy without interruption or distraction. Advertising in both commercial and private media communications (soon possibly even through our cell phones), and its ubiquitous visibility both indoors and out, is an often unwelcome intrusion into our private as well as our public spaces. Certain kinds of advertising intrude on the personal sensibilities of many of us in especially offensive ways; for example, abrasive, loud, hard-sell pitches; the enormous volume of junk mail advertising appearing without prior consent in our e-mail inboxes; pornographic online advertising that almost seems calculated to offend most of us; unsolicited advertising faxed to us (at our involuntary cost and expense); direct marketing phone calls at inconvenient times; direct mail ads clogging our mailboxes; and advertising that forces conscientious parents to closely monitor their children's TV watching because they have good reason to suspect that the ads specifically designed to catch the attention of children are for products that will be harmful to them.

A further objectionable aspect of consumeritis as it may affect us individually is the stimulus it gives to product proliferation and marginal product innovation, including what some call planned obsolescence. After we have found a product that suits our particular needs and wants, we may find that we cannot continue to enjoy the special benefits it offers to us because it has become obsolete in a relatively short time. If it becomes worn out, we are of course free to purchase its successor innovation, but almost always at an increased cost we would prefer not to incur at all. This has become more and more common with respect to rapidly advancing products like computer software and other sophisticated technological innovations. Marketers of such products regularly announce their obsolescence and replacement offerings. One of these recent announcements confessed, "All too often, products are discontinued as a result of business decisions that do not adequately include the customer's perspective." Moreover, such evidently planned obsolescence is not confined to high-ticket items; it is a common part of the marketing of ordinary retail purchases. Expiration dates found on many products may not necessarily be tied to actual hazards.

The cumulative effects of all the preceding harms, ranging from little daily inconveniences to actual and potential ill health and life-threatening dangers, add up to considerable impairment of the quality of our individual personal lives. Consumeritis has changed the character of our daily lives in so many ways by reinforcing the American culture of buying and selling, and by increasing pressure for the getting in "getting and spending," that many of us—particularly younger people—may not even realize what we are missing. This may be the greatest harm collective consumeritis is doing to us as individuals: it has operated to transform our culture so thoroughly into a culture of buying and selling that the particular effects discussed in the preceding can be seen to be only threads of a new and disabling fabric with which our individual lives have been clothed. Consumeritis has so surrounded and cluttered our lives with external things and their pursuit that it leaves less and less room for introspection and self-examination, activities that are essential to our fullest possible individual development. It is a debilitating attack on our inner lives and psychological well-being.

These effects of consumeritis on us as individuals can be separated from their effects on us as social beings only as a matter
of thought, not in reality. To be an individual with a distinctive
identity partly means, as we have suggested, to be a person who
has made choices about his or her social role and, in the words of
Alan Ryan quoted earlier, "habitual allegiances to people, places,
and values." Our individuality is largely defined by the degree
and character of our concern with community. The Greeks have
a saying expressing this notion. To put it in English: "He who
does not participate in common affairs we do not consider inac-
tive, but *useless*." Two of the world's most insightful writers on
democracy and liberty, de Tocqueville and John Stuart Mill, as
Ryan says:

> would have been deeply astonished to be told that a con-
> cern for community was incompatible with a concern for
> individuality. If asked whether they wanted us to have
> deep attachments—to our friends, families, towns, and
> nations, with their particular histories and quirks—or
> whether they wanted us to pursue our individual inti-
> mations of the good life, drawing on the resources of the
> whole world and the whole of human culture, they would
> certainly have answered "both."

To the extent consumeritis affects us as individuals, it thus
also affects us as members of the families to which we are related
by blood or marriage, as well as the broader family of communities we inhabit or participate in. Its injuries therefore necessarily
have multiplier effects. Such effects are the subjects we consider
next, beginning with the effects of consumeritis on our families
by blood or marriage.

Effects on Families and Family Life

*Marriage is comprised of two solitaries
who protect, border, and salute one another.*
—Rainer Maria Rilke, *Letters to a Young Poet* (1908)

*All happy families are the same;
but every unhappy one is unhappy in its own way.*
—Leo Tolstoy, *Anna Karenina* (1876)

"Love and marriage, love and marriage, go together like a horse and carriage. This I tell you, brother: 'You can't have one without the other.'" These words from a hit song of the 1950s may evoke some nostalgia for old-timers. By the 1970s, this was not an anthem of popular culture, which was better exemplified by the Beatles' hits "Let Me Hold Your Hand" and "All the Lonely People," or the Rolling Stones' widely popular "I Can't Get No Satisfaction."

In 1998, 2.2 million couples married in the United States, while 1.1 million couples divorced. By 2000, 58 million married couples were separated and there were over 21 million divorces. People between the ages of 25 and 39 make up 60 percent of all divorcees; none of these had even been born during the period when popular American culture had it that "you can't have love without marriage." The connection between love and marriage has not been altogether abandoned in American mores. A second marriage, Samuel Johnson is reputed to have said, represents "the triumph of hope over experience," and more people today are in a second marriage than in a first. On the other hand, the longer-range historical fact is that love and marriage have not always been so closely associated as they were in the United States in the 1950s. For many centuries, marriage was more commonly a property arrangement between families than a consequence of love between the bride and groom. More generally, depending on the personality of the parties, marriage was not so universally expected to follow from love until about the mid-twentieth century. In a lecture about the causes of the rise in the U.S. divorce rate beginning in the 1960s, the anthropologist Margaret Mead pointed out how the notion that people in love must get married was in large part a post–World War II cultural development:

> There are many reasons why so many marriages end in divorce now. As recently as the 1940s, it was widely understood that some people are suited for marriage, and some are just not. Marriage is a kind of vocation, like economics. And not everybody can do that either. But after World War II, with all the GI's returning from the war—love- and woman-starved—there grew such a general passion for the idea of marriage that people began to lose sight of the obvious fact that marriage is not for everybody.
>
> There is another reason growing out of World War II that divorce has become so common. Before the war, married couples often lived with their parents. So, before the war, if you and your spouse had a quarrel, there was usually someone else you were living with, a parent or grandparent or uncle or aunt, who was family and cared about you, who could help patch things up. And babysit your children while the two of you went off somewhere to patch things up yourself. But after the war, those same GI's found that their war experiences made returning home to live with their parents no longer as comfortable as they had imagined it would be. And, when they did marry, they wanted to live in their own homes. So there was a great building boom after the war, and by the 1950s, the almost universal ideal was a home of your own in the suburbs with a two-car garage.
>
> The problem with that has turned out to be that if you have a home of your own in the suburbs, and your parents and your grandparents and your aunts and uncles

are still living in the city, then you really have to take
care of many things on your own that you could formerly rely on your extended family to help you to do. So
the pressures of the nuclear family have built up and are
now exploding. It is true that if you live in an extended
family situation, you have less privacy. But you also have
a lot of help for all the problems that marriage and your
children may bring home to you. So we have lost something in our gain of greater privacy—which often means
not privacy but isolation—and that loss has contributed
to the high rate of divorce.

Mead's insight into the reasons so many divorces were happening in the late 1960s has even greater force and relevance today.
As the statistics clearly indicate, marriage is difficult for most
of us, and divorce has become relatively easy. (In the maverick
opinion of Mead, who was married and divorced three times, it
was "idiotic to suppose that because a marriage has ended, it's
failed.") The pressures married couples feel in their relationships
are, of course, compounded by the pressures they experience apart
from the demands of marriage itself. Financial pressures most
of all. Consumeritis plays a substantial part in the escalation of
these pressures to the point that they may become intolerable
strains on a marriage.

Since the consumeritis epidemic appears to have begun in
the mid-1980s, when personal consumer expenditures began a
sharp rise as a percentage of both GDP and disposable income,
it is no surprise that PCE now adversely affects marriages from
their very beginning. "The Effects of Debt on Newlyweds and
Implications for Education," a study by researchers at Utah State
University, published in 2005, reports that "entering marriage
with consumer debt has a negative impact on newlywed levels of marital quality"; and that "debt brought into marriage is

especially troublesome as couples struggle with financial issues in early marriage." Moreover, the number one cause of divorce in the United States is financial pressure. As consumer debt continues its alarming growth rate (it has doubled in less than ten years), these pressures will intensify; they may greatly intensify if, as is expected, credit interest rates rise substantially. The first and most obvious adverse effect of consumeritis on families is, therefore, that it may contribute substantially to the breakup of marriages; and if the breakup is early, it may even thereby prevent families from being formed. These are effects we cannot afford to ignore if we wish the United States to thrive as a decent civil culture.

> Marriage is central to our culture. Marriage legally confers many hundreds of benefits, but that is only its material aspect. Marriage is an institution, the public expression of lifelong commitment based on love. It is the culmination of a period of seeking a mate, and, for many, the realization of a major goal, often with a build-up of dreams … rituals, families coming together, vows, and a honeymoon. Marriage is the beginning of family life, commonly with the expectation of children and grandchildren, family gatherings, in-laws, Little League games, graduations, and all the rest. Marriage is also understood in terms of dozens of deep and abiding metaphors: a journey through life together, a partnership, a union, a bond, a single object of complementary parts, a haven, a means for growth, a sacrament, a home. Marriage confers a social status—a married couple with new social roles. And for a great many people, marriage legitimates sex. In short, marriage is a big deal.

Just how big a deal marriage is may be inferred from the fact that, according to the U.S. General Social Survey (among other surveys), the single most important factor affecting people's happiness is the quality of their family relationships. When these go awry, most other things tend to fall apart, especially for children of divorced parents. In fact, "divorce has been identified as the clearest reason for rising youth suicide in the United States." The breaking up of families and their fracturing into single-parent homes has also been a significant contributor to juvenile crime. By 1996, the number of children being raised in single-parent families rose to about 18 million, and divorce accounted for most of this. Studies have found that "one of the most reliable indicators of juvenile crime is the proportion of fatherless children." (In 1995, about seven million children five- to fourteen-years-old were regularly left unsupervised.)

Its contribution to marital separation and divorce is not the only injury consumeritis inflicts on our children; it also does continuing injury to children after their parents have separated or divorced, and has harmful effects on child raising by married couples who are not even broken up. This reality is reflected in the title of a book by a child developmental and clinical psychologist, Diane Ehrensaft: *Spoiling Childhood: How Well-Meaning Parents Are Giving Children Too Much—But Not What They Need.* As Ehrensaft writes:

> Children are typically miserable when their parents separate, and nothing will make up for it. The goal is not to divert the child with good things, but to offer support for the child to get through the inevitable deprivation regarding the loss of the family as he or she knew it. It is … a time to help a child develop resiliency, rather than to force happiness in the face of bad circumstances that are out of the child's control.

Ehrenesaft is not only concerned about harm done by the overindulgence of divorced or separated parents who give their children things to compensate for the pain of a broken marriage;

her analysis includes similar harm done by parents who buy things for their children because they don't have—or give—their children enough time to meet their real family needs. She frames her observations about this situation by referring to movies not entirely dissimilar from *Clueless*:

> We all know the canned movie plot of the wealthy, overindulged child with mansion, servants, horses in the stable, but no parents available to love or attend to their son or daughter. Full of riches, empty of love. *Increasing concern has surfaced that this plot has left the movie screen and is now the plight of the average middle-class American child....* Showering the children with goods can serve as a bargaining chip in love, in which parents gratify what they think is their child's every whim in order to say: "I love you and I hope you love me." The paradoxical consequence, however, is that they end up leaving the child deprived of the experience of wanting something and of the security of knowing we love them whether a room is filled with toys or not....
>
> [Children] can also speak in tongues that need to be deciphered, as when the overindulged child says, "I don't want that anymore," after every granted wish. Translation: "That's not the bucket that needs to be filled. None of this will make me happy because it's really something else I want from you, like telling me, 'No, you can't have everything you want,' or 'Maybe it's not the doll you want but a telephone call from your daddy or a little extra time with me.'" Bells should go off in any situation where you feel you are giving so much but your child is resistant to receiving your gifts. Your child may well be signaling to you to stop overgratifying and start attending to other of his or her needs. (emphasis added)

Movies with scenarios depicting overindulged children of materialist parents have not yet left the screen. This scenario is included in the 2005 movie *Charlie and the Chocolate Factory*, based on the 1964 book of that name by Ronald Dahl and starring Johnny Depp as Willie Wonka. One of the children invited to the chocolate factory who does not win Willie Wonka's grand prize is a spoiled little girl ("Daddy, I want another pony") whose expectation of always getting what she wants teaches her father that he will be a better parent if he says no to her demands from time to time. Ehrenstadt observes that many overindulgent parents know "deep in their hearts" that giving things to their children is often an attempt to compensate for doing too little for them in ways that will better assist their growth, and thereby demonstrate more care for their well-being—and more authentic love for them. Such parents no doubt include many of those who spend more time shopping than playing with their children.

Lack of good parenting may be even more serious when it compounds the injury done to a child by a broken marriage. A comparison of children of divorce with children whose families are legally intact shows that children of broken homes are more likely to become depressed or delinquent. This has further consequences in reducing the ability of children to behave in socially acceptable ways. Over the past forty years, as divorce rates have accelerated, the number of juvenile court cases handled has more than doubled. A careful research correlation of divorce and juvenile crime using a set of data from 1957 to 1990 concluded that a 1 percent increase in the divorce rate yields nearly ½ percent (0.488%) increase in juvenile crime. During this same period, the juvenile crime rate increased more than two and a half times, from 19.8 to 51.0 per thousand. The data obtained in this study provides clear support for the hypothesis "that the breakdown of the American family has been a contributor to the increasing juvenile crime rate." It has also evidently been a significant contributing factor to alcoholism. A UK study found that "higher levels of alcohol consumption, heavy drinking and problem drinking were found for those who had experienced parental divorce in childhood."

The chain linking consumeritis to increased family break-ups, child and teenage depression, impairment of emotional growth, juvenile crime, and alcoholism is not a long one. Excess consumption, decreased savings, and a materialistic culture facilitated by increased consumer credit now commonly lead to levels of consumer debt and financial pressures that are one of the leading causes, if not the leading cause, of marital dissatisfaction and divorce. These pressures almost certainly cause similar adverse effects on other forms of personal commitment short of marriage.

We are not, of course, making the claim that consumeritis is the only major cause of divorce; we do assert that when it afflicts one or both parties to a marriage, it seriously exacerbates the effects of all the others. Succeeding at marriage is not easy. "For one human being to love another," Rilke writes, "is perhaps the most difficult task of all, the epitome, the ultimate test. It is that striving for which all other striving is merely preparation." I can testify from my own experience how accurately Rilke described marriage with those words. I divorced and then remarried the same woman (our divorce was unsuccessful). As of the time of this writing, we have celebrated the forty-second anniversary of our first marriage to each other and the twenty-first anniversary of the last. It was only at the last ceremony that I was mature enough to understand the true significance of the marital vow, without the thought that "I can always get a divorce if it doesn't work out." The most authentic marriage is one that is truly a commitment "for better or for worse." The kind of heart and mind and spirit it takes to give this very difficult vow real meaning became apparent to me some time after our divorce, in the course of reflecting on other experiences that demanded commitment.

Beginning in my mid-thirties, I often went mountain climbing in the late summer or early fall. I was inspired to do that after my first experience, climbing Mt. Shasta, a 14,132-foot peak in California. When I reached the summit, I was awed by the silence, a silence I had never heard before. It put the entire world in a new perspective for me, detaching me from the noise and hurly-burly of day-to-day life below. From the vistas at the peak, I also acquired a new respect and wonder for the beauty of creation, and I wanted to repeat these experiences as frequently as practical. I later came to learn that a satisfying mountain-climbing experience did not always require reaching the summit, especially when prudence dictated that going farther would be folly. In such cases, the stopping point could be satisfying enough. Attaining the summit, however, is a mountain climber's usual goal.

The way to the summit of a high mountain is almost always arduous. High altitudes are breathtaking in more than one respect, and much above ten thousand feet, almost every step of the way can be a painful effort. It is also often frustrating. A climber may think he's about to reach the summit only to find he's reached a false summit and must go much farther to attain his goal. With a very high mountain, this can happen many times, and a climber may be compelled to go on and on and on again if he is to reach the summit. On many of these climbs, I have been able to look down on the mountain-climber's lodge at or near the base of the mountain's higher reaches. After repeated false summits, especially, I have sometimes asked myself, Why am I putting myself through all this trouble and pain when I could be down at the lodge drinking hot toddies and just having some fun?

This thought completely evaporates and, indeed, seems

absolutely inane once I have finally reached the summit. This, in my experience, is a metaphor for a successful marriage. The labor and pain invested in getting to the summit of a mountain is generously repaid by the view from the top. In fact, the labor and pain constitute an essential part of the beauty and richness of the mountain-climbing experience, just as they are part of the satisfactions of an enduring marriage. We become friends with others, perhaps most of all, as a result of the experiences we share with them. The more we are able to suffer with our chosen life partners the "slings and arrows that outrageous fortune brings," the more well-married we are to them. After more than forty-two years of marriage (among which my life partner and I include our respective experiences of the divorce), I am not completely certain that we have reached the summit, but we have reached a point from which neither of us is any longer tempted to descend.

> Let me not to the marriage of true minds
> Admit impediments. Love is not love
> Which alters when it alteration finds,
> Or bends with the remover to remove:
> O, no! It is an ever-fixed mark ...

In getting to such a point in a marriage, we need all the help we can get. Deprived especially, as Margaret Mead reminded us, of the likely help of an extended family in the United States of the twenty-first century, every impediment to keeping the faith implied in our marriage vows makes the journey even more difficult than it is inherently. Consumeritis, promoted and fueled by commercial advertising morning, noon, and night, and almost everywhere we look here beneath the mountain, keeps in view the material comforts and temptations of the lodge far beneath us every step of the way. We may therefore conclude, not only from this metaphor but from the facts set out in this and preceding chapters, that if American culture were not so dominantly a culture of buying and selling, if it did not encourage our materialism at the advertising rate of nearly $1,000 per person per year, more marriages would remain intact, more families would stay together and have a chance to thrive, our children would be less depressed, and juvenile crime and alcoholism would not be at their high levels; they would even be likely to decrease. America's consumer culture is not only too much for our own good as individuals; it is far too much for the good and well-being of marriage, families, and family life; and we need to do something about it. This is a conclusion that both classical liberals and conservatives can rally round. As Edward Luttwak, a former Reagan administration official now with the Center for International and Strategic Studies, has written:

> The contradiction between wanting rapid economic growth and dynamic economic change and at the same time wanting family values, community values, and stability is a contradiction so huge that it can only last because of an aggressive refusal to think about it ... I want to conserve family, community, nature. Conservatism should not be about the market, about money. It should be about conserving things, not burning them up in the name of greed.

Luttwak is emphatic about the contradiction implicit in typical "conservative" speeches that laud the unrestricted market as the best mechanism for rapidly increasing American wealth while at the same time saying, "we have to go back to old family values, we have to maintain communities."

> It's a complete non sequitur, a complete contradiction, the two of course are completely in collision. It's the funniest after-dinner speech in America. And the fact that this is listened to without peals of laughter is a real problem ...

America is relatively rich, even Americans that are not
doing that well are relatively rich, but America is very
short of social tranquility, it's very short of stability. It's
like somebody who has seventeen ties and no shoes helping himself to another tie. The U.S. has no shoes as far as
tranquility and the security of people's lives is concerned.
But it has a lot of money. We have gone over to being a
complete consumer society, a 100 percent consumer society. And the consequences are just as one would predict
them. Mainly lots of consumption, lots of goodies and
cheap things, and a lot of dissatisfaction.

The text of the passage in the book *Affluenza* from which
these words of Luttwak are quoted, adds that

human beings are more than consumers, more than stom-
achs craving to be filled. We are producers as well, looking
to express ourselves through stable, meaningful work. We
are members of families and communities, moral beings
with interest in fairness and justice, living organisms
dependent on a healthy and beautiful environment. We
are parents and children. Our affluenza driven quest for
maximum consumer access undermines these other values.

If, as Tolstoy said, "all happy families are the same," they
are at least the same in being families united and unified by
their respect for the individual pursuits of happiness each family member may enjoy. They are also no doubt the same in sharing values that go beyond materialistic pursuits likely to put
their families' security at serious risk. The abundant number
and range of materialist temptations our culture of buying and
selling so feverishly promotes, on the other hand, helps to make
each unhappy family—while it lasts—unhappy in its own way.
Given the seriously damaging effects consumeritis has on us as
individuals and on families and family life in the United States,

how can it fail to have seriously damaging effects on the communities in which we live and of which we are a part? This is the subject we will next explore.

Effects on Community

When Cher Horowitz, in the film *Clueless*, first begins to find reasons to admire Josh (with whom she is falling in love), she is influenced by him to think of ways to be helpful to others instead of having, as her only direction, the way to the mall. At first Cher misunderstands what this might mean, and begins "doing good" by trying to help others become just like her, a doll baby in the most fashionable clothes. She awakens eventually (as described earlier) to the fact that different people have different qualities that deserve nurturing in their own way, and she sees a much deeper and more satisfying possible relationship between her maturing individuality and the communities to which she belongs. Cher thus becomes less of a consumer and more of a "citizen," a word that unfortunately no longer enjoys the respect it had before consumeritis struck the United States, a self-respecting member of a civil society appreciating the rights and duties that true citizenship implies. James Kunstler, author of *The Geography of Nowhere,* says:

> We've mutated from citizens to consumers in the last sixty years. The trouble with being consumers is that consumers have no duties or responsibilities or obligations to their fellow consumers. Citizens do. They have the obligation to care about their fellow citizens, and about the integrity of the town's environment and history.

The Harvard political scientist Robert Putnam has devoted his career to the study of "social capital," the connections among people that bind a community together. He observed that the quality of governance varies with the numbers of people in such things as voter turnout, newspaper readership, and membership in choral societies. Recently, he captured the public's imagination by concluding that far too many Americans are "bowling alone"; compared to a generation ago, more people are bowling, but fewer of them bowl in leagues. This phenomenon and its implications are addressed by the authors of *Affluenza*:

> Once a nation of joiners, we've now become a nation of loners. Only about half of the nation's voters typically vote in presidential elections. Only thirteen percent reported attending public meetings on town or school affairs, and PTA participation has fallen from more than twelve million in 1964 to seven million in 1995. The League of Women Voters' membership is down forty-two percent since 1969, and fraternal organizations like the Elks and Lions are endangered species.
>
> Volunteering for Boy Scouts is off twenty-six percent since 1970, and for the Red Cross, sixty-one percent. Overall, a record [number of] Americans are volunteering, but many of them do it "on the run," in shorter installments, so the total time volunteered has actually declined. The "fun factor" is a major stimulant in volunteering. If it's not fun, forget it. A 1998 study on volunteering revealed that thirty percent of young adults volunteered because it was fun, compared to eleven percent who said they were committed to the cause.
>
> Putnam concedes that membership has expanded in newer organizations such as the Sierra Club and the American Association of Retired Persons. But most members never even meet, he points out—they just pay their dues and maybe read the organization's newsletter.

The percentage of Americans who volunteer their services for community causes dropped from 54.4 percent to 44 percent in the period from 1989 to 2000; it further decreased to 28.8 percent in the period from September 2003 to September 2004.

That's a decrease of nearly 50 percent since 1989 in the portion of Americans who volunteer for service to their communities. In its December 2004 issue, the *Bureau of Labor Statistic News* says, "Among those who had volunteered at some point in the past, the most common reason given for not volunteering in the year ended September 2004 was lack of time (45.0 percent) … Lack of time was the most common reason for persons in all age groups except those age 65 and over, who reported health or medical problems as the primary reason." What is the probability that consumeritis plays a significant role in the perceived lack of time increasing numbers of people have for volunteering their services to the community? And what are the most likely explanations for any such role?

Consider, first, a news story that appeared in 1995 and the poem it inspired me to write. A headline on the front page of the *San Francisco Chronicle* on September 14, 1995, read, "Automation, E-Mail, Encourage Isolation—a Less Social Society Is Becoming Shy." The story summarized the findings of a university study about increasing social isolation, reading in part, "Growing numbers of those people standing silently in line at the ATM and pumping their own self-service gas are probably victims of America's 'silent, anonymous epidemic.'" And here's the poem.

A TALE OF LIFE IN AMERICA
or JOHN ALONE

John Alone awoke
To his radio clock
(Long after the sun arose
but his blinds were closed
And there was nothing else to wake him).
John Alone showered and dressed
And listened to the radio.

He heard how hard the traffic was, and so
John Alone took the subway car in silence
(no one talked to him).
John Alone waited at the ATM,
While others did their business;
And then, when John Alone arrived
At his comfy cubicle,
He read his ready e-mail
And listened to his messages,
While upon his desk he heard
the whirring of his fax.
And then
John Alone listened to the Recorded Message Option menu
So thoughtfully provided by his correspondent.
And
when he went to pay his overdue computer generated bill,
John Alone's Answering Machine spoke clearly to the callers
Who did not know the number of his beeper.
And after John had left his messages in return,
He turned to do his business,
Processing words as well he could.
His silent day's work done,
John Alone returned to his subway seat
and rode back home in silence.
John Alone found it hard to choose
Whether he should watch TV tonight
Or play computer bridge.
So he chewed upon the thought
And dined upon his microwave,
A special Cordon Bleu
Of filet in shallot gravy,
And fell asleep to dream
Of flesh and blood and maybe.
Then John Alone awoke
To his radio clock
(Long after the sun arose,
but his eyes were closed
And there was nothing else to wake him).

Consider, second, that among people in rich countries, those in the United States work the longest hours; they work much longer than Europeans.

> In most countries and at most times in history, as people have become richer they have chosen to work less. In other words they have decided to "spend" a part of their extra potential income on a fuller private life. Over the last fifty years Europeans have continued this pattern, and hours of work have fallen sharply. But not in the United States. We do not know fully why this is. One reason may be ... more satisfying work, or less satisfying private lives.

We do know, however, that the incidence of depression in the United States has been steadily increasing. Indeed, according to an American association of medical professionals, "the number of patients treated for depression increased significantly during the economic boom of the 1990s." The National Institute of Mental Health has reported that "approximately 18.8 million American adults, or about 9.5% of the U.S. population aged 18 and over in a given year have a depressive disorder." We also know that over the past twenty-five years, Americans have been spending themselves more and more deeply into debt largely as a result of their increasing personal consumption expenditures. Is it any wonder that an increasingly depressed, overworked, debt-ridden, shy, alienated, and isolated adult American population finds increasingly less time (or energy) to volunteer their services to the community?

Consider, third, the social research findings summarized in chapter 2 confirming the hypothesis that "materialists are unhappy because their focus on material goals conflicts with their other goals," especially their social relationships with others. In the American culture of buying and selling, our priorities have become so thoroughly skewed toward getting and spending that an increasing number of Americans have been giving themselves less and less time for the pleasures of leisure and general sociability, let alone for community volunteerism. The psychological definition of a "materialist," as we have pointed out, is a person whose psychic energy is disproportionately interested in things and their symbolic derivatives—wealth, status, and power based on possessions—and therefore whose life consists mainly of experience with the material dimension of life.

Consider, finally, the drama of Cher's transformation in *Clueless*. Her change followed her falling in love with Josh, taking her out of her childish and egoistic self, and leading her to see things from a more adult and fulfilling perspective. Her new perspective included a greater concern for the dignity and well-being of others, the perspective of a citizen of her community. This is neither the perspective of a consumer nor that of a John Alone, isolated from his own natural social yearnings by the deadening habits of an increasingly technological, depersonalized society. Cher's transformation was, moreover, an achievement that *grew out of her depression*, which helped awaken her to the fact that it was time for a change in her life.

The importance of depression is recognized by everyone in the field of mental health. Some psychologists have claimed that "more human suffering has resulted from depression than from any other single disease affecting mankind." As in Cher's case, however, depression can be a signal of our need for change, and can present us with an opportunity for growth. I have experienced this in my own life. In the period immediately following my divorce, I became deeply depressed, as divorced men commonly do. I was fortunate enough not to turn my depression in the direction of the mall, as some research suggests unhappy people may do. Instead, I volunteered for the San Francisco Suicide Prevention 24-hour crisis line; this work enabled me to learn a lot about depression, better understand and appreciate the sufferings of others, and give some of them a needed listening ear. That helped get me through my own depression in several ways. When depression struck me particularly acutely, I spent the very early hours of the morning at the Suicide Prevention Center offices with other members of the crisis-line community until my own crisis had passed. This experience taught me much about how community can contribute to the enrichment of a person's individual life and growth in a pursuit of happiness. And it didn't cost me anything but bus fare.

One of the encouraging, wonderful things about the people of the United States is that we have traditionally shown that we do care about others. With the Marshall Plan for example, Americans provided billions of dollars for the reconstruction of Europe in the aftermath of World War II, not only for reconstruction of our allies' countries but also the countries of our former enemies, in what was perhaps the most generous act of international community in world history. And that humanitarianism earned us the admiration and respect of the entire world. We have lost much of this credit with the rest of the world in recent years, but this traditional American sense of caring for others remains evident in America's young people. Between 1980 and 2001, the percentage of high school seniors who participated in community affairs or volunteer work rose from 23.9 percent to 33.9 percent, an increase of nearly 50 percent, and an almost exact reverse of the decrease in adult volunteerism in the period from 1989 to 2004. As these still generous and idealistic young people enter the American culture of buying and selling as adults, the probability is that unless we can cure or mitigate the effects of consumeritis, their sense of community and citizenship will be consumerized out of them.

Consumeritis has shown itself to be an enemy of community and the highest obligations of citizenship. It is almost, in some respects, a betrayal of humanistic American civil society as it has shown itself to be in the past, and as it may be again—at its best. Too many Americans still fail to appreciate, or appreciate fully, the damage consumeritis is doing to our pursuits of happiness and the dangers it poses to our economic lives. For those especially who do not yet appreciate its damaging effects, perhaps this book, and particularly its next chapter, will offer some help so they will no longer remain—how shall we say it—clueless?

Notes

105 Clueless, *a film released by Paramount in 1995*   Produced by Robert Lawrence and Scott Rudin, written and directed by Amy Heckerling (Paramount Films, 1995).

Jane Austen's novel, Emma, *whose first sentence is*   Jane Austen, *Emma* (1816), (London: Collins Clear-Type Press, 3rd ed., 1953), 19.

109 *We must embrace struggle*   Rainer Maria Rilke, *Letters to a Young Poet* (1908), (hereafter *Letters*), (San Rafael, CA: New World Library, 1992), 63.

On the Waterfront   The movie was produced by Sam Spiegel, directed by Elia Kazan, and written by Malcolm Johnson and Budd Schulberg (Columbia Pictures, 1954). Marlon Brando plays the boxer Terry Malloy, with Rod Steiger cast as his brother.

111 *the desire to own the most currently popular athletic shoe has actually led to homicide*   The source of the following quoted commentary is Rick Telander and Mirko Ilic, "Senseless: In America's Cities, Kids Are Killing Kids over Sneakers and Other Sports Apparel Favored by Drug Dealers; Who's to Blame?" *Sports Illustrated*, 72:20, May 14, 1990. "Sneakers and team jackets are hot, sometimes too hot. Kids are being mugged, even killed for them…. In America's cities, kids are killing kids over sneakers and other sports apparel favored by drug dealers…. Is it the shoes? … For 15-year old Michael Eugene Thomas, it definitely was the shoes. A ninth grader at Meade Senior High School in Anne Arundel County, Maryland, Thomas was found strangled on May 2, 1989. Charged with first degree murder was James David Martin, 17, a basketball buddy who allegedly took Thomas's two week old Air Jordan basketball shoes and left Thomas's barefoot body in the woods near school … [T]here have been plenty other such crimes. Not only for Air Jordans, but also for other brands of athletic shoes, as well as for jackets and caps bearing sports insignia—apparel that Michael Jordan and other athlete endorsers have encouraged American youth to buy. "The killings aren't new. In 1983, 14-year-old Dewitt Duckett was shot to death in the hallway of Harlem Park Junior High in Baltimore by someone who apparently wanted Duckett's silky blue Georgetown jacket. In 1985, 13-year-old Shawn Jones was shot in Detroit after five youths took his Fila sneakers. But lately the pace of the carnage has quickened. In January, 1988, an unidentified Houston boy, a star athlete in various sports, allegedly stabbed and killed 22 year old Eric Allen with a butcher knife after the two argued over a pair of tennis shoes in the home the youths shared with their mothers. Seven months later a gunman in Atlanta allegedly robbed an unnamed 17 year old of his Mercedes-Benz and Avia high tops after shooting to death the boy's 25 year old friend,

Carl Middlebrooks, as Middlebrooks pedaled away on his bike. Last November, Raheem Wells, the quarterback for Detroit Kettering High, was murdered, allegedly by six teenagers who swiped his Nike sneakers. In Baltimore last summer 19-year-old Ronnell Ridgeway was robbed of his $40 sweatpants and then shot and killed. In March, Chris Demby, a 10th grader at Franklin Learning Center in West Philadelphia, was shot and killed for his new Nikes. In April 1989, 16-year-old Johnny Bates was shot to death in Houston by 17-year-old Demetrick Walker after Johnny refused to turn over his Air Jordan high tops. In March, Demetrick was sentenced to life in prison. Said prosecutor Mark Vinson, 'It's bad when we create an image of luxury about athletic gear that it forces people to kill over it.'"

113 *All too often, products are discontinued as a result of business decisions*   Quoted from "Xilinx: Products Obsolescence Policy," at *www.xilinx.com/xcell/x123/x123_14.pdf* (accessed October 5, 2005; site now discontinued).

114 *would have been deeply astonished to be told that a concern for community*   Alan Ryan, "The Magic of I," in *The New York Review of Books*, April 28, 2005.

115 *Love and marriage, love and marriage, go together like a horse and carriage*   The song "Love and Marriage," popularized by Frank Sinatra, was written by Sammy Cahn and Jimmy Van Heusen in 1955 for a TV musical adaptation of a play that has become an American classic, *Our Town*, written in 1940 by Thornton Wilder (1897–1975).

In 1998, 2.2 million couples married in the United States   The marriage, separation, divorce, and related statistics in this paragraph are taken from the "Frequently Asked Questions" section of *The Divorce Center*, reprinted from divorcePeers.com at *www.divorcecenter.org/faqs/stats.htm* (accessed October 3, 2005).

the triumph of hope over experience   attributed to Samuel Johnson (1709–1784) in *Boswell's Life* (1770).

116 *There are many reasons why so many marriages end in divorce now*   Margaret Mead (1901–1978) was a distinguished American anthropologist and writer. Her most famous and controversial book is *Coming of Age in Samoa* (1928), an exploration of sexual mores on whose reliability later anthropologists cast serious doubt. Dr. Mead was also a popular and controversial lecturer on contemporary social issues; she was named "Mother of the Year" by *Time* magazine in 1968. The statement attributed to her is adapted from an unpublished book, *Voices of Light*, by Harrison Sheppard, and is based on his recollection of a talk he heard Dr. Mead give at a hotel in New York in the late 1960s.

117 *The Effects of Debt on Newlyweds and Implications for Education*   Linda M. Skogrand et al., *Journal of Extension*, vol. 42, no. 3, Article no. 3RIB7 (June 2005), *www.joe.org/joe/2005june/rb7.shtml*.

118 *the number one cause of divorce in the United States is financial pressure*   See William Branigin, "Consumer Debt Grows at Alarming Pace: Debt Burden Will Intensify When Interest Rates Rise," *The Washington Post* (January 2004), *www.msnbc.msn.com/Default.aspx?id=3939463&p1=0;* and Selena Maranjian, "Living on Borrowed Dimes," *The Motley Fool: Fool.com* (March, 2004), *www.fool.com/news/commentary/2004/commentary040304SM.htm:* "Another downside to debt is divorce. You're probably aware that roughly half of all marriages today end in divorce, but did you know that the top reason that people end up divorcing is financial? Do you think that debt might be part of the problem here? Me, too."

Marriage is central to our culture   George Lakoff. *Don't Think of an Elephant: Know Your Values and Frame the Debate* (White River Junction, VT: Chelsea Green Publishing, 2004), 46.

the single most important factor affecting people's happiness   In *Happiness*, 63.

119 *divorce has been identified as the clearest reason for rising youth suicide*   In *Happiness*, 79.

The breaking up of families and their fracturing into single-parent homes   Kate Bartkis, Kristin Cahayla, and Christi Ulrich, "Do Break-Ups Cause Break-Ins?" (hereafter "Break-Ups") Muhlenberg College study, supervised by Dr. Arthur Raymond, *Issues in Political Economy: Undergraduate Student Research in Economics*, vol. 9 (Elon University and Mary Washington College, Allentown, PA: Mary Washington College Press, July 2000), 8.

number of children being raised in single-parent families   Dr. Tom O'Connor, "Has There Been an Increase in Juvenile Ruthlessness?" (Wesleyan College, NC: MegaLinks in Criminal Justice, 2005), *faculty.ncwc.edu/toconnor/juvjusp.htm#ESSAY* (accessed November 2005).

the proportion of fatherless children   Ibid.

In 1995, about seven million children five- to fourteen-years-old   Kristin Smith, "Census Bureau Says 7 Million Grade-School Children Home Alone," *United States Department of Commerce News* (Washington, D.C.: Economic and Statistics Administration and Bureau of the Census, October 31, 2000).

Spoiling Childhood: How Well-Meaning Parents Are Giving Children Too Much—But Not What They Need   Diane Ehrensaft, Ph.D. (New York: Guilford Press, 1997); the passages quoted from the book are at pp. 165–168.

120 *Charlie and the Chocolate Factory*   Warner Bros, 2005, directed by Tim Burton, screenplay by John August, based on Ronald Dahl's book of the same name (New York: Alfred A. Knopf, 1964). *Willie Wonka and the Chocolate Factory*, Paramount Pictures, 1971, directed by Mel

Stuart and starring Gene Wilder as Willie Wonka, was the first movie based on the Dahl book.

121 *A comparison of children of divorce with children whose families are legally intact*   All the data cited in this paragraph, with the exception of those relating to alcoholism, come from *Break-Ups*, 2. The UK study relating to "higher levels of alcohol consumption" is cited in William Lay and Derek Rutherford, *Families as a Cause of Alcohol Problems* (Eurocare, 1996–2005; hereafter *Families*), *www.eurocare.org/projects/familyreport/english/famen_p15.html* (accessed November 2005).

122 *For one human being to love another*   *Letters*, 65.

124 *Let me not to the marriage of true minds*   William Shakespeare, *Sonnets*, no. 116.

125 *As Edward Luttwak, a former Reagan administration official now with the Center for International and Strategic Studies*   The quotations of Edward Luttwak and the passage quoted on pages 125 to 126 of the text are in *Affluenza*, 50.

128 *Once a nation of joiners*   See *Affluenza*, 60–61.

The percentage of Americans who volunteer their services   The data in this paragraph come from "Value of Volunteer Time," *Independent Sector* (2004), *www.independentsector.org/programs/research/volunteer_time.html* and the U.S. Department of Labor, *Bureau of Labor Statistic News* (December 2004), *www.bls.gov/news.release/volun.nro.htm*.

131 *In most countries and at most times in history*   For supporting data, see *Happiness*, 50.

Indeed, according to an American association of medical professionals   "Ten Years Later, Greater Access to Treatment Did Not Increase Cost of Depression," *OBGYN Headline News* (January, 2004), *www.obgyn.net/newsheadlines/headline_medical_news-Depression-20040128-0.asp*.

The National Institute of Mental Health has reported   "The Numbers Count: Mental Disorders in America," *National Institute of Mental Health* (2001), *www.nimh.nih.gov/publicat/numbers.cfm*.

132 *Some psychologists have claimed that*   See, for example, the seminal and classic study of depression by Aaron Beck, M.D., *Depression: Causes and Treatment* (Philadelphia, PA: University of Pennsylvania Press, 1967), 41. Beck also points out that "complete recovery from an episode of depression occurs in 70–95 percent of the cases. About 95 percent of the younger patients recover completely." Beck, 55.

I became deeply depressed, as divorced men commonly do   See, for example, *Families*, 15: "There is evidence that divorcees of all ages are at greater risk of premature death than married people. This has been shown for every country with accurate health statistics. For men between the ages of 35 and 45 the risk is doubled ... Divorcees, especially men, have higher mortality from cardiovascular and cerebrovascular disease, cancer, suicide, and accidental death. The strong association between marital breakdown and subsequent ill health both mental and physical has led some to argue that divorce as such should be a key target in strategies for improving public health."

133 *the percentage of high school seniors who participated in community affairs* These data come from the National Center for Education Statistics—Indicator 36: Community Affairs and Volunteer Work, "Youth Indicators, 2005," at *nces.ed.gov/programs/youthindicators/Indicators. asp?PubPageNumber=36* (accessed October 13, 2005).

Clark Gable as Rhett Butler and Vivien Leigh as Scarlett O'Hara in *Gone with the Wind* (MGM, 1939)

4

U.S. and Global Economics of Consumeritis: Risks and Opportunities

I believe only in Rhett Butler.
The rest doesn't mean much to me.
—Clark Gable, as Rhett Butler
in *Gone with the Wind*

After all, tomorrow is another day.
—Vivien Leigh, as Scarlett O'Hara
in *Gone with the Wind*

ONE OF THE greatest and most popular American movies of the twentieth century was *Gone with the Wind*, adapted from the 1936 Pulitzer Prize–winning novel by Margaret Mitchell. The film, which won ten Oscars—a record at the time—was released by MGM in 1939, the same year that *The Wizard of Oz* was released. It was also the same year that World War II began in Europe.

Gone with the Wind is the story of the American Civil War written from a Southerner's perspective. Its drama turns on the reverses of fortune suffered by slave-owning Southern aristocrats as a result of the war, and their recovery during the period of Reconstruction. The film was long enough to be presented in two parts, with an intermission. At the very end of the first part, when the heroine, Scarlett O'Hara, is at the depth of her poverty and misery as a result of the ravaging of her father's beloved plantation, Tara, by Northern troops, she is seen in a field, desperately digging for a radish to eat. She plucks a scrawny vegetable from the earth and, in rage at her condition, and in an expression of her determined will to survive and recover her pre-war prosperity, she raises her fist to the sky and declares, "As God is my witness, I'll never be hungry again!"

This climactic scene appears after the depiction of the epic burning of Atlanta, Georgia, where the author Margaret Mitchell was born. Atlanta's destruction by William T. Sherman, a Union general, prior to his march to the sea, was one of the events of the Civil War most bitterly recalled by Southerners for generations after, and certainly until the time Margaret Mitchell's novel appeared. The film also depicts the early post–Civil War Reconstruction era, during which Scarlett uses her beauty, charm, and guile to captivate the men she needs to help her regain wealth and restore Tara to its pre-war condition; these men include a Charleston buccaneer, Rhett Butler (played by Clark Gable), whom she marries. Her enduring love for another man eventually alienates Butler, and when he announces he is leaving her, Scarlett asks what will become of her if he does. Butler famously replies, "Frankly, my dear, I don't give a damn." As she weeps, Scarlett thinks of her love for Tara and of her father saying to her, "Land is the only thing that matters." The movie ends with Scarlett's determined words: "Tomorrow is another day."

In the annals of history, the destruction caused by the ravages of all-out war have always posed not only the immediate horrors of death and awful physical injury for its duration but incalculably great economic losses for the people who survive it. The economics of recovery from war is a complex matter, and without at least some external assistance, it can be expected to be a prolonged, painful, and arduous process. The Reconstruction period in the South after the Civil War was facilitated by the arrival of opportunistic Northerners—the carpetbaggers—and while their capital was needed for recovery, they were not welcomed by most Southerners (giving the determined Scarlett *her* opportunities). The case of World War II—the most horribly destructive war in human history, causing the deaths of perhaps 50 million people, and the devastation of cities throughout Europe and Asia—was different. The recovery of nations and peoples was, in light of that devastation, almost miraculously swift. Rapid economic recovery was made possible by the generosity of the United States toward its former enemies in both Europe and Asia. We have previously mentioned the Marshall Plan, but the benign U.S. occupation and administration of Japan in the early post-war period was an equally significant factor in helping Japan to become the prosperous nation it is today. American policy in the post–World War II period was thus consistent with what Winston Churchill defined as the "Moral of the Work" in his book *The Second World War*:

In War: Resolution
In Defeat: Defiance
In Victory: Magnanimity
In Peace: Good Will

No matter how helpful American magnanimity and good will may have been to the peoples of Asia and Europe after World War II, however, their achievement of recovery was, after all, made possible by their own will and determination. It also took a great deal of European and Asian labor, economic expertise, skill, and foresight to accomplish their recovery as swiftly as they did. In sum, it takes a combination of political and human will and determination, as well as prudent economic analysis, to help advance and assure a community's well-being in periods of economic pressure.

The extraordinarily high level of American borrowing to

fuel its consumeritis is leading to unprecedented economic pressures on the United States. Economic savvy, national political will, and individual determination must therefore all be kept in mind as we consider the potentially challenging effects of consumeritis on America's future in a global economy, and the risks and opportunities that present themselves to us as individuals in anticipation of that future.

As to considerations of economic savvy, the Scottish essayist Thomas Carlyle (1795–1881) called the study of economics a "dismal science," which is how many people—perhaps even some economists—think of it. The modern global economy is so complex that economists often disagree about the right answers to some of the most basic questions about possible future economic developments. This was especially the case after World War II. Harry Truman, the first post–World War II U.S. president, was so frustrated by the advice his economists gave him that he reportedly hoped to find "a one-handed economist," considering that virtually every piece of advice he was given by the experts was that "on the one hand" *this* could happen, and "on the other hand" *that*. If Harry Truman were alive today and asked his economics experts to tell him what the future effects of continuing consumeritis would be on the American economy, on the one hand, they might agree about some matters; on the other hand, they might substantially disagree about other matters. But the situation may not be as dismal as it was immediately after World War II. As one economist has recently written:

> The practice of economics has advanced immensely since the days of Truman, not so much because of tremendously unique and innovative ideas (no concepts as seminal as Adam Smith's "invisible hand" or Ricardo's "comparative advantage" have been articulated), but because of advances in techniques of formal and empirical

research and the greater availability of relevant and useful information. This makes it harder to substantiate arguments that are wild or completely ideological.

With this encouragement, we now examine the ideas about consumeritis and our economic future on which economists generally agree, those on which they disagree, and the risks and opportunities with which we are presented, considering not only the opinions of the economists, but also the political possibilities and the liberty we each have as individuals to make our own self-determined choices.

Economists' Agreements about Continuing Consumeritis

*Money is a guarantee that we may
have what we want in the future.
Though we need nothing at the moment,
it insures the possibility of satisfying
a new desire when it arises.*
—Aristotle, *Nichomachean Ethics* (4th cent. BC)

He who pays the piper gets to call the tune.
—Old Proverb

There was no doubt a time when all economists would have been inclined to agree that when you run out of money, you can't buy anything, and, moreover, you shouldn't. When Scarlett O'Hara begins her efforts to return to prosperity, she can't afford to buy a new dress; so she makes an elegant one out of the fabric of her window curtains. It is, as we all know, no longer the case that you can't buy anything without ready money. For most of us, running out of cash when we want to buy something only means that we will have to charge it: on the seller's trust, for example, if he knows us; or on a store account or on a credit card; or by taking out a loan from a friend, a relative, the seller, a bank, or a loan company. There was, however, a time within living memory when we Americans didn't do that so often, except to buy a house or a car, or to make a business investment. The fact is that the United States in the twenty-first century runs largely on credit, *big* amounts of credit. As of this writing, the 2005 U.S. government deficit is projected to approach $423 billion, or 3.5 percent of GDP. In contrast, in 2000, the United States had a $245 billion *surplus*, amounting to about 2.5 percent of GDP (see fig. 4.1). In fact, the United States absorbs at least 80 percent of the savings that the rest of the world does not invest at home.

The banks and the lenders, at least at this writing, couldn't be happier about American borrowing, especially in real estate loan financing markets. As Robert D. Manning, author of *The Credit Card Nation,* has written, "In the old days, the best customer was someone who could pay off their loan. Today the best client of the banking industry is someone who will never pay off their loan"—but continue to pay interest on it indefinitely. As we mentioned in chapter 1, apart from real estate loans, private consumer debt totaled over $2 *trillion* in 2004, of which credit-card debt was nearly $820 billion. In that same year, the U.S. external current account deficit stood at $665 billion. The current account deficit represents the difference between capital accounts from American exports to other countries (paid *to* the United States in foreign currencies) and capital accounts for foreign imports to the United States (paid *by* the United States in U.S. dollars), and the difference between foreign purchases of U.S. currency and securities, and U.S. purchases of foreign monies. In 2004, the United States exported $1.5 trillion worth of goods and services, but imported $1.76 trillion worth. In the same year, foreigners bought an amazing $900 billion in U.S. long-term bonds. Foreign central banks are now financing three-quarters of the $665 billion current account deficit. In 2004, $1 trillion of foreign money flowed into the United States, funding private economic activity at a rate as large as in any previous year. While it's no longer accurate to say that when you run out of money you can't buy anything (because you can get it on credit), it is accurate to say that if you run out of money *and* credit, you can't buy anything, or at least you shouldn't when finding additional credit is very costly.

Current account deficits, like any other debt, must be paid back at some point. Nations, like individuals, usually have to consume less in order to pay off their loans, and this can be painful for each. But there is a key difference in the case of reductions in national spending: it can mean recession. As the population and the national government stop spending, firms slow down production and cut costs, including labor costs. To avoid this scenario, an orderly, gradual transition toward savings and away from increased debt is therefore generally less painful for everyone. Otherwise, the charge cards and loan potential we have recently been enjoying so much for our personal consumption will eventually either become maxed to the limit, *or* any credit remaining available to us will be offered at higher—perhaps very much higher—interest rates. These scenarios signify household pain. The more households that share these fates, the greater will be the drop in consumption in the entire economy, representing a recessionary pressure. Just how many households encounter these setbacks at the same time depends on how abruptly the interest rate changes. A gradual rise in the interest rate would imply that households shift away from consumption one by one, in which case we may tiptoe our way around a recession. A sudden rise, however, would require that many households would have to make that shift simultaneously, coupling pain at the household level with the generalized pain of recession.

If this is what will actually happen, then what will households do about paying off all the conveniently available credit debt they have accumulated, much of which was being paid by incurring greater debt? Well, unless they have the means to up their income in a short time by an extraordinary amount, it could mean bankruptcy. Or losing their homes by a foreclosure. Or both. At the least, it will probably bring an end to using home equity for new loans. Whether this is likely to happen and, if so, how soon, is something economists do not agree about. But they all agree, for reasons as plain as $3 - 4 = -1$, that the mounting debt has to stop at some point and reverse itself if Americans and their national government are not to be charged higher interest rates for the mounting riskiness of their borrowing. If the United States were a poorer nation, it would be vulnerable to the type of creditor pressure that led to financial crises in Mexico in 1994, in Russia in 1998, in Brazil in 1999, and in Argentina in 2002; and the International Monetary Fund (IMF) would have forced us to rein in our spending. As Herb Stein, who was chairman of the Council of Economic Advisers from 1972 to 1974, said, "If something cannot go on forever, it will stop." Moreover, our enormous debts are not just public debt, which, in a sense, we owe to ourselves—and especially to our children. Since private U.S. savings are now so low, the money that Americans are borrowing is mostly foreign savings, fueling our high rate of private consumption. As Menzie D. Chinn, a professor of economics, explains:

> In essence, the federal government has been borrowing at very low rates—lower than any other private or government entity—and then providing those resources in the form of a tax cut to households to consume at the government's expense. This is not prudent long-term policy when the government itself faces a set of daunting liabilities on the horizon, from guarantees on pension benefits to Medicare and Social Security.

The largest part of our borrowing is in loans given to us by China and Japan. And he who pays the piper gets to call the tune. American policymakers are relying in large part on the hope that neither China nor Japan will call a tune to which we cannot dance fluidly. This is one of the main reasons that John Snow, the U.S. secretary of the treasury, during a visit to China in October 2005, urged the Chinese government to facilitate consumer credit in China so that "Chinese families would be able to spend more money, buy more goods and perhaps reduce China's huge surplus with the United States."

How might this situation affect Americans in the near and longer term? Imagine the following situation as one microcosmic example of how concern about the present debt and deficit situation might be troubling to us: A couple in their early thirties, with an infant child, has just bought their first home. They've agreed that the mother will interrupt her own career for two years or so until their child can be cared for in nursery school. They can handle their variable interest mortgage payments, but they have also taken on a lot of debt to furnish the house. They live in the suburbs of the city where the young father works, so they are also making payments on a second car. Their monthly medical insurance payments are high. Or consider this second illustration: An older married couple has a first mortgage and a home equity line of credit, both at a variable interest rate, and a new car payment on a hybrid. He is near the limit of the business line of credit he has to keep his business overhead payments current. The couple also has a fair amount of credit-card debt. On the asset side, they have some funds invested toward their retirement, and the husband has a modest Social Security benefit. But the sum of their investments and Social Security is not yet enough to maintain their standard of living if and when the man can no longer earn income. Finally, this older couple also has two grandchildren, ages ten and sixteen, for whom they'd like to help their daughter provide the best possible advanced education and some of the little luxuries that will add pleasure to their childhood and adolescence. While the man continues to work in his own business, he has no prospect of any great addition to his income in the near future. He is, therefore, understandably a little nervous about the present deficit and high debt situation in the United States. His anxiety follows from the fact that almost all economists agree that higher interests rates are on the way sooner or later, essentially for the reasons we've just explained. A rise in interest rates could be dramatic if our foreign debts were called, or if Asian countries either sold off large amounts of U.S. Treasury notes (which is not very likely) or reduced their large purchases of them (which would be more likely).

If interest rates spike fairly quickly, that could mean trouble for both families: the elder as the husband no longer earns income from his business, and the younger because they can anticipate that their financial needs are likely to grow as their family does. So what do economists say about the possibility of a rapid increase in interest rates in the near term? They disagree. Let's look at their disagreements.

Economists' Disagreements about Continuing Consumeritis

> *Money, and not morality,*
> *is the principle of commercial nations.*
> —Thomas Jefferson, Letter (1810)

These words are being written in October 2005. By the time this book is published sometime in 2006, a need to halt and then reverse increasing American debt and deficits may already have become apparent through significant increases in interest rates, either modest and gradual, or sudden and severe. This is one of the critical things about which economists disagree: whether a virtually inevitable increase in interest rates will come sooner or later, and whether it is more likely to be gradual and tolerable or sudden, sharp, and traumatic.

The more optimistic economists, among whom is the chairman of the Federal Reserve Board, Ben S. Bernanke, believe that high American debt and consumption are more a sign of economic strength than of weakness. Bernanke has argued that the low rate of American savings is attributable partly to (1) a "global savings glut" produced by the high savings rate of Asian countries, and (2) "the rise in the global supply of savings [as a result of] the recent metamorphosis of the developing world from a net user to a net supplier of funds to international capital markets." It has been Bernanke's corollary view that

> in particular, during the past few years, the key asset-price effects of the global saving glut appear to have occurred in the market for residential investment ... The expansion of U.S. housing wealth, much of it easily accessible to households through cash-out refinancing and home equity lines of credit, has kept the U.S. national saving low—and, indeed, together with the significant worsening of the federal budget outlook, helped to drive it lower.

What Bernanke is saying is that many Americans are using growth in their home equity as a form of savings and have been willing to continue to go into debt and increase their consumption by borrowing against the increased valuation of their real estate, which permits them to continue to forestall saving in ordinary ways for "the rainy day" they don't see coming. Bernanke is also optimistic about the process of ultimate adjustment of the U.S. trade imbalance and current account deficit. He believes that this will be "medium term or even long-term in nature, suggesting that the situation will eventually begin to improve." His conclusion is that "fundamentally, I see no reason why the whole process should not proceed smoothly," but he cautiously adds that

> the risk of a disorderly adjustment in financial markets always exists, and the appropriately conservative approach for policymakers is to be on guard for any such developments.

In other words, even an optimistic chairman (who was an FRB governor at the time he made the statement) wants us to remain aware of the possibility that interest rates could rise sharply as a result, for example, of foreseeable possible changes in the economic policies of the countries—particularly the Asian countries—who are financing our borrowing in such large amounts. He therefore also recommends government policies "to increase household saving in the United States, for example by creating tax-favored saving vehicles." Bernanke pointed out that while this would have no dramatic effect on the trade imbalance and the U.S. current account deficit,

> increasing U.S. national saving from its current low level
> would support productivity and wealth creation and help
> our society make better provision for the future.

So, again, even the optimistic chairman of the FRB wants us to keep in mind the rainy day that could be coming. Although Bernanke is not alone in his optimistic view that an upward adjustment in interest rates can be a gradual and smooth process, he admits that his view of the causes of the dearth in U.S. savings and his positively encouraging analysis is "unconventional."

The more conventional and prevailing view held by economists is not as encouraging. In a remarkably lucid exposition of the causes, implications, and potentially serious adverse consequences of the U.S. debt situation, Menzie D. Chinn, a professor of public affairs and economics at the University of Wisconsin and former member of the President's Council of Economic Advisors (2000–2001), expounded the view held more generally by economists in his paper "Getting Serious about the Twin Deficits." The twin deficits to which Chinn refers are the current account deficit and the U.S. budget deficit. Chin begins his exposition by pointing out that at the end of 2004, U.S. debt to the rest of the world exceeded its assets by about $2.5 trillion—21 percent of its GDP, a proportion unmatched by any other major developed economy. He further introduces his critical analysis of the U.S. economic situation with the following:

> It would be nice to say that this [indebtedness] situation has started to improve, but in fact the opposite has happened ... Since 2000, the value of the net foreign debt accumulated has been unparalleled. The main culprits in this recent surge are the enormous increases in the current account deficit that largely resulted from the return of the government's budget deficit. The current account balance—the sum of the trade balance and what the U.S. earns from its assets abroad—was about negative 5.7 percentage points of GDP in 2004. The budget balance—the gap between government tax revenues and total spending—was also negative last year, amounting to 4.7 percentage points of GDP. The simultaneous emergence of the two deficits during the mid-1980's led to the characterization of this phenomenon as the "twin deficits" issue, because both economic theory and empirical observation suggested a link between the two gaps.

Chinn points out that "the absolute magnitude of the [current account] deficit [$665.9 billion] is unprecedented because the U.S. looms so large in the international economy." Using figures provided by the Bureau of Economic Analysis, he shows how closely linked the account deficit is to the U.S. net international investment position (see fig. 4.2). About one-third of this deficit is attributable to U.S. imports of foreign oil. Chinn states the prevailing view that

> since the U.S. cannot continue increasing its indebtedness to the rest of the world at this pace—at some point, global investors will tire of holding ever-larger amounts of American debt—the size of the current account deficit is not sustainable.

Chinn makes three recommendations to curtail the deficit.

His highest recommended priority is reducing the growth rate of U.S. government spending and raising its tax revenues. Doing this, he points out, "will curtail overall spending in the economy and thereby reduce the U.S. role as the world's consumer of first resort." Second, he urges substantial reduction of imports of foreign oil. Third, he urges U.S. leaders to remain engaged in the formulation of East Asian policies relating to revaluation of their currencies against the dollar:

> Once East Asian currencies have strengthened noticeably, central bank purchases of U.S. Treasury securities will decline, along with the flow of savings to the United States. U.S. interest rates, savings, and investment will move toward long-run rates, reducing pressure on the trade deficit.

In the absence of such measures, Chinn asserts, the trend toward increasing trade and budget deficits "will not self-correct painlessly." Noting that the Federal Reserve began raising short-term interest rates in mid-2004, Chinn says that, eventually, "higher interest rates will cool consumer spending. But until growth of consumption spending slows down, imports will tend to remain high," and "policymakers can expect the energy [oil] component of the trade deficit to remain large indefinitely."

In his paper, Chinn then addresses the optimistic views expressed by Bernanke and other economists. Chinn acknowledges that Americans "may have a pleasant surprise if global growth booms and Europe and Japan finally run current account deficits." Chinn cautions us, however, that "it doesn't make sense to gamble on this happening [because] such hopes have been dashed before." More specifically, Chinn refutes the Bernanke "saving glut" argument by pointing out that

> this argument would be more convincing if GDP growth
> were being maintained by investment rather than consump-
> tion and, more importantly, if lending to the U.S. took the
> form of purchases of stock and direct investment. Instead,
> a large proportion of capital flowing to the U.S. takes
> place in the form of purchases of U.S. government securi-
> ties—not purchases of American stocks or direct invest-
> ment in its factories ... The fact that foreign central banks
> are doing so much of the lending suggests that the profit
> motive is not behind the ongoing flows to the United States.

The inference is that the Asian central banks' purchases of U.S. Treasury bonds are artificially shoring up the value of the dollar. Purchases of Treasury bonds strengthen the dollar because they increase the demand for U.S. dollars. Issuing the Treasury bonds without a matched demand, however, would weaken the value of the dollar because it increases the supply of dollars. China, as well as other export-oriented Asian economies, buys T-Bills to keep the dollar strong and thus make it easier for holders of dollars to buy Chinese goods. This implies that capital flows into the United States not so much because foreigners want to build malls but because they want to keep selling their goods to us in our malls. Under these circumstances, if present trends continue, the con-sequences are disturbing indeed. Citing the results of a study by the economists Nouriel Roubini and Brad Stetser, Chinn quotes projections that the ratio of debt to GDP could rise to nearly 90 percent by 2015.

> This means that the U.S. would need to devote up to nearly
> 90 percent of its income in that year to pay off its debt to
> the rest of the world. If, instead, the trade deficit were to
> continue to rise—albeit at a lower pace than it has—to
> around 8.5 percent of GDP, the debt ratio would rise to
> over 100 percent.

While acknowledging that the savings glut view "has some intellectual merit," Chinn adds that there is "reason to suspect that much of its newfound popularity stems from how it conveniently absolves U.S. elected officials from taking action." He concludes that

> the conventional wisdom is more plausible: there is a savings *scarcity* in the U.S., driven largely by the federal budget deficit, and it is this savings drought *in the United States* that has been sucking in excess savings from the rest of the world for most of the past five years ... To the extent that the savings glut argument has held some elements of truth ... we have much to fear from an end to that glut. If East Asian investment, which has been unnaturally low since 1977, rebounds, interest rates will rise at exactly the same time as U.S. national savings is declining ... The collision of expanding demand for credit here and abroad will lead to much higher interest rates in the future.

Here may be Chinn's most disturbing conclusions about the twin deficit situation:

> The arguments for a benign view of the deficit ... do not stand up to scrutiny. U.S. citizens and foreign governments *do* need to worry about the current account deficit. The U.S. faces a wide variety of possible outcomes, *with the most dire having a significant likelihood.* One real possibility entails the satiation of global investors' appetite for U.S. Treasury securities, combined with an endless vista of government budget deficits.... In the absence of action, the government's financing needs will increase over time, meaning that more debt will be issued at a faster and faster pace. Foreigners do not have an infinite appetite for treasuries, so yields [interest rates] will have to rise ... or the dollar will plummet. (second emphasis added)

Toward the end of his paper, Chinn addresses the question of how these factors will play out in the broader economy; that is, for example, how they might affect the two hypothetical families we described earlier. He says:

> With interest rates spiking, the housing sector will experience a sharp correction. Since much of the typical American household's wealth is in the form of housing, less wealthy consumers in particular will suddenly be forced to cut back on their spending. The weakening dollar will put upward pressure on import prices, which will then confront the Fed with a choice between accommodating the shock and stifling inflationary pressures. To the extent that the Fed opts for greater price stability, interest rates will have to rise by even more. All of these events will result in a deep recession. Although the likelihood of a "disorderly adjustment" is small, the potential consequences are so troubling that the possibility of economic disruption cannot be ignored. In addition to the threat of rising unemployment and declining income, sharp movements in asset prices and interest rates could also threaten the stability of the financial system … The question is whether [markets] are up to the task of distributing risks when low-probability events occur. This open question should in itself give some additional weight to the case for action now, to avoid putting the world economy in the position of finding out the answer…. There is a looming crisis.

We now have before us both economists' hands on the table. On the one hand, we are told by some of the experts that there is not too much to worry about, but there is a little. Essentially, they say there is no reason to worry because markets know best; and markets know the United States is one of the best places in the world to invest and so they are comfortable sending their "glut of savings" to the United States. If markets did not adhere to this logic, then interest rates would have risen by now. On the other hand, we are told by most of the experts that there is some reason to worry a lot. They are less confident that markets are wise in their evaluation of the entire global situation. They believe that an actual crisis is looming, considering the entire global situation (including factors not discussed in detail here, but also related to the twin deficits). Can we afford, like Rhett Butler, to say frankly that we "don't give a damn"? The authors of this book don't think so. We believe that if we are to think and act responsibly and prudently, we need to consider *now* the risks and opportunities the economists' views present to us. We will now do this.

The Risks and Opportunities We Now Face

At the conclusion of *Gone with the Wind*, Rhett Butler has left Scarlett O'Hara, and Scarlett is thinking about tomorrow. Our sympathies are mostly with her for a number of reasons. Rhett Butler has told us that he doesn't believe in love, that he really only believes in himself. "The rest," he says, "doesn't mean much to me." Scarlett, on the other hand, does believe in love. She has in fact discovered that she loves Rhett, and it was her earlier love for another man that had alienated Butler. The other man, Ashley Wilkes (played in the film by British actor Leslie Howard), also believes in love—and in family. Scarlett also believes in family; in fact, she is rescued from her despair at Butler's departure by thinking of her father and his attachment to Tara (an attachment Scarlett shares partly for her family's well-being), and by thinking of the future, about which she is now concerned. In a dialogue earlier in the film, Ashley tells Scarlett that when circumstances change radically, "Those who have brains and courage come through all right. Those who haven't are winnowed out." Scarlett shows that she has brains and courage in her strategies to recover from the defeat of the South, and at the end of the movie, she is continuing to think, determinedly, about tomorrow. In the economic situation Americans now face, those with brains and courage will try to do the same.

We asked one of the consulting economists for this book, Andres Centeno, how he viewed the economists' disagreements about the likely consequences of continued excess consumption and American debt. He replied, "Think of a situation where an unexploded bomb has dropped on your property. Some people tell you 'There is nothing to worry about. If the bomb was going to explode, it would have done so when it hit the ground.' (This is why Alan Greenspan has called the enduring low interest rates a 'conundrum.' Under ordinary economic processes, interest rates should, as of the time of this writing, already have gone up considerably.) Others tell you 'This is a bomb! It can explode, and there is good reason to suppose that, sooner or later, it will.' If you hear these contrary arguments, will you stay close to the bomb? Or will you get out of its way and try to have it defused?"

To anyone with brains (with or without courage), the answer will be obvious. Even the optimistic economists agree we should get out of the way of the potential explosion of interest rates as they may affect us. As Bernanke has said, "Increasing U.S. national saving from its current low level would support productivity and wealth creation and help our society make better provision for the future." This advice strongly suggests that, in the face of the enormous risks that even the optimistic FRB chairman acknowledges, we should cut our consumption and increase our savings if we are to use our brains.

The call to use our brains is one thing; the call for courage is another. It is a call to see an opportunity for us as individuals in this situation: the opportunity to enjoy, in Auntie Mame's phrase, more of life's "banquet" than consumeritis and the pleasures of consumption offer. It is an opportunity to look within ourselves and use our own imaginations (as James Barrie urged Peter to do) to help us discover the pursuits of happiness of which we are capable, especially if we redirect our energies from materialistic pleasures, as Cher did in *Clueless*, toward the nonmaterialist dimensions of life. It is an opportunity, because these dimensions offer much deeper and more enduring satisfactions. It is also an opportunity to "look behind the curtain," as Dorothy did in *The Wizard of Oz*, and become more aware of the deceptions—the lies, both explicit and implicit—of commercial advertising constantly urging us to spend more money on things to increase a kind of "happiness" that usually turns out to be empty. It is, finally, an opportunity to recognize, as Humphrey Bogart recognized in *Key Largo*, that "more" of the Rocco kind is not the kind of "more" we really need or want to identify ourselves with.

It has been pointed out that people tend to follow the economic practices and policies of the government. When the government spends more, people tend to do so; when it spends less, people tend to economize. This simply follows from the fact that government fiscal expansion (either from tax cuts or increased spending or both) stimulates the economy. The stimulus adds demand to the economy, which motivates firms to expand output, which increases demand for labor, which increases employment, which increases wages, which increases spending. Some economists argue that people will be wise when unsustainable cuts or spending occurs, and will realize that they must save more since they anticipate that taxes will probably have to go up to finance fiscal expansion. This dampens the effect of the stimulus. This matter is still hotly debated among the some of the most talented economists.

On the other hand, when experts virtually unite in saying that government spending at present levels may not only be unsound and risky but may reasonably be seen to be absolutely stupid, people with brains should not want to follow that kind of practice or policy. The good news in all this is not only that reducing our consumption and increasing our savings will help us to stop increasing our debts and thereby reduce the risk of personal bankruptcy from overspending (including the risk of forfeiting our homes in a foreclosure), but that we are being presented with great incentives and an opportunity to enhance the quality of our lives. By recognizing that the level of our getting and spending may now be too much for our own good, and acting wisely on that recognition, we may be able to do more than we have ever done before to increase our own security and the security of our families, and—perhaps most important of all—we may find the energy and imagination we need to better secure for ourselves and those we love our American rights to life, liberty, and the pursuit of happiness.

A part of this opportunity may be realized by reducing our dependence on oil, as Chinn has recommended, and our related American automobile extravagances. This means of prudently reducing our consumption may not only add to our own energies in pursuits of greater happiness but is also necessary to help halt the damage consumeritis has been doing to the physical environments we live in, and to the earth's ecology, whose balance and beauty in some parts of the globe are now also—all too sadly—gone with the wind. These destructive consequences of consumeritis are the topics we discuss in the next chapter.

Notes

141 *One of the greatest and most popular American movies of the twentieth century* The movie was *Gone with the Wind* (MGM, 1939) produced by David O. Selznick, directed by Victor Fleming, with screenwriting credit to Sidney Howard; and starring Clark Gable, the British actors Vivien Leigh and Leslie Howard, and Olivia DeHavilland. While in production, the film actually had several screenwriters and directors.

adapted from the 1936 Pulitzer Prize–winning novel by writer Margaret Mitchell Margaret Mitchell (1900–1949) was awarded the Pulitzer Prize for her novel *Gone with the Wind* in 1937, the year after it was published.

144 *Harry Truman, the first post–World War II U.S. president, was so frustrated by the advice his economists gave him* Harry S. Truman (1884–1972) was the thirty-third president of the United States (1945–1953). The origins of the frequent attribution of the statement about the "one-handed economist" to President Truman are obscure, but it is still frequently made; see, for example, *The Economist*, November 13, 2003, "The one-handed-economist: Paul Krugman and the controversial art of popularizing economics." The statement is also attributed to Herbert C. Hoover (1874–1964), the thirty-first president of the United States (1929–1933), in the form, "Please find me a one-armed economist so we will not always hear 'On the other hand …'" in, for example, Simon James and Robert Parker, *A Dictionary of Business Quotations* (New York: Simon & Schuster, 1990), 45.

The practice of economics has advanced immensely since the days of Truman Andres Centeno, Department of Economics, University of San Francisco, San Francisco, California, in an e-mail dated October 16, 2005, to coauthor Harrison Sheppard concerning an early draft of the beginning of this chapter. Ricardo's "comparative advantage" (also referred to as "relative advantage") is part of the basis for all international economics. It is a principle holding that the total amount of wealth of two nations can be increased through trade even if one nation has no absolute advantage, that is, even if one nation is not as productive as the other in any industry. Adam Smith had argued that it was absolute advantage that brings about gains from trade, but Ricardo proved this intuition inaccurate.

146 *As of this writing, the 2005 U.S. Government deficit* The financial figures stated in this paragraph and the next, including the account deficit estimates, but excluding the last sentence (see the note immediately below), come from the following sources: (1) Brad Stetser and Nouriel Roubini, "How Scary Is the Deficit? Our Money, Our Debt,

Our Problem," *Foreign Affairs,* July/August 2005; and (2) "The Global Savings Glut and the U.S. Current Account Deficit," *Remarks* by Federal Reserve Board Governor Ben S. Bernanke, published in the April 14, 2005, Federal Reserve Board update of a speech given by Bernanke on March 10, 2005, at the Sandridge Lecture, Virginia Association of Economists, Richmond, Virginia (hereafter Bernanke).

In fact, the United States absorbs at least 80 percent of the savings that the rest of the world does not invest at home Nouriel Roubini and Brad Stetser, "Will the Bretton Woods 2 Regime Unravel Soon?" p. 2. This paper was written for the symposium "Revived Bretton Woods System: A New Paradigm for Asian Development?" organized by the Federal Reserve Bank of San Francisco (and University of California, Berkeley), San Francisco, February 4, 2005.

As Robert D. Manning The quotation comes from "Consumer debt grows at alarming pace: Debt burden will intensify when interest rates rise," *MSNBC,* at *msnbc.com/Default.aspx?id=3939463&pl=0* (accessed October 19, 2005).

148 *In essence, the federal government has been borrowing at very low rates* Menzie D. Chinn, "Getting Serious about the Twin Deficits," *Council of Foreign Relations,* September 2005, 9.

149 *John Snow, the U.S. secretary of the treasury, during a visit to China* Edmund L. Andres, "Snow Urges Consumerism on China Trip," *New York Times,* October 14, 2005.

151 *The more optimistic economists, among whom is the chairman of the Federal Reserve Board, Ben S. Bernanke* See Bernanke, cited above.

152 *Getting Serious About the Twin Deficits* This is a paper Menzie D. Chinn prepared for the Bernard and Irene Schwartz series on *The Future of American Competitiveness,* published in September 2005, by the *Council of Foreign Relations* (CSR No. 10). All the quotations of Chinn that follow are from this paper.

Earth from Apollo 17, NASA, 1972

5

The Environmental Wasteland: Pollution, Waste, Litter, and Global Warming

> *April is the cruelest month,*
> *Breeding lilacs out of the dead land,*
> *Mixing memory and desire,*
> *Stirring dull roots with spring rain.*
> —T. S. Eliot, *The Waste Land* (1922)

> *The major cause of the continued deterioration of*
> *the global environment is the unsustainable pattern*
> *of consumption and production,*
> *particularly in industrialized countries.*
> —United Nations, *Agenda 21* (1992)

WINGED MIGRATION IS undoubtedly one of the most aesthetically captivating films ever made. Released in the United States in 2003 (the original French version, *Le Peuple Migrateur,* was first shown in Europe in 2001), it documents the migration of birds from pole to pole, through and above all seven continents, and over forty countries around the globe. As one reviewer put it, "The movie is, in three words, beautiful beautiful beautiful." The beauty of the film is not only in its marvelous, graceful, and often poignant depiction of the

flight and migration of birds but in what it shows us of the exqui-
site and delicate beauty of the terrain, waters, and climates of
the planet: its plains, hills, and mountains; its lakes, seas, and
oceans; its arctic expanses and fertile fields; and the play of sun
and shadow on the magnificent vistas perceived from a bird's
eye view around the globe. It is a film, as another reviewer wrote,
that is "as humbling as it is remarkable."

Winged Migration is humbling in what it reveals about the
extraordinary stamina, sensitivity, and intelligence of Earth's
winged species. (One species of bird migrates from the North to
the South Pole and back every year; pelicans will embrace human
beings with affection—with what intelligence may be an open
question.) The film is also humbling in its symphonic depiction
of the planet we inhabit with other living creatures; a depiction
of how vulnerable we, they, and the earth can be to the depredations of humankind's industrial effluvia; and a depiction of the
ecological havoc thoughtlessness and greed can cause. In other
words, it artfully suggests what we have to lose if we act ignorantly,
carelessly, or disrespectfully of the earth's ecology.

One of the sadder consequences of humankind's extraordinary technological achievements as we have progressively mas-
tered and exploited nature during the past century has been a
growing disrespect for it—to our growing peril. The book of
Genesis 1:1–3 poetically tells us:

> In the beginning God created the heaven and the earth.
> And the earth was without form, and void; and dark-
> ness was upon the face of the deep. And the Spirit of God
> moved upon the face of the waters. And God said, Let
> there be light: and there was light.

Traditional veneration for the sublimity of nature in the
Western world was reflected in the well-known biblical saying,

"The earth is the Lord's, and the fullness thereof, the world and they that dwell therein" (Psalms 24:1), and in a corresponding respect for the designs of nature as part of a cosmic ordering in which human beings should seek and find a proper and harmonious place. Religionists who have heretically turned their backs on this tradition, and chosen instead to believe that the earth is made for the use of humankind alone, ignore the primacy that was accorded to "the laws of nature" in the most venerable writings of the Judeo-Christian canon, and the respect for "Nature and Nature's God" that was expressed by the Enlightenment thinkers who composed our Declaration of Independence. Pride in our scientific achievements has lessened the force of our classical respect for nature. On the other hand, the picture of the earth from the moon captured by astronauts and man-made satellites has become a modern icon, reminding us of the fragility of our gloriously blue, white-clouded planetary home as seen from outer space. Too many people—including some who should know better—are, however, unaware or too little aware or even disregardful of how vulnerable our planet can be to human interference with its ecology. Many people were first alerted to this fact in 1962 by Rachel Carson's book *Silent Spring,* which documents such depredations as the injury pesticides have done to birds, ending their songs as signals of the coming spring in many places.

A seminal insight that may help us appreciate our cosmic interdependence on nature—as opposed to unthinking acceptance of the delusion that our advanced technology may permit us to tyrannize it with impunity—is consideration of the common roots of the words "ecology" and "economy," and the essential relationship of those words to the household. The Greek word *oikia* signifies things "relating or belonging to a house or household." "Economy" essentially signifies the management, governance, or rule of the household, whether that of a family, a city, a nation, or of the global community. The biological extension of economy is "ecology," the branch of biology that deals with the relationship of living organisms to their environment. As these etymologies indicate, a household, its economy, and its environment are so closely interrelated that the character or quality of one necessarily affects the character and quality of the others. The need to integrate and harmonize the operation of our households with the whole of our economic lives and our environments has become an urgent matter. The present chapter explores this necessity in detail.

T. S. Eliot termed April the "cruelest month" because of the revivifying effects of spring on our dormant passions. For cruelty, however, even unwelcome stirrings of passion cannot match in depth, scope, or magnitude the cruelty that the diseconomies of consumeritis have been inflicting on us, on other living creatures, and on the planet's ecological balance. Residents of villages, towns, and cities in or near highly industrialized areas are already acquainted with one manifestation of that cruelty, whose name is a word coined in the twentieth century: the combination of smoke and fog called smog, which can literally choke us to death. This and similarly far-reaching adverse effects of consumeritis on living, breathing creatures and the planet's ecology were ignored for a long time by American policymakers. But the situation has become so serious that many who have so far been deaf to urgent calls to remedy it, and blind to the effects of the air pollution around them, are beginning to heed the demands of environmentalists for corrective action. Our overuse of oil and gas-fueled transportation has been the chief culprit implicated in the particular cruelty of air pollution, and it is one of consumeritis's most directly destructive effects. America's romance with the gas-fueled automobile has become so disproportionate to the imperatives of sound economy and ecology that it has demonstrably become too much for our own good; it is one of the chief aspects of consumeritis that need to be corrected. We will therefore begin our exploration of the interrelationship of the household, the economy, and the environment, and the adverse effects of excess consumption on each of them, both locally and globally, with car consumeritis.

Car Consumeritis

> *Come away with me, Lucille,*
> *in my merry Oldsmobile.*
> —Gus Edwards and Vincent P. Bryan,
> "In My Merry Oldsmobile" (1905)

America's romance with the automobile began more than a century ago. As its very name implies, the automobile gave a new mobility to Americans: the freedom of the road. Over time, it helped to make it increasingly difficult "to keep them down on the farm" as it brought rural and urban life closer together. The automobile's liberation of rural Americans captured the imagination of songwriters almost as soon as the horseless carriage was a recognizable vehicle. We have seen how Henry Ford's mass production and innovative automobile consumer financing in the 1920s had major effects on American society, and made substantial contributions to American industry and affluence. In 1990, I visited a farm in southern Illinois on an excursion with the photographer Jock McDonald, who has been photographing images of rural village life around the world to preserve a visual record of its diminishing vestiges, and to depict the common humanity threaded through its diversity. We had the opportunity to meet the grand matron of the rural county we were visiting, a woman over one hundred years old who still clearly had her wits about her. I asked her what she thought was the greatest change she had witnessed in her long life, and there was no hesitation in her response. "Oh," she said with certainty, "I can remember the day I first saw an automobile coming down that road," pointing toward the highway leading to her farm. "That changed everything."

Now, in the twenty-first century, it is difficult for most of us to imagine what life would be like without cars and trucks and buses and motorcycles. With the exception of the railroad, used mainly for long-distance travel, late nineteenth- and early twentieth-century Americans had to rely almost entirely on their own legs or on horses to get around the countryside. The automobile not only provided an innovative mode of local travel, it radically accelerated the pace of daily life in virtually all its dimensions. Just try to imagine how different the pace and quality of our daily lives would be if we could get around only on foot or by horse or horse-drawn carriage. (The difference might not be altogether for the worse.)

Today many American commuters routinely travel distances by car or bus that, a century ago, they would have planned as carefully as we now plan our vacation travels. I can recall, as late as the 1950s, before the development of the federal interstate highway system, how our family's sixty-five mile drive from Philadelphia to Atlantic City for summer vacations was considered a significant journey. Millions of Americans now commute that distance daily to and from their jobs. In 2003, Americans drove an average of nearly ten thousand miles *per capita* (not per driver). According to the 2004 American Community Survey of the U.S. Census Bureau, more than three out of four American workers (over 101 million, or almost 78 percent of the total U.S. workforce) commuted to work every day by *driving alone* in a car, truck, or van. Only 10 percent of American workers (13,183,471) carpooled, and less than 5 percent (5,978,055) used public transportation. A little more than three million workers (2.38 percent) walked to work, while about five million (4 percent) worked at home. The high percentage (78 percent) who drive to and from work alone is an extravagance that is a matter of public concern for many reasons, and the percentage has been increasing steadily. Twenty-five years ago, in 1980, the percentage was 64.4 percent, representing a growth in the period 1980–2004 of about 14 percent or, on average, more than half a percent a year.

Our dependence on the automobile for transportation, even in our cities, continues to grow. In 1965, there were nine cars on the road for every ten licensed drivers. In 1971, the number of licensed drivers and licensed motor vehicles were about equal. By 2003, there were over 231 million licensed motor vehicles (excluding motorcycles and military vehicles) for 195 million licensed drivers, or almost 18 percent more vehicles than licensed drivers (see table 5.1). (This excess is, of course, partly accounted for by commercial vehicles.) In 2003, licensed drivers constituted almost 87 percent (196,165,666) of the U.S. population of driving age (225,953,387). No urban or suburban American needs to have statistics cited in order to be aware of the problems of traffic congestion these figures indicate.

Americans' overreliance on the automobile is far more than just a source of daily inconvenience; there were about forty-three thousand traffic-related fatalities in the United States for each of the years 2002 and 2003. In fact, more Americans have been killed in traffic accidents than in all the wars the United States has fought since 1776. Though the overused automobile has added to the hazards of daily living from accidents, and to its inconvenience from traffic congestion, it is doing even more harm to us directly from its contribution to air pollution. Carbon monoxide is a primary air pollutant, produced by combustion in the auto engine. It has been estimated that about seventy thousand people in the United States die each year from causes directly related to air pollution.

As we have already suggested, smog is especially implicated in this elevated morbidity and mortality. Smog, which is formed by chemicals emitted by vehicles and power plants, is the most widespread air-quality problem in the United States. A study of ninety-five urban areas found that a small increase in the average smog level over seven days can lead to a 0.5 percent rise in deaths on the seventh day.

> The increase in deaths after a smoggy week is "relatively small," says Arden Pope, an air-quality researcher at Brigham Young University in Provo, Utah. "The concern is that exposure is ubiquitous and the number of people affected is large. You take a small risk and spread it out over huge numbers of people, and you end up with a fairly large impact."

The EPA says that smog levels above 84 parts per billion threaten public health, and levels in many urban areas exceed 90 parts per billion on warm, sunny days. One of the more disturbing attributes of smog is its potentially damaging genetic effects. Recent studies of air pollutants caused by emissions from steel plants and automobiles suggest that genetic changes caused by air pollution may be inherited. Studies examining the effects of these pollutants on the DNA of mice showed that mice populations whose parents were exposed to the pollutants inherited twice as many mutations as mice from unexposed populations.

As decent human beings, if we clearly understood that emissions from our own automobiles were responsible for contributing to the serious illnesses or deaths of others—perhaps members

of our own families, our circle of friends, or our local communities—from agitated asthma, bronchitis, emphysema, lung
and heart disease, or other respiratory allergies, wouldn't we be
more inclined to use our own motor vehicles less and rely more
on carpools and public transportation? There is no escaping the
conclusion that emissions from our own individual automobiles,
vans, trucks, and motorcycles are having precisely that effect. In
recognition of this reality, we may each wish to consider how we
might economize and ecologize our motor vehicle use.

Jane Jacobs has pointed out in her book *Dark Age Ahead* that
ecological ignorance has destroyed past empires and civilizations;
it could do so again. American ignorance of the environmental
damage caused by excess automobile usage is largely the willed
ignorance of denial. Many of us just don't want to see that the
fault lies in ourselves. We are free, however, to reject denial and
change willed ignorance into greater self-knowledge. To do this,
we need only remember to see ourselves and our households as
integral parts of our communities, and acknowledge the contribution we can choose to make to our own environments, to the
health of our families and friends, and, not so incidentally, to our
own physical and economic health as well. Americans who cling
to dependence on gas-guzzling automobile travel and overuse it,
despite the evidence of its harmful effects, may be exhibiting less
affection for human beings than pelicans do, particularly since
there are available alternatives that require little or no sacrifice of
personal convenience (as described in chapter 8) such as hybrid-
fueled vehicles, carpooling, and public transportation.

The ecological damage American overconsumption causes
through release of pollutants into the air we breathe also gives
new meaning to the phrase "ugly American." Per capita carbon-
dioxide emissions in the United States are more than twice those
of the United Kingdom and Japan and nearly three times that of

the European Union; see fig. 5.1 and the discussion in chapter 7 of the adverse effect the U.S. refusal to sign the Kyoto Treaty on global warming has had on world opinion. It gives the people of other cultures—including Europeans—good reason to disdain "the American way." The author Jeremy Rifkin, president of the Foundation on Economic Trends in Washington, D.C., is another informed American observer who urges us to stop indulging in willful ignorance and take a realistic look at what we are doing to ourselves. In his recent book, *The European Dream: How Europe's Vision of the Future Is Quietly Eclipsing the American Dream,* he concludes that American patterns of excess consumption may amount to a death wish.

> The American Dream is largely caught up in the death instinct. We seek autonomy at all costs. We overconsume, indulge our every appetite, and waste the Earth's largesse. We put a premium on unrestrained economic growth, reward the powerful and marginalize the vulnerable ... We consider ourselves a chosen people and, therefore, entitled to more than our fair share of the Earth's bounty ... We have become a death culture.
>
> What do I mean by "death culture"? Simply this. No one, and especially no American, would deny that we are the most voracious consumers in the world. We forget, however, that consumption and death are deeply intertwined. The term "consumption" dates back to the early fourteenth century and has both English and French roots. Originally, to "consume" meant to destroy, to pillage, to subdue, to exhaust. It is a word steeped in violence and until the twentieth century had only negative connotations. Remember that as late as the early 1900's, the medical community and the public referred to tuberculosis as "consumption." Consumption only metamorphosed into a positive term at the hands of twentieth century advertisers who began to equate consumption with choice....

Today, Americans consume upwards of a third of the world's energy and vast amounts of the Earth's other resources, despite the fact that we make up less than 5 percent of the world's population. We are fast consuming the Earth's remaining endowment to feed our near insatiable individual appetites.

The problem of our excessive use of energy from fossil fuels is not merely an economic matter; it includes growing threats to the ecology of the entire planet because of its continuing contribution to global warming. "Global warming," which may pose unprecedented disruption of our planet's ecological balance, refers to a measurable increase in the average temperature of the earth's atmosphere that has occurred during the past century.

According to the National Academy of Sciences, the Earth's surface temperature has risen by about 1 degree Fahrenheit in the past century, with accelerated warming during the past two decades. There is new and stronger evidence that most of the warming over the last 50 years is attributable to ... the buildup of greenhouse gases— primarily carbon dioxide [a primary byproduct of auto emissions], methane, and nitrous oxide. The heat-trapping property of these gases is undisputed ... Energy from the sun drives the Earth's weather and climate, and heats the Earth's surface; in turn, the Earth radiates energy back into space. Atmospheric greenhouse gases (water vapor, carbon dioxide, and other gases) trap some of the outgoing energy, retaining heat somewhat like the glass panels of a greenhouse. Without this natural "greenhouse effect," temperatures would be much lower than they are now, and life as known today would not be possible. Instead, thanks to greenhouse gases, the Earth's average temperature is a more hospitable 60°F. However, problems may arise when the atmospheric concentration of greenhouse gases increases.

> Since the beginning of the industrial revolution,
> atmospheric concentrations of carbon dioxide have
> increased nearly 30%, methane concentrations have
> more than doubled, and nitrous oxide concentrations
> have risen by about 15%. These increases have enhanced
> the heat-trapping capability of the Earth's atmosphere....
> Scientists generally believe that the combustion of fossil
> fuels and other human activities are the primary reason
> for the increased concentration of carbon dioxide ... Fos-
> sil fuels burned to run cars and trucks, heat homes and
> businesses, and power factories are responsible for about
> 98% of U.S. carbon dioxide emissions, 24% of methane
> emissions, and 18% of nitrous oxide emissions. Increased
> agriculture, deforestation, landfills, industrial production,
> and mining also contribute a significant share of emis-
> sions. In 1997, the United States emitted about one-fifth
> of total global greenhouse gases.

The EPA predicts that by 2100, in the absence of emissions
control policies, carbon dioxide concentrations will be 30–150
percent higher than today's levels. Consistent with EPA's predictions, greenhouse gas levels continue to climb, and the evidence
is now undeniable that the threat is real and unprecedented. A
front page story in the *San Francisco Chronicle* on November 25,
2005, headlined "Greenhouse gas levels highest ever measured,"
reports such evidence. Recent studies based on drillings of Ant-
arctic ice reveal the millennial history of global temperatures;
these studies show that this warming is not cyclical (i.e., part
of the swings in climate from ice ages to temperate periods) but
unprecedented in the earth's long ecological history; thus, these
studies refute those who dismiss the global warming threat.

Among the most significant risks associated with continued
global warming, which causes melting polar ice caps to continuously increase the volume of water in the oceans, is the threat it

poses to our coastal cities. Economic prosperity largely depends on international commerce. Most international ports are located at sea level and are therefore at risk of being flooded by rising sea levels. Such floods could lead to global crises of unprecedented proportions. An abrupt flooding of key world ports and highly populated coastal areas could result simultaneously in many disasters of the magnitude suffered by parts of Asia because of the Indian Ocean tsunami in 2004 and by New Orleans in the hurricane floods of 2005. The social and political instability to the point of anarchy, the possibility of famine, and the potential for chaos resulting from massive refugee populations around the globe are horrible to contemplate. Contrary to the skeptical view referred to above, recent scientific evidence clearly supports the conclusion that these grim possibilities are not science-fiction fantasies but potential consequences of the real threats we face if the pace of global warming is not abated or reversed during this century. Among other things, such reversal would require that we keep in mind the likely effects of our own household economies (especially as they relate to motor vehicle usage) on the lives and well-being of other households. We are already pretty much aware of the extent to which our use of oil and gas-fueled vehicles has become increasingly costly and less economical. Our excess consumption of nonrenewable energy sources is, as Rifkin suggests, a form of consumeritis that threatens the economic and ecological future of the entire world. It is to this subject we now migrate, aiming for a clear, unsmoggy view of the terrain we are about to cover.

Too Little Energy: Nonrenewable Resources and Consumeritis

Even when a bird walks,
we see that it has wings.
—A. M. Lemierre, *Fastes* (1775)

Finding a way to reconcile economic development
with the limited biological and mineral resources
available on a small planet, especially without
compromising the planet's life-support functions,
is the fundamental challenge of our generation.
—Edgar Hertwich, "Consumption
and Industrial Ecology"

Even though *Winged Migration* mostly just shows birds flying, the film has many poignant moments. These include glimpses of the arduous fight for survival that animates the migration of birds; the natural obstacles of wind, rain, and snow they must struggle against in their flight; and the inhospitable terrains of desert, ocean, and ice on which they must from time to time alight to regain their strength. Nature has equipped winged creatures with what they need to overcome these natural obstacles. Perhaps the most painful moments of the movie are those that show the man-made obstacles to survival for which winged creatures are unprepared by nature, obstacles such as oceanic oil spills, polluted swamps, and ground filled with oil and other industrial effluvia. Whether they can survive these threats is far more a matter of chance than of nature, and scenes of their death-defying struggles in unnaturally contaminated environments are therefore especially poignant. From a human perspective, there is some irony in these scenes. As Colin Campbell has written in *Forecasting Global Oil Supply*, "Few would deny that the world runs on oil." Just as its negligent management can be life threatening to creatures of the sky and sea, its negligent and short-sighted management is now threatening to compromise the quality of our own continued survival as a technologically advanced society.

> Industrial ecology has mainly been conceived with improving the efficiency of production systems. But addressing consumption is also vital in reducing the impact of society on its environment ... [Some experts argue] vehemently that the scale of consumption in modern society is both environmentally and psychologically damaging, and that we could reduce consumption significantly without threatening the quality of our lives.

If it is fair to say the world runs on oil, we have to face the question, What will be done when we run out of it? Indeed, as Campbell has observed:

> The critical issue is not so much when oil will eventually run out, but rather when production will reach a peak and begin to decline, which will represent a major watershed for the world's economy.

Our present overuse and overdependence on oil has therefore created a double-barreled risk and opportunity for American consumers. We can risk (1) lowering our standard of living and (2) the further degradation of our environment. Or we can (1) find ways to live better by consuming less and (2) thereby simultaneously reduce our negative impact on the environment.

Oil presently provides about 40 percent of global energy needs and about 90 percent of the world's transport fuel. A cogent and persuasive analysis of the past, present, and future state of the world's oil production and supply is set out by the M. King Hubert Center for Petroleum Supply Studies. The center predicts that oil production will begin its decline around the year 2010. On the basis of a global survey and analysis of the relationship between oil discoveries and peak oil production following discovery since 1930, the Hubert Center analysis concludes, "It is evident that the world will have to learn to use less, much less, which should not be difficult given the current waste." An earlier article by Colin Campbell, "Peak Oil: A Turning for Mankind," distills the following conclusions from the realities of U.S. and global oil discovery, production, and consumption:

> The fundamental driver of the 20th century's economic prosperity has been an abundant supply of cheap oil ... The United States is perhaps the most vulnerable to the coming crisis having farther to fall after the boom years, which themselves were largely driven by foreign debt and inward investment.... The U.S. has to somehow find a way to cut its demand by at least five percent a year. It won't be easy, but as the octogenarian said of old age "the alternative is even worse."... This is clearly revealed by even the simplest analysis of discovery and production trends. The inexplicable part is our great reluctance to look reality in the face and at least make some plans for what promises to be one of the greatest economic and political discontinuities of all time. Time is of the essence. It is later than you think.

The dimensions of this crisis and the foreseeable problems it will create if not properly addressed were reflected in the August 2005 issue of *National Geographic* in a cover story devoted to its possible solutions. The story, titled "After Oil: Powering the Future," examines the dangers of what it calls our oil addiction, and notes, consistent with the Hubert analysis, that

> every 24 hours California's Carson Refinery produces seven million gallons of gasoline—only 14 percent of the state's daily diet. Oil is king, but with supplies tight and production expected to peak in the next few decades, the future depends on finding an heir.

The Hubert–Campbell analyses are so unequivocal about the dimensions and certainty of the coming energy crisis, and the necessity for reduced oil consumption that they might give readers the impression that there can be no debate about their conclusions. But there is a continuing debate about them, despite the clear evidence relied on by the Hubert Center and the inferences it logically draws from the available relevant data. This debate and the urgent necessity for a meeting of the minds among the debaters are delineated in two articles in a recent issue of the *Journal of Industrial Ecology.* The first article, "Consumption: It Is Time for Economists and Scientists to Talk," begins from an environmental perspective, pointing out that

> the U.S. National Academy of Sciences, the British Royal Society, the United Nations Environmental Program, the U.S. President's Council on Sustainable Development, and notable leaders from almost every sector have identified unsustainable consumption and production as the root causes of ecological degradation. Agenda 21, the 1992 Earth Summit's final report, observes that "the major cause of the continued deterioration of the global environment is the unsustainable pattern of consumption and production, particularly in industrialized countries."

The article concludes by stating the necessity for a "new path" that "must be supported by elected officials, economists, and private sector leaders willing to face the conundrum of our times: that increased consumption is literally bringing our biological home into ruin and yet, without consumption, millions fear for their security." These fears—concerns about jobs if our nonrenewable energy consumption is systematically reduced— indicate the axis of the debate the article discusses: the debate between scientists who warn about the predictable depletion of our petroleum resources and economists who worry about the adverse economic effects of reduction in consumption. The elements of this debate inevitably lead to the question posed by the title of the second article: "Live Better by Consuming Less?" a close, extended analysis of the issues. It notes the emphatic view of one of the proponents for the conventional economic side of the argument, namely that "the desire to moderate consumption or to establish a normalizing network of needs is naïve and absurd moralism." In its concluding discussion, the article cogently summarizes the clashing philosophical perspectives that form the deepest bases for debate between eco-humanists on the one hand, and two branches of the opposing view (characterized as proponents of "consumption-as-evolution" and "consumption-as-meaning").

> The eco-humanist view of consumption as a social pathol-
> ogy arises as a dialectical response to the conventional
> economic insatiability of *wants.* In place of insatiability,
> the eco-humanists place sufficiency in the satisfaction of
> *needs,* and they emphasize the social and psychological
> dangers of materialism. The consumption-as-evolution
> avenue warns against any simplistic adoption of this per-
> spective by emphasizing the evolved nature of consumer
> behaviors, whereas the consumption-as-meaning school
> attacks the eco-humanist approach for failing to account
> for the symbolic nature of material goods. It emphasizes
> the vital social and cultural roles that consumer artifacts
> are called upon to play. (emphases added)

You may recognize members of the "consumption-as-mean-ing" school as disciples of Thorsten Veblen's analysis of the social significance of conspicuous consumption, that is, as a sign of mastery and social status. You may likewise recognize members of the "consumption-as-evolution" school as disciples of Adam Smith, holding on to the invisible hand of self-interest as the most reliable mechanism for social progress consistent with individual liberty. The eco-humanists are represented by scientists and petroleum experts who insist on the necessity for economy in consumption and a shift to renewable energy sources;

the authoritative, disinterested national and international public agencies, among others, named in the first article quoted above; and all those who are concerned about the ecological damage done by our overconsumption of energy. Acknowledging the force and vitality of the opposing views, the author of "Live Better by Consuming Less?" poses the ultimate question:

> How should we now construe the idea that it is possible to live better by consuming less? Should this simply be abandoned as an unrealistic reading of a much more complex situation? Or is there still room for maneuver in negotiating a less materialistic society that is also capable of delivering improved well-being?

The author's final answer to these questions is consistent with the theses of this book (especially as articulated in chapter 2) that American overconsumption is not in fact advancing American happiness; that the materialistic excesses we enjoy are really too much for our own good; and that most Americans are capable of appreciating this fact for themselves and finding ways to elevate their pursuits of happiness beyond materialism. The article "Live Better by Consuming Less?" concludes:

> The insight that a certain amount of consumer behavior is dedicated to an (ultimately flawed) pursuit of meaning [that is, securing happiness mainly through materialistic pursuits] opens up the tantalizing possibility of devising some other, more successful and less ecological damaging strategy for pursuing personal and cultural meaning.
> This is not, in any sense, a simple task … It is a fundamentally social and cultural project, which will require sophisticated policy interventions at many different levels … Nonetheless, it remains a very real possibility that we could collectively devise a society in which it is possible to live better (or at least as well as we have done) by consuming less, and become more human in the process.

The expansion of our humanity—foreseen as a possibility by the author of that article, by us, and by many other humanists who wish to promote greater respect for our planet's balanced ecology—would also include more conscious concern about the ways in which excess consumption has been despoiling our environment and creating wastelands where once there was fertility and beauty. It is to the creation of these consumeritis-generated wastelands that we now turn our attention.

Consumeritis and the Wasteland

Winged Migration gives us only a few fleeting glimpses of the pollution of natural environments by oil spills and industrial discharges. There is some encouraging news about the frequency of such incidents: according to the U.S. Coast Guard, "there is a general downward trend in the number of spills over 1,000 gallons." Most of us have, however, seen televised news reports from time to time of the catastrophic effects of large oil spills on marine life and seabirds. When such spills do occur, they are ecological disasters. The *Exxon Valdez* incident in 1989 is the most spectacular example. In that incident, the American oil tanker *Exxon Valdez* collided with a reef, causing an oil spill that polluted 1900 square kilometers of Alaskan coastline, killing approximately 250,000 sea birds, 2,800 sea otters, 250 bald eagles, and possibly 22 killer whales. More recently, in January 2003, two oil tankers, the *Vicky* and the *Tricolor*, collided, causing oil spills from the *Vicky* to flow into the sea and reach French and Belgian shores. At the end of that month, another ship collided with the *Tricolor* wreck, causing the *Tricolor* also to leak at least 1,000 tons of oil. Nearly 10,000 seabirds washed up on the Belgian shore from the effects of these spills and were collected on Belgian beaches, more than half of them dead.

Many Americans may react with horror and righteous indignation at these foreign ecological disasters, and congratulate themselves on their innocence of such environmental disasters, attributing them to negligent seamen and avaricious oil producers. But not so fast. The damage and losses ordinary Americans are causing from the waste products of their consumeritis is, in the aggregate, greater than the damage done and losses caused by these occasional marine catastrophes. We are, moreover, doing this damage with our litter on land and in and near waterways. Americans throw away about 35 billion aluminum cans every year. If all of these cans were recycled, we would save an amount of energy equivalent to 150 *Exxon Valdez* oil spills annually. In our description of the excesses of consumeritis in chapter 1, we cited the almost unbelievable amount of waste our consumer society generates—enough, it has been said, to fill a line of garbage trucks every year reaching halfway to the moon. Unfortunately, this waste is not entirely disposed of as collected garbage for landfill or incineration; much of it is also distributed as litter in our city streets, parks, and forests, and on our riverbanks, lakeshores, and beaches.

On average, each man, woman, and child in the United States generates 4.5 pounds of solid waste a day; cumulatively, that's over a billion pounds or half a million tons of daily waste. Americans will thus, on average, leave a lifetime legacy of 112,410 pounds of trash. The wastefulness indicated by this volume of trash is suggested by the fact that the average American consumer uses nearly 20 tons of raw materials each year, twice that of the average Japanese or European. One child born in the United States adds more to consumption and pollution over his or her lifetime than do thirty to fifty children born in developing countries. The food Americans throw away could, if transportable, alleviate much world famine. Americans throw away about 10 percent of the food they buy at the supermarket, dumping the equivalent of more than 21 million shopping bags full of food into landfills every year. In the aggregate, nearly a ton of waste materials per person in the United States is deposited in landfills each year, creating billions of cubic yards of wasteland. While landfill space is plentiful on the national level, some areas of the United States, particularly the heavily populated East Coast, have less landfill capacity and higher landfill costs. The largest component of waste (40 percent) is paper and cardboard; about 8 million tons of magazines alone are dumped annually into landfills in the United States. Much of this paper waste comes from junk mail, an apotheosis of commercial waste. About 44 percent of junk mail is never opened or read, and Americans toss out 2 million tons of junk mail annually (at a hauling cost of $320 million). If a million people ordered their junk mail stopped, we'd save about 1.5 million trees a year.

Recycling, which includes composting, is, however, one of the greatest environmental success stories of the late twentieth century. It diverted more than 72 million tons of materials away from landfills and incinerators in 2003, up from 34 million tons in 1990—doubling in just ten years. Recycling a ton of aluminum saves the equivalent of 2,350 gallons of gasoline, or the amount of electricity used by the typical home over ten years. Recycling a six-pack of aluminum cans may save enough energy to drive a car five miles; just one recycled aluminum can saves enough electricity to operate a TV for three hours.

In contrast to our recycling progress, litter remains an important environmental issue. As John Kenneth Galbraith remarked, our quest for "private opulence has led to public squalor." While 94 percent of the public identify litter as a major environmental problem, people still litter.

> Litter discarded in streets and parks can travel through
> storm water to our bays and oceans, where it can cause

harm to wildlife ... Removing litter from the environment costs everyone money. Litter is a threat to public
health. It attracts vermin and is a breeding ground for
bacteria ... Litter can be a fire hazard ... Litter attracts
litter. It sends out a message that people do not care for
the environment and that it is acceptable to litter.

The damaging effect of our litter on wildlife is a growing
problem.

Birds, mammals, and reptiles can be injured or killed by
the trash we throw away. The magnitude of the problem
is growing every day, especially because some types of
litter do not readily disintegrate and therefore remain in
the environment as a threat for decades.... The amount
of litter that ends up spoiling the beauty of the natural
environment is not surprising considering the amount
of waste we produce: Glass bottles, plastic packaging, tin
cans, newspaper, cardboard, and other types of garbage
litter urban and rural landscapes everywhere.

Unfortunately, our environmental litter is not limited to
urban and rural landscapes. It extends to the depths of oceans
and to the highest reaches.

When a climbing party reached North America's highest
peak [Mt. McKinley], they found a pile of partially eaten
food, foil wrappers from freeze-dried meals, plastic bags,
and other trash left behind by previous climbers.

In the 1960s, the chairman of the Federal Communications
Commission, Newton Minow, characterized American television
programming of the time as having become "a vast wasteland."
The relentless, progressive commercialization of that wasteland, reinforced by what is appropriately called *junk* mail, has,
in a more than merely poetic sense, contributed to making the
United States itself in some respects a vast wasteland of material excess, pollution, garbage, and litter. Some progress is being

made against the extension of this wasteland, but not enough to ensure our own future good. We urgently need to consider and adopt the best practical remedies available to help us rescue ourselves from ourselves; and we need to learn how we may restore a greater harmony among our households, our economies, and our environments, both local and global. (Chapter 8 of this book discusses what some of those remedies might be.)

The stilled birds of Rachel Carson's *Silent Spring,* the oil-soaked birds of Alaska and the Belgian Coast, the birds in flight in *Winged Migration,* and the pelicans—all should remind us of the need to care more about our environment and the effects its degradation and pollution are having not only on other living creatures but on our fellow humans at home and abroad. Even if we acquire the social and political will to act on such needs, how can we determine whether the public officials we elect will enact and enforce laws that will be faithful to such a will for change? This has been made especially difficult and problematic because the political landfill occupying much of the vast wasteland of television has by now been thoroughly corrupted by the advertising techniques that fuel consumeritis. The same kind of dream-making that is the leading principle of commercial advertising effectiveness is now endemic to American political campaigning. It is to this pervasive commercialized corruption of the American political process that we now turn our attention.

Notes

165 *The major cause of the continued deterioration of the global environment* The epigraph, from the United Nations *Agenda 21*, Chapter 4.3
(1992), was quoted and cited by Betsy Taylor in "Consumption: It Is
Time for Economists and Scientists to Talk," *Journal of Industrial Ecology*, vol. 9, issues 1–2 (Winter–Spring 2005), 14.

*Winged Migration is undoubtedly one of the most aesthetically capti-
vating films* Released in the United States by Sony Pictures in 2003,
Winged Migration, the English version of *Le Peuple Migrateur* (2001),
was directed by Jacques Perrin; codirected by Jacques Cluzard; produced by Christophe Barratier; and written by Jean Dorst, Stephanie
Durand, Guy Jarry, Jacques Perrin, Valentine Perrin, and Francis Roux.
The English-language version was narrated by Jacques Perrin and Phillipe Labro.

The movie is, in three words Jeffrey Chen, November 24, 2003, in *www.
windowtothemovies.com/af2003-2.html#wingedmigration*. Chen writes,
"*Winged Migration* is sparsely narrated, showing almost nothing but birds
flying. It's less a nature documentary than it is a movie that offers a transcendent experience through achieving a spiritual unity with nature ...
The movie is, in three words, beautiful beautiful beautiful."

166 *It is a film, as another reviewer wrote, that is "as humbling as it is
remarkable"* Joe Baltake, "'Winged' is a Soaring Achievement in Filmmaking," *Sacramento Bee*, June 13, 2003.

167 *the most venerable writings of the Judeo-Christian canon* In addition
to the Old Testament sayings quoted in the text, one may also refer to
Thomas Aquinas's *Summa Theologica* as a seminal part of the canon
infused with an overriding respect for "Natural Law."

*Many people were first alerted to this fact in 1962 by Rachel Carson's
book* Rachel Carson, *Silent Spring* (New York: Houghton Mifflin,
1962).

168 *But the situation has become so serious* See, for example, the front
page story in the October 14, 2005, issue of the *San Francisco Chronicle*,
"A national conversation on conservation: Environmentalists hope the
time is now." The story begins, "It took $3-a-gallon gasoline, the promise
of record home heating bills this winter and the White House rolling
out a conservation campaign ... to give environmentalists something
they've been craving for years."

169 *Come away with me, Lucille* Gus Edwards and Vincent P. Bryan wrote
the song "In My Merry Oldsmobile" in 1905.

photographer Jock McDonald Jock McDonald, born in Vancouver, Canada, in 1961, is a San Francisco, California, photographer whose *Rurals*

collection has been exhibited in galleries and museums in the United
States, Mexico, and Cuba, and published in printed media throughout
the world, perhaps most notably in *The Human Condition* (New York:
Graphis, 1995).

171 *more Americans have been killed in traffic accidents than in all the
wars* According to *Death Statistics Comparison* (UnitedJustice.com
Staff, *Death Statistics Comparison,* Radok Corporation, 1998–2005), the
number of deaths from car accidents has averaged 42,116 for the last
nineteen years in the United States. That's over eight hundred thousand
deaths in less than twenty years. From these figures it may be inferred
with certainty that the death toll from car accidents since the automobile's mass production in the 1920s has greatly exceeded the 1.2 million fatal war casualties estimated on the authority of Hannah Fischer,
American War and Military Operations Casualties: Lists and Statistics
(Washington, D.C.: Navy Department Library, July 13, 2005).

172 *Carbon monoxide is a primary air pollutant* Bernie Fischlowitz-Roberts,
"Air Pollution Fatalities Now Exceed Traffic Fatalities by 3 to 1," Earth
Policy Institute (Washington, D.C.: Earth Policy Institute, 2002), *www.
earth-policy.org/Updates/Update17.htm* (accessed February 7, 2006).

   Smog, which is formed by chemicals The data in this paragraph come
from "Urban smog causes immediate rise in deaths from heart disease,
lung disease," *News Target: Daily news and commentary on natural health,
wellness, planetary health and medicine, www.newstarget.com/002508.
html* (accessed November 8, 2005).

   *One of the more disturbing attributes of smog is its potentially damag-
ing genetic effects* Reference to the reported studies of the transmitted
mutating effects of air pollution on the DNA of mice may be found in
Kate Ruder, "Air Pollution Causes Genetic Mutations," *Genome News
Network, www.genomenewsnetwork.org/articles/2004/05/13/airpollution.
php* (accessed November 8, 2005).

173 *Jane Jacobs has pointed out* Jane Jacobs, *Dark Age Ahead.* (New York:
Random House, 2004), 14–15. Jacobs writes: "Mesopotamia, the so-called
Fertile Crescent of the Tigris and Euphrates rivers—traditionally thought
to be the site of the biblical Garden of Eden—in historical terms has
centered on the fabled city of Baghdad. For some nine thousand years,
starting in about 8500 B.C.E., almost every major innovation adopted
in ancient Europe had originated in or very near the Fertile Crescent:
grain cultivation; writing; brickmaking; masonry engineering, and
construction; the wheel; weaving; pottery making; irrigation…. [T]he
Fertile Crescent was the seat of the ancient world's earliest empires:
Sumer, Babylon, Assyria…. By 115 C.E., Mesopotamia had been con-
quered by Rome and became a Roman province … [T]he lead was lost
through environmental ignorance. In ancient times, much of the Fertile Crescent and eastern Mediterranean was covered with forests. But

to obtain more farmland and more timber, and to satisfy the plaster industry's relentless demands for wood fuel, the forests were cut faster than they could regenerate. Denuded valleys silted up, and intensified irrigation led to salt accumulation in the soil. Overgrazing by goats, allowing new growth no start in life, sealed the destruction. The damage had become irreversible ... by 400 B.C.E. What escaped earlier has been done in recently: 'The last forests in modern Jordan ... were felled by Ottoman Turks during railroad construction just before World War I. Most of the last wetlands, the great reed marshes of southern Iraq, with their complex ecology of plants, mammals, insects, birds, and human beings too—the "Marsh Arabs" who had occupied these lands for some five thousand years—fell to a drainage scheme undertaken for political reasons by Saddam Hussein in the 1990's, creating another barren, salt-encrusted desert.'" Jacobs's quotations are from Jared Diamond's book, *Guns, Germs, and Steel* (New York: Norton, 1997, paperback 1999).

174 *The author Jeremy Rifkin* The passage quoted may be found on pages 379–380 of Rifkin's *The European Dream* (New York: Jeremy Tarcher/ Penguin, 2005).

175 *According to the National Academy of Sciences* The extended quotation is from an Internet publication of the U.S. Environmental Protection Agency, at *yosemite.epa.gov/oar/globalwarming.nsf/content/climate.html* (accessed December 2, 2005).

178 *Too Little Energy: Nonrenewable Resources and Consumeritis* While the title of this section refers to nonrenewable resources generally, in the interest of brevity its discussion focuses our consideration on petroleum products. Many of the sources cited in its text and notes do, however, also discuss excess consumption of other nonrenewable energy sources such as coal.

Finding a way to reconcile economic development This epigraph is from Edgar Hertwich, "Consumption and Industrial Ecology," *Journal of Industrial Ecology*, vol. 9, issues 1–2, 2005. *mitpress.mit.edu/journals/ JIEC/v9n1_2/jiec_9_1-2_001_0.pdf* (accessed March 2, 2006).

As Colin Campbell has written Colin Campbell, "Forecasting Global Oil Supply 2000–2050," *Hubert Center Newsletter* (2002). (hereafter *Hubert*)

179 *Industrial ecology has mainly been conceived with improving the efficiency* Tim Jackson, "Live Better by Consuming Less?" *Journal of Industrial Ecology*, vol. 9, Winter–Spring 2005, 19.

The critical issue is not so much when oil will eventually run out See *Hubert*.

A cogent and persuasive analysis of the past, present, and future state of the world's oil Ibid.

The fundamental driver of the 20th century's economic prosperity has been an abundant supply of cheap oil Colin Campbell, "Peak Oil: A Turning for Mankind," *Hubert Center Newsletter,* April 2001.

181 *the U.S. National Academy of Sciences, the British Royal Society* Betsy Taylor, "Consumption: It Is Time for Economists and Scientists to Talk," *Journal of Industrial Ecology,* vol. 9, Winter–Spring 2005.

182 *The eco-humanist view of consumption as a social pathology* Tim Jackson, "Live Better by Consuming Less?" *Journal of Industrial Ecology,* vol. 9, Winter–Spring 2005.

184 *there is a general downward trend in the number of spills* "Polluting Incident Compendium: Cumulative Data and Graphics for Oil Spills 1973–2001," United States Coast Guard, *www.uscg.mil/hq/g-m/nmc/ response/stats/Summary.htm* (accessed February 8, 2006). This site also includes detailed oil-spill data and tables showing the following for 1973–2001: Total Number of Spills by Spill Size; Oil Spills in U.S. Waters Over 1,000 Gallons; Total Volume of Spills By Spill Size (Gallons); Total Number of Spills by Waterbody; Total Volume of Spills by Waterbody (Gallons); Total Number of Spills by Location; Total Volume of Spills by Location (Gallons); Total Number of Spills by Source; Total Volume of Spills by Source (Gallons); Total Number of Spills by Type of Oil; Total Volume of Spills by Type of Oil (Gallons); Total Number of Spills by Coast Guard District; Total Volume of Spills by Coast Guard District (Gallons).

The Exxon Valdez incident This account of the *Exxon Valdez* incident comes from Enzler, *Environmental Disasters* (hereafter Lenntech), (Delft, The Netherlands: Lenntech Water Treatment & Air Purification Holding B. V., 1998–2005), *www.lenntech.com/environmental-disasters. htm.*

two oil tankers, the Vicky and the Tricolor, collided This account of the *Tricolor* oil spills comes from Lenntech, and the statistical account of the damage is extracted from "Birds victim of oil pollution during the *Tricolor* incident," *Management Unit of the North Sea Mathematical Models* (Belgium: Department VI of the Royal Belgian Institute of Natural Sciences, 2002–2005), *www.mumm.ac.be/EN/Management/ Nature/event_birds.php.*

185 *Americans throw away about 35 billion aluminum cans every year* "Solid Waste Factoids," Oregon Department of Environmental Quality, at *www. deq.state.or.us/wmc/solwaste/cwrc/edpro2.html* (accessed November 22, 2005) (hereafter DEQ). Unless otherwise annotated, statistics in this section relating to recycling energy ratios and waste equivalents are taken from this source.

On average, each man, woman, and child in the United States generates 4.5 pounds of solid waste The waste data in this paragraph is derived from various sources cited in DEQ.

186   *Recycling, which includes composting, is, however, one of the greatest environmental success stories*   "Frequently Asked Questions about Recycling and Waste Management," *U.S. Environmental Protection Agency Municipal Solid Waste Website* at *www.epa.gov/epaoswer/non-hw/muncpl/faq.htm* (accessed February 14, 2006).

   As John Kenneth Galbraith remarked   As quoted in *Affluenza*, 146.

   While 94 percent of the public identify litter as a major environmental problem   This statistic and the quotation that follows comes from *Litter, An Environmental Education Program of the Prague Post Endowment Fund*, vol. 4, no. 9. February 19, 2003.

187   *Birds, mammals, and reptiles can be injured*   This statement is from "Environmental, Chemistry & Hazardous Materials News, Information & Resources," *EnvironmentalChemistry.com* (accessed November 22, 2005).

   When a climbing party reached North America's highest peak   G. Tyler Miller, Jr., "Living in the Environment, 1990," as quoted in DEQ.

   Newton Minow, characterized American television programming of the time as having become "a vast wasteland."   Newton Minow, then chairman of the FCC, made this comment in "Television and the Public Interest," a speech given to the National Association of Broadcasters on May 9, 1961.

Orson Welles as Charles Foster Kane and Joseph Cotton as Jedediah Leland in *Citizen Kane* (RKO and Mercury Productions, 1941)

6

The Political Costs of Consumeritis: Threatened Loss of Citizenship and Civil Liberty

Bread and circuses (Panem et circenses).
—Juvenal, *Satires X* (AD 125)

Presidential campaigns rely almost entirely
on the entertainment and
advertising techniques of television.
—Russell Baker

ITIZEN KANE, WHOSE original working title was "John Citizen," was released by RKO Pictures in 1941. It is generally acknowledged to be a masterpiece of filmmaking. Produced, directed, and co-written by Orson Welles at age twenty-four, it ignored conventional cinematic techniques and provided a host of innovations in photography, lighting, and subject matter. The movie tells the story of Charles Foster Kane, a rich young man who builds a newspaper empire and sacrifices his professed ideals on the altar of yellow journalism. The film portrays Kane as a grasping, vain, selfish, and ambitious man who dies alone on a vast Florida estate among his art treasures. There had never been another picture like *Citizen Kane*. It openly satirized a wealthy and powerful living American—William Randolph Hearst, the owner of a newspaper empire whose inflammatory editorial policies were the epitome of yellow journalism, and who, at one time, considered running for president. The power and originality of the film made Orson Welles (who cast himself as Kane in the film) the most praised and criticized man in Hollywood.

True to life in many ways, *Citizen Kane* showed the power of mass media to form public opinion. In one exchange in the movie, a woman says to Kane, "Really, Charles, people will think—" and Kane finishes the sentence by saying "—what I tell them to think." In one memorable scene, Kane receives a cable from a reporter named Wheeler whom he has sent to Cuba to report on the situation there, hoping to find evidence of downtrodden Cubans rebelling against their Spanish governors so Kane can instigate a war between the United States and Spain. Kane asks an assistant to read the cable:

> Bernstein (reading): "Girls delightful in Cuba. Stop. Could send you prose poems about scenery, but don't feel right spending your money. Stop. There is no war in Cuba, signed Wheeler." Any answer?
> Kane: Yes. "Dear Wheeler: you provide the prose poems. I'll provide the war."

The following dialogue takes place later between Kane and a friend, Jed Leland (played by Joseph Cotton):

> Kane: Are we going to declare war on Spain, or are we not?
> Leland: *The Inquirer* [Kane's newspaper] already has.

In the days before television, Kane understands the manipulative inaccuracies of all mass media. He advises a friend, "Don't believe everything you hear on the radio."

By the 1950s, television, which had grown to become the most popular American mass medium, was already beholden to commercialism. This corruption had led Edward R. Murrow, the most highly respected radio and television journalist in the United States at the time, to say that television was

> being used to distract, delude, amuse, and insulate us [when it] can teach, illuminate, even inspire. But it can do so only to the extent that humans are determined to use it to those ends.

As we have pointed out, televised commercial advertising is the chief fuel of American consumeritis, accounting for nearly 20 percent of advertising sales in all media. The effectiveness of television's commercial advertising techniques has helped transform American politics from reliance on debates about substantive issues to competition for the most stirring sound bites and image-making consumer appeal. Packaging presidential candidates as commercial products might be considered an insult to the American electorate—except that Americans are buying it. It works. Campaign managers who have observed the effectiveness of commercial advertising want their candidates to benefit from the habits commercial advertising has engendered in the public through appeals to contrived tastes and appetites. Commenting on the important role television played in John F. Kennedy's political success, Gretchen Rubin, in her recent book *Forty Ways to Look at JFK,* observes:

> It's one of the curious characteristics of television that, in a kind of cynosure effect, no matter how lofty or insipid the context, the mere sight of a face on TV significantly increases an audience's interest, and the more the image is repeated, the more attractive it becomes. After [John F.] Kennedy's appearance at the 1956 Democratic National Convention, female college students surrounded his car shouting, "We love you on TV!"

Image building played little part in the earliest days of the American republic. George Washington was a highly aloof man who despised appeals to public passions and sentiment, as did the cantankerous John Adams, our second president. The early era of American politics was, however, not free of political rhetoric or even (foreshadowing today's negative campaigning) vitriolic mudslinging. The brutality and coarseness of some journalistic character assassination of the period may have surpassed today's. Our third president, Thomas Jefferson, —a man of genius appropriately venerated as the principal drafter of the Declaration of Independence, a man Tocqueville called "the greatest living democrat" of the age—was not above denigrating the character of his political opponents, though he did so covertly. Secret agents acting on his behalf smeared his political rivals with strategically placed newspaper articles. But in deference to the high standards set by his predecessors, Jefferson himself strictly maintained the appearance of probity. Notwithstanding use of mudslinging in early presidential politics, and some image making, the American political process continued in the main to focus on substantive matters throughout the nineteenth century. Abraham Lincoln followed the advice of a little girl and grew a beard to improve his appearance a month before the election of 1860, but he won the presidency chiefly because of his position on the issues.

At the turn of the twentieth century, leading Democratic and Republican presidential candidates were still able to avoid or minimize public appearances, and to rely mainly on their substantive political positions to win office. William McKinley, for example, notoriously stayed at home, often visible on his front porch receiving convention delegates, during most of the presidential campaign of 1900. As late as the 1940s, political campaigning continued to be conducted chiefly by the candidates' debates about the issues of the day. President Harry Truman seemed to most Americans to be a "little man" in comparison to his pre-

decessor, Franklin Delano Roosevelt. Truman surprised almost
everyone by his upset election to the presidency in his own right
in 1948, not by "selling himself," but by "giving hell" to a Repub-
lican-dominated Congress for its inaction on matters of concern
to the post-war American electorate.

In 1952 and 1956, Dwight D. Eisenhower, a popular World War
II leader of the D-Day invasion and Allied campaign in Europe,
was considered a sure winner in both races against Adlai Stevenson of Illinois. (Eisenhower had been asked by both the Democratic and Republican parties to be their candidate for president
in 1952). The campaign slogan "I Like Ike" was in an old political
tradition, but it was also an effective sound bite, with Madison
Avenue advertising influences. In fact, Eisenhower's campaign
for reelection in 1956

> was the first presidential campaign which relied heavily
> on political television commercials. After the election,
> "[President Harry] Truman, referring to the effects of
> political advertising ... commented that it was the first
> time in 148 years that a president had been elected with-
> out carrying a Congress with him."

Commercialized presidential campaign tactics escalated
dramatically in the 1960s. When John F. Kennedy was preparing
his first election campaign for a Massachusetts Congressional
seat in 1946, his father, Joseph P. Kennedy, told his family that
to get his son elected president, "We're going to sell Jack like
soap flakes." In 1960, John F. Kennedy was elected as America's
first Catholic president. The success of selling JFK was substantially assisted by the Kennedy-Nixon debates, the first televised
debates between presidential candidates. While voters who listened to the first debate on the radio felt that Richard Nixon
had won, Nixon's tense, drawn, five-o'clock-shadow appearance

on TV so contrasted with JFK's confident, charismatic, tanned handsomeness that Kennedy was proclaimed the clear winner in the competition for consumer—er, that is, voter—appeal by those, including professional campaign observers, who saw the debate on television.

By his second run for the presidency in 1968, Nixon had learned his lesson. He engaged as one of his top campaign advisors—and later his first White House chief of staff—H. R. Haldeman, a man with more than twenty years of experience with the J. Walter Thompson advertising agency. As a result of his commercial advertising experience and expertise, Haldeman was credited with revitalizing Nixon's public image. It is therefore no wonder that, following Nixon's presidential victory in 1968, a best-selling book by the author Joe McGinniss describing the campaign was titled *The Selling of the President*. Richard Nixon has the distinction of being the first elected president to put experts in commercial advertising at the core of his administration's operations, as well as being the only U.S. president to resign from office. (His resignation was, in fact, the direct result of the events known as Watergate, relating to his amoral political campaign practices.)

By 1972, selling presidents like soap flakes had become the standard for presidential campaigning, but many voters were at first turned off by the spectacle. Voter turnout in 1972 decreased by nearly 10 percent from the 1968 election, from 60.8 percent to 55.2 percent, and has (with the exception of the 1992 election when there were three major candidates) generally decreased since (see fig. 6.1).

> People in today's society are becoming more and more apathetic about voting; voter turnout in recent elections has hit an all-time low. In addition, people are becoming increasingly disinterested in spending time researching

the various candidates and their platforms. Why exert
effort to seek out independent information when one can
simply turn on the radio or television and get barraged
with all sorts of political rhetoric?

As we have suggested, the shift in American politicking—
from emphasis on substantive issues to competition for appeal
to the irrational preferences of voters—is a direct outgrowth of
American commercialism and the successful marketing techniques feeding consumeritis. Its escalating importance bears
an inverse relationship to the relevance and health of typical
American political discourse. Political professionals and their
advertising experts now habitually exploit the transformation
of the American electorate from a body of citizens to a mass of
consumers. If we were a sensibly aroused citizenry, we might be
angry enough about this to wish for a Harry Truman to give most
politicians hell for their commercial demagoguery and negative political campaigning (about which, more below). But this
exploitation of the electorate's commercial conditioning is now
so universal that we may be condemned to suffer forever, in the
manner of Orwell's *1984*, with television's political Big Brother
imagery, propaganda, and mass appeal.

Thoughtful political observers such as George Anastaplo
acknowledge the benefits of television, but point out the ways in
which the injuries it has done to American political and cultural
life now appear clearly to outweigh its benefits in critical ways.

> Some see the American people, in tens of millions,
> elevated politically and culturally by the mass media.
> Such elevation, others reply, is not good for these mil-
> lions; they cannot become truly enlightened; they are
> much more likely to become frustrated. Most peo-
> ple, it seems to me, have not been elevated; rather,
> their cultural life, as well as their politics, has become
> inferior to what it had been, and their thinking less

disciplined and more sentimental than it need be ...

This social indictment of television can be summed up thus: Each of us is constantly addressed by television apart from the others, and yet none of us is ever really spoken to. The ability to read, and hence to think and to join in serious common discourse, suffers. Every kind of association is filtered through the camera and stripped of its humanity. The community is depreciated while a hollow privacy is emphasized; communal tastes are reduced to the lowest common denominator and then shamelessly catered to. Spectacle replaces theatre; feeling replaces thought; image replaces character. The world shaped by television is an empty one, starved and frenetic, dreamlike and debilitating. It can be expected to culminate eventually in a crippling mediocrity and perhaps even in tyranny.

Anastaplo's description of the "vast wasteland" television has become, and its sorrowful effects on American communal, social, political, and cultural life, echoes the chilling prediction of Alexis de Tocqueville, quoted in the first chapter of this book, about what thorough-going materialistic individualism in American democracy might lead us to; that is, to a benevolent-seeming political order that "stupefies" us.

I seek to trace the novel features under which despotism may appear in the world. The first thing that strikes the observation is an innumerable multitude of men, all equal and alike, incessantly endeavoring to procure the petty and paltry pleasures with which they glut their lives. Each of them, living apart, is as a stranger to the fate of all the rest; his children and his private friends constitute to him the whole of mankind. As for the rest of his fellow citizens, he is close to them, but does not see them; he touches them, but he does not feel them; he exists only in himself and for himself alone; and if his kindred still remain to him, he may be said at any rate to have lost his country. Above this race of men stands an immense and tutelary power, which takes upon itself alone to secure their gratifications, and to watch over their fate ... Such power does not tyrannize, but it compresses, enervates, extinguishes, and stupefies a people, till it is reduced to be nothing better than a flock of timid and industrious animals, of which the government is the shepherd.

Tocqueville wrote this at the beginning of the nineteenth century, long before the invention of television, which, as Anastaplo has pointed out, operates successfully to reinforce the alienation of individuals from their community. The connection Anastaplo makes between the effects of television on American cultural life and its consistency with the possible rise of tyranny through its erosion of our sense of community—was a connection foreseen by Tocqueville, even though, in the passage just quoted, he avoided the direct imputation of a tyrannous future for the American polity.

No vice of the human heart is so acceptable to [despotism] as selfishness; a despot easily forgives his subjects for not loving him, provided they do not love one another.... Despotism, then, which is at all times dangerous, is more particularly to be feared in democratic ages.

To the extent, in other words, that we are successfully encouraged by our commercialized television culture to focus habitually on our individual pleasures and wants to the neglect of our sense of community ties and obligations, we make it easier for the government to manipulate us to behave the way tyrants prefer their subjects to behave; that is, without regard to the welfare of the community as a whole and the well-being of others. The great magnitude and power of the forces working on us to perpetuate and extend a change from community awareness to isolated individualism and political ignorance is evident in the growth of campaign advertising expenditures during the past two generations. Between 1952 (when the majority of voters said "I Like Ike" with their ballots) and 1988, campaign spending in the United States grew fifteenfold. The growth of commercial political television advertising since 1972, the year of Richard Nixon's reelection, has been enormous (see fig. 6.2). The amount of money spent on political television ads in the nation's one hundred largest media markets in 2004 was over $1.6 billion, more than double the $771 million spent in 2000, the previous presidential election year. The commercial political advertising this money bought substantially eclipsed serious political reporting and journalistic coverage on television.

> The deluge of ads swamped the meager campaign coverage that most local [TV] stations offered. According to the Lear Center News Archive, in presidential battleground states, a half-hour of local news averaged almost six minutes of campaign advertising, but only three minutes of campaign news. Forty-five percent of all campaign stories were about strategy or horserace, while only 29 percent focused on campaign issues. Ad watch stories, which truth-check the political commercials, made up less than one percent of campaign stories in the study's sample.

From its beginnings in the 1950s, political campaign advertising borrowed the techniques of commercial advertising, but the character and substance of political advertising have progressively degenerated during the past quarter century.

> Prior to the 1980's candidates usually used issue or image ads at the beginning of a campaign to establish their positive image and then used negative ads at the end of the campaign to attack the opponent. However, these strategies were abandoned in the 1980's. A significant trend in today's political advertising is the increasing use of

negative political advertising. In today's political campaign, candidates, either challengers or incumbents, use
negative ads from the beginning of a political campaign.
After examining more than 1,100 political commercials
[one political consultant] asserted ... "If there is a single
trend obvious to most American consultants, it is the
increasing proportion of negative political advertising....
At least a third of all spot commercials in recent campaigns
have been negative, and in a minority of campaigns half
or more of the spots are negative in tone or substance."

Would it be unfair to characterize this development as indicating that political campaign advertising now generally oscil-
lates between candidate "dream-making" through positive
images on the one hand, and increasing negative "nightmaring"
on the other, leaving little room for discussion of down-to-earth
realities or serious political discourse? The kind of commercialized dream-making now typical of political advertising reflects
a serious decline in political ethics since television first became
an important factor. Though he used television to great political
effect, President Kennedy still allied himself with a higher vision
of a president's responsibilities to voters in his campaign appeals.

Walking through the White House grounds, Kennedy
reflected, "A politician is a dream merchant." After a
moment, he added, "But he must back up the dream."

American political candidates now evidently feel compelled
to conduct their campaigns on the basis of perceived consumer
preferences, and position themselves in TV ads as commercial-
like products rather than as aspiring statesmen taking detailed
positions on issues that may distinguish them from other candidates. A sound-bite culture characterizes political advertising
almost as much as it does commercial advertising—and, in sad

fact, even television news. This makes it extremely difficult (perhaps impossible) for televised substantive political discussions to take place for even a small portion of the time bought for positive and negative sound-bite political commercials. The loss of vigorous, substantive political debate is a loss of the lifeblood of democracy. Winston Churchill, the great wartime prime minister of England, was one of only three people made honorary citizens of the United States by Congress in recognition of his incomparable service to the cause of human liberty. Though Churchill's father was the son of an English duke, his mother was American, and Churchill believed in the democratic process as conceived by America's founders.

> He believed passionately in democracy, and he believed that the vitality of democracy depended upon the serious discussion by an informed electorate of opposed philosophies and a real choice between rival visions of the future. [He] would have been appalled at the reduction of complex issues to sound bites and the trivialization of debate that has occurred since [his] death.

The continuation of televised political debate between presidential candidates—however choreographed, filtered, and orchestrated they might be compared, for example, to the Lincoln-Douglas debates—remains one of the few examples of significant televised politics that may permit comparison of candidates based on an in-depth examination of their respective views (depending, of course, on the exact formats adopted and the skills of third-party moderators and questioners).

The commercialized character of American political campaign advertising is open and visible to everyone. But it may mask a more general, devious, and pernicious shift in the character of American political life from what the founders hoped it could be.

As we have pointed out, Richard Nixon was the first American president to put experts in commercial advertising at the core of his administration's operations. This signified more than political reward to Nixon's campaign staffers; it also signaled the routine elevation of commercial advertising techniques to the presentation and treatment of political issues of high public concern. Our consumerized society has thus promoted not only the regular "selling of the president" during presidential campaigns but, by adopting commercial advertising techniques for the selling of positions on the issues, it has effectively abandoned that "marketplace of ideas" the First Amendment was designed to protect, and substituted in its place the spin typical in the marketplace of merchandise. Careful scrutiny of press releases now regularly issued by the White House and state governors throughout the nation should largely confirm this conclusion.

In sum, the prevalent commercial techniques of political campaign advertising and their extension to partisan treatment of public issues suggests that political discourse of the kind that accurately informs the public's political choices is steadily diminishing, perhaps to near extinction. This is a tragic loss for our democratic republic, progressively increasing the likelihood that our American government will be placed in the hands of politicians whose real interests are not in the general public good but in personal power and service to those private special interests that are their real constituencies (whether or not they earnestly believe that the real business of America is business). This would be tragedy in the classic sense: the downfall and destruction of greatness through a tragic flaw. As we point out in chapter 8, the Internet's capacity to provide voters with information beyond that provided by misleading sound-bite political advertising may reduce the probability that this disaster will be realized. But no matter how much the possible future of the Internet may justify our faith and hopes, we should ask ourselves the following questions about our political condition as citizens of the United States of America in the twenty-first century:

- To what extent has our political apathy and pursuit of narrow self-interests tended to make us, increasingly, "a nation of timid and industrious sheep, of which the government is the shepherd"?

- Are we, as Tocqueville predicted we might, so thoroughly glutting ourselves with "the petty and paltry pleasures" of our affluent materialistic society, and have we as individuals become so highly insensitive to the duties of community, that it may rightly be said of most Americans that they have "lost their country"?

- Is our increasing identification of ourselves as consumers rather than as citizens an effective abdication of our rights and duties as citizens of a democratic republic, especially through our continued tolerance and acceptance of ersatz political discourse and its emphases on image making and sound-bite rhetoric?

- What remains within our power to elevate the character of American political discourse, thereby better avoiding the gradual subversion of our republic by candidates for public office who seek power and service to private special interests above public service?

- Do we care enough about the well-being of our democratic republic to give politicians hell for doing more to manipulate us as consumers than inform us as citizens?

Some may justifiably believe that the American republic as our founders envisioned it is already lost, or nearly so. Thomas Jefferson hoped that our government would be administered, and our political candidates chosen, from a "natural aristocracy of virtue and talent." He feared, as Tocqueville did, the kind of political demagoguery that could lead our nation to incline toward tyranny. The First Amendment to our Constitution was designed to protect freedom of speech and assembly from interference by the federal government, and later, through the Fourteenth Amendment, from state government as well. The First and Fourteenth Amendments thus guarantee the people of the United States the right to engage in political discourse and debate without interference from their governments. The guiding assumption, or premise, of the First Amendment, is that uncensored political debate would help protect and preserve all other rights accorded by the Constitution to the people, and also thereby help to preserve our republican form of government. But these protections lose their meaning if people surrender their right to significant political debate, failing to insist that they hear significant political debate and discourse among those who seek their votes for public office. Demagoguery—which includes the offer of bread and circuses to distract the public from political awareness—is made far easier with mass media, and especially television, than it ever was in the eighteenth or nineteenth century. The need, therefore, for an intelligent and insistent exercise of our First and Fourteenth Amendment rights is now more important than ever, but politicians are being permitted largely to evade real political discourse in their election campaigns, and even in official pronouncements.

Through the proven power of advertising techniques to seduce rather than to persuade, campaign advertising may be seriously misleading uninformed voters to vote against their own interests—and against the public good. As these words are written, our federal administration continues to claim that the aim of the war being fought by us in Iraq is to help bring elective democracy to the Middle East. To what extent do the methods by which we get to know our own political candidates provide a sound model for less democratic peoples? How is American consumeritis and its infection of elective politics viewed by the international community? How do the people of other nations perceive the consumer culture described in these pages? To what extent, and in what ways, do their perceptions affect international security? In what ways does our consumer culture promote friendship, and in what ways does it promote enmity, with the people of other nations around the globe? These questions are explored in the next chapter.

Notes

195   *Bread and circuses (Panem et circenses)*   A Latin phrase indicating the bribes held out to the populace by wealthy politicians; probably first recorded by Juvenal in *Satires X* (125 AD).

Presidential campaigns rely almost entirely   Russell Baker, "The Entertainer," in *The New York Review of Books*, November 3, 2005.

Citizen Kane, *whose original working title was*   Released by RKO Pictures in 1941, *Citizen Kane* was produced and directed by Orson Welles, with a screenplay by Herman J. Mankiewicz and Orson Welles.

196   *By the 1950s, television, which had grown to become the most popular American mass medium*   See Gretchen Rubin, *Forty Ways to Look at JFK* (New York: Ballantine Books, 2005) (hereafter Rubin). On pages 135–136, she writes, "In 1950, 11 percent of American families owned a television, and only ten years later, that number had mushroomed to 88 percent—while only 78 percent had a telephone." A critical analysis by George Anastaplo of the pernicious effects of television on the American public invites us to consider those effects and the reasons for television's popular appeal. He writes, "The remarkable success of television since the Second World War in sweeping all before it should make us wonder what there is that makes it so attractive." See page 264 in George Anastaplo, *The American Moralist: On Law, Ethics, and Government* (Athens, OH: Ohio University Press, 1992) (hereafter Anastaplo).

197   *It's one of the curious characteristics of television*   See Rubin, 137.

198   *The early era of American politics*   For examples of the raucous tone of early American political debate, consider the following from Ron Chernow's *Alexander Hamilton* (New York: Penguin Press, 2004. 391–392): "The sudden emergence of parties set a slashing tone for politics in the 1790's. Since politicians considered parties bad, they denied involvement in them, bristled at charges that they harbored partisan feelings, and were quick to perceive hypocrisy in others. And because parties were frightening new phenomena, they could be easily mistaken for evil conspiracies, lending a paranoid tinge to political discourse." Another source (Paul Reynolds, "US campaign begins to get dirty," *BBC News*, February 18, 2004, news.bbc.co.uk/2/hi/americas/3493277.stm) furnishes the following specific examples of this "paranoid tinge" and the extremities to which partisan political debate went in the early years of the American republic. "One of the most vitriolic elections was in 1828 " John Quincy Adams was nicknamed 'The Pimp' by the campaign of his opponent General Andrew Jackson, based on a rumour that he had once coerced a young woman into an affair with a Russian Nobleman when he had been American ambassador to Russia. Adams' supporters hit back with a pamphlet which claimed: 'General Jackson's mother

was a common prostitute brought to this country by British soldiers! She afterwards married a mulatto man with whom she had several children of which number General Jackson is one!!' Jackson won anyway. And just to show that this kind of thing goes right back to the start of American campaigning, we have the election of 1800 in which Thomas Jefferson was accused of favouring the teaching of 'murder, robbery, rape, adultery and incest.' Jefferson won. He did not teach the offending subjects."

Abraham Lincoln followed the advice of a little girl   Abraham Lincoln (1809–1865) was the sixteenth president of the United States (1861–1865). In October 1860, "An eleven-year-old girl who lived in Westfield, New York, wrote Lincoln an artless letter in which she told him he would look better with a beard. Soon after, he grew one." See Paul M. Angle and Earl Schenck Miers, eds., *The Living Lincoln: The Man, His Mind, His Times, and the War He Fought, Reconstructed from His Own Writings* (Rutgers, NJ: Barnes & Noble Books, 1992), 357.

At the turn of the twentieth century, leading Democratic and Republican presidential candidates   Stephen Douglas, running against Abraham Lincoln in the 1860 presidential election, was "the first presidential candidate in American history to make a nationwide tour in person." See Paul F. Boller, Jr., *Presidential Campaigns* (New York: Oxford University Press, 1984, 101) as quoted by Doris Kearns Goodwin in *Team of Rivals: The Political Genius of Abraham Lincoln* (New York: Simon & Schuster, 2005), 274. The precedent Douglas set was not followed by other presidential candidates until the twentieth century.

William McKinley, for example, notoriously stayed at home   William McKinley (1843–1901) was the twenty-fifth president of the United States (1897–1901). "During the presidential campaign of 1900, the Republican McKinley, running for a second time against the Democrat William Jennings Bryant, conducted a 'front porch campaign,' receiving hand-picked delegations on the verandah of his house in Canton, Ohio, hearing their carefully censored speeches of support, and delivering in reply selected passages of patriotic platitudes." Samuel Eliot Morison, *The Oxford History of the American People* (New York: Oxford University Press, 1965), 809.

President Harry Truman seemed to most Americans to be a "little man"   Harry Truman (1884–1972) was the thirty-third president of the United States (1945–1952). As to Truman being a "little man," in his autobiography, *Present at the Creation*, Dean Acheson, Truman's secretary of state, had this to say: "If he was not a great man, he was the greatest little man the author of this statement had ever seen."

199 *Dwight D. Eisenhower, a popular World War II leader*   Dwight D. Eisenhower (1890–1969) was the thirty-fourth president of the United States (1953–1961).

The campaign slogan "I Like Ike"   Compare, for example, Eisenhower's campaign slogan "I Like Ike" to the contemporary automobile advertising campaign slogan "See the USA in your Chevrolet." The ninth president of the United States, William Henry Harrison, also a popular U.S. army general, similarly ran his campaign for the presidency in 1840 with the slogan "Tippecanoe and Tyler too." "Tippecanoe" was Harrison's popular nickname (as "Ike" was Eisenhower's). John Tyler was the vice-presidential candidate who ran with Harrison, succeeding him as the tenth president after Harrison's death from pneumonia one month after his inauguration, in which he gave the longest inaugural speech in U.S. history, outdoors in the pouring rain.

Eisenhower's campaign for reelection in 1956   The quotation following, with citations omitted, comes from Chang, Park, and Shim, "Effectiveness of Negative Political Advertising," December 1998 (hereafter Chang *et al.*), at *www.scripps.ohiou.edu/wjmcr/vol02/2-1a.HTM*. At the time the article was written, Won Ho Chang was a professor and the director of the Stephenson Research Center at the University of Missouri's School of Journalism; Park was a public relations specialist with the LG Corporation in Seoul, Korea; and Shim was a graduate student at the University of Missouri School of Journalism.

When John F. Kennedy was preparing his first election campaign   John F. Kennedy (1917–1963) was the thirty-fifth president of the United States (1961–1963).

"We're going to sell Jack like soap flakes."   Rubin, 159, citing Hamilton, *JFK: Reckless Youth*, 812.

While voters who listened to the first debate on the radio   See Rubin, 137: "After the first debate, radio listeners thought Nixon had won or tied with Kennedy, but TV viewers disagreed: on television, Kennedy, with his cool, handsome, and confident demeanor, beat the sweaty, uneasy Nixon. Kennedy's TV appearances gave him a dramatic boost."

200 *By his second run for the presidency in 1968, Nixon had learned his lesson*   Richard M. Nixon (1913–1974) was the thirty-sixth president of the United States (1969–1973).

a best-selling book by the author Joe McGinniss describing the campaign   Joe McGinniss, *Selling of the President 1968* (New York: Simon & Schuster, 1969).

but many voters were at first turned off by the spectacle   The amorality of Nixon's and Haldeman's campaign tactics were clearly established in the Watergate scandal after Nixon's 1972 reelection, which eventually led to his resignation as president in 1973, and H. R. Haldeman's imprisonment in 1975 for obstruction of justice.

People in today's society are becoming more and more apathetic   Jon Gould, Chicago, USA, from "The Debate Room: Political Television Advertisements," at *www.etext.org/Zines/Intl_Teletimes/Teletimes_ HTML/debate_room_9402.html* (accessed February 10, 2006).

201   *Orwell's 1984, with television's political Big Brother imagery*   George Orwell, *1984* (New York: New American Library, 1961).

Some see the American people, in tens of millions,   Anastaplo, 268–269.

202   *I seek to trace the novel features under which despotism may appear*   Tocqueville, *Democracy in America*, vol. 2, chapter 4, Everyman ed., 102.

203   *No vice of the human heart is so acceptable*   Ibid.

204   *Between 1952 (when the majority of voters said "I Like Ike" with their ballots) and 1988*   Chang et al., 1.

The deluge of ads swamped the meager campaign coverage   See "Local Stations Are Big Winners in Campaign 2004: TV Broadcasters Rake in More than $1.6 Billion in Political Advertising," *The Political Standard,* December 2004.

Prior to the 1980's candidates   Chang et al., quoting Larry Sabato, *The Rise of Political Consultants: New Way of Winning Elections* (New York: Basic Books, 1981), 165–166.

205   *Walking through the White House grounds*   Rubin, 156.

206   *He believed passionately in democracy*   Richard Holmes, *In the Footsteps of Churchill* (New York: Basic Books, 2005), 298.

207   *Careful scrutiny of press releases*   See, for example, Michael Massing, "The End of News?" *The New York Review of Books,* December 1, 2005, 23–27, reporting on the Bush administration's covert funding and support for partisan radio and TV commentators favoring the administration's position. The article analyzes the decline of objective news reporting and the continuing decline in newspaper readership (especially among the young); it begins: "In late September [2005], the Government Accounting Office—a nonpartisan arm of Congress—issued a finding that the Bush administration had engaged in 'covert propaganda,' and thereby broken the law, by paying Armstrong Williams, a conservative commentator, to promote its educational policies." The article also cites analysis of the news release by the U.S. Department of Education "No Child Left Behind Video News Release and Media Analysis" [B-304228], September 30, 2005, and "Dead Wrong," an hour-long CNN television report on the Bush administration's false claims about the existence of weapons of mass destruction in Iraq as its justification for going to war.

209 *The First Amendment to our Constitution*   For a definitive examination
of the purposes of the First Amendment, see George Anastaplo, *The
Constitutionalist: Notes on the First Amendment* (Dallas, TX: Southern
Methodist University Press, 1971; reprinted by Lexington Books in 2005),
and George Anastaplo, *The Amendments to the Constitution: A Commentary* (Baltimore, MD: The Johns Hopkins University Press, 1995).

Salvatore Cascio as the young Salvatore and Philippe Noiret as Alfredo in *Cinema Paradiso* (Cristaldifilms, Les Filmes Ariane, RAI, TFI Films Productions, 1989)

7

Consumeritis and International Insecurity: *Cinema Paradiso* and Global Inferno

*Movies offer us a transformed reality in which
the body is stripped of its material bonds
and becomes united with our essential
nature as centers of consciousness.*
—Colin McGuinn, *The Power of Movies* (2006)

Here's lookin' at you, kid.
—Humphrey Bogart as Rick to Ingrid
Bergman as Ilse in *Casablanca* (1942)

WHENEVER I TRAVEL to another country, I always include as part of my visit going to a local theater to see a film, whether or not it is in English or has English subtitles. My experiences have never failed to be both entertaining and instructive. I always enjoy at least parts of the movie because I go to a film that locals have told me is a good one. Good movies are produced in a universal language, the language that justifies our saying that "a picture is worth a thousand words."

Cinema Paradiso, Good Movies, and the
Export of American Culture

Cinema Paradiso, the first film by the Italian director Giuseppe Tornatore, is a joint Italian and French production with the original dialogue in Italian and English. It is, among other things, a profoundly moving celebration of the magical enchantment of movies. It won an Oscar, seventeen other prestigious cinema awards, and eleven other nominations; and it was a popular success in the United Kingdom, Italy, France, Germany, Sweden, Finland, Iceland, Argentina, Chile, Hong Kong, Singapore, and many other countries.

Cinema Paradiso is the story of a boy named Salvatore (called Toto as a child, and played by three different actors portraying his childhood, his adolescence, and his adulthood), and his relationship to an old movie projectionist named Alfredo (played by the French actor Phillipe Noiret). Alfredo nurtures Toto's love of movies and encourages him to grow beyond the confines of the small Sicilian village in which Toto was born and raised, helping motivate him toward his eventual success as an Italian filmmaker in Rome. *Cinema Paradiso* has been called "a beautiful film about the love of movies and life." In an early scene, Alfredo projects a movie that is introduced with a scene-setting written narrative on the screen. One of the men in the audience turns to another and asks, "What does it say?" The other replies, "I'm illiterate." The first exclaims, "You too?" This vignette is one of Tornatore's tributes to movies and how they speak a human language more universal than the written.

The reason I invariably go to a movie theater when I am traveling abroad is not only because I love good movies but also because it enables me to share in the sentiments of the people in the place I am visiting; to understand something about their sensibilities and attitudes; and to become, at least for a while, a little less of a foreigner to the people in whose country I am a guest. I recall a pleasurable experience similar to Alfredo's delight in the young Toto's love of the movies: observing the raucous fun children in the audience were having watching the British comedy *Clockwise* with John Cleese, when my wife, Joy, and I saw it on a rainy Saturday afternoon in Dublin, Ireland. Joy and I also first saw Federico Fellini's *Satyricon* shortly after it opened in Rome, and were caught up, when the box office opened, in the Roman audience's stampede into the theater in exuberant anticipation of the great film they knew they were about to see. In Havana, Cuba, I went to a movie satirizing the difficulties of life in Cuba and its complex relations with the United States, and was enlightened to witness the marvelous capacity of Cubans to laugh at themselves despite the serious difficulties they have been compelled to live in as a result of the U.S. boycott of Cuba under the Castro regime. The congenial orderliness and courtesy of New Zealanders was evident in the commodious comforts of the movie theater in Christ Church ("the most British city in the world outside of England"), where Joy and I went to see *Head in the Clouds*. I regret never having gone to a movie in China, although Joy and I had the pleasure of waltzing in the same ballroom in Shanghai in which the last, deposed Chinese emperor was depicted waltzing in Bernardo Bertolucci's fine movie, *The Last Emperor* (the first Western feature movie the Chinese government permitted to be filmed in China).

Good movies are produced in a universal language for which Hollywood rightfully takes much credit. The earliest feature movies are generally credited to the imagination of three French filmmakers, George Méliès and the brothers Auguste and Louis Lumière, and film directors in other countries have created innovative film genres. Charlie Chaplin and Douglas Fairbanks, though best known as American filmmakers, were originally

English performers, and (with Mary Pickford) were the first internationally acclaimed movie stars. Likewise, Britain's Alfred Hitchcock (though also best known as an American director) gave suspense mystery new tempo and intrigue, and England's David Lean (*Lawrence of Arabia*) brought new amplitude to film epic. Sweden's Ingmar Bergman (*The Seventh Seal; Wild Strawberries; Fanny and Alexander*), Japan's Akira Kurosawa (*Seven Samurai; Ran*), Spain's Luis Buñuel (*The Discreet Charm of the Bourgeoisie; Obscure Object of Desire; Tristana*), Germany's Fritz Lang (*Metropolis; M; The Woman in the Window*), France's Jean Renoir (*The Grand Illusion; The Crime of Monsieur Lange*), and India's Satyajit Ray (*Pather Panchali*), for further examples, are each credited with an originality and influence that at least approaches the creation of genres. The most seminally influential beginnings of the "language" of popular cinema and its techniques were, however, creations of the Hollywood film industry, most notably of D. W. Griffith. Griffith is credited with directing as many as 536 films, writing 228 films, and producing 541, most of them in the first quarter of the twentieth century.

The filmmakers of other countries have produced superior films in some genres, but American movies remain, on the whole, the world's favorites. *Cinema Paradiso* confirms both these observations. As to genre, no one surpasses the Italians, for example, in producing the kinds of film melodramas that make us weep with joy and pathos like *Cinema Paradiso*, Vittorio DeSica's *Bicycle Thief*, Federico Fellini's *Amarcord* (which is also partly about movies), or Roberto Benigni's *Life Is Beautiful*. As to Hollywood's persistent primacy, American film and TV tape rental exports to other countries, which exceeded $10 billion in 2004, more than quadrupled in the period 1992–2004. They also constitute more than 15 percent of the total U.S. private services export trade balance and more than 3 percent of total U.S. private service exports (see figs. 7.1–7.3). *Cinema Paradiso* is overwhelmingly dominated by references to American movies. The film shows photographs, movie posters, and film clips depicting the following American movie stars and movies, and includes dialogue referring to them:

> Humphrey Bogart and Ingrid Bergman (in *Casablanca*) and Lauren Bacall; John Wayne (in *Stagecoach* and *Shepherd of the Hills*); Charlie Chaplin (in two film clips); Clark Gable and Vivien Leigh (in *Gone with the Wind*, with repeated references to Gable as a surrogate for Toto's mustached father); Greta Garbo, Tyrone Power, Buster Keaton, Joan Crawford, and Eric Von Stroheim (as both an American and German film figure); Louis Hayward (whose swashbuckler and pirate movies enchanted me as a kid); Walt Disney's *Snow White*; Spencer Tracy (several times, in *Dr. Jekyll and Mr. Hyde,* and with Katharine Hepburn; Rita Hayworth ("What a build!" Toto exclaims, and his companion, seizing Toto's binoculars, insists "Me too!"); Laurel and Hardy; Kirk Douglas (in the Italian-made *Ulysses*); and Gary Cooper, James Stewart, Henry Fonda, Cary Grant, Jane Russell, Errol Flynn, Marilyn Monroe, and Rudolph Valentino.

Cinema Paradiso shows and tells us some of the most significant things about the cultural importance of movies and their global influence. Alfredo says to Toto that he likes what he does, despite the little pay and large discomforts of the heat of summer and cold of winter he suffers in his small projection booth,

> because it grows on you. You hear people giggling and laughing. Then you're happy too. It makes you feel good to hear them. Like you're the one who makes them laugh, who makes them forget their troubles. That part I like.

The old projectionist tells the adolescent Salvatore, "Life isn't like in the movies. It's harder." But he has also shown the child Toto "*Abracadabra,* and we pass through walls," a statement that is both literal and metaphorical. Perhaps quoting an uncredited movie character, Alfredo also says to Salvatore, "If you have no faith in me, have faith in what you see." This gives movies a transcendent spiritual meaning, reflecting Alfredo's previously telling Toto, referring to a difficult real-life situation they witness, "You live on hope."

Our delight in good movies, and the profound emotional impact of the film medium, is depicted in *Cinema Paradiso* by showing us audience reactions at the Cinema Paradiso movie house, reactions to American Westerns, gangster movies, murder mysteries, adventure stories, comedies, and musicals. The film shows us the audience's sobered shock at newsreel film of soldiers frozen dead in the snow and ice around Stalingrad in World War II; their rejoicing at the undoing and arrest of a villain; the tears that can flow from watching poignant scenes of family joys and sorrows; and the erotic thrills of many, many love stories—with passionate kisses censored by the local priest but preserved by Alfredo for Salvatore's adult enjoyment, and as Alfredo's own farewell kiss to the child he loved as much as any father could love.

The story of *Cinema Paradiso* is, however, much more than the story of a deeply loving relationship between a boy and an old man, although the drama of that relationship and its end is what most immediately brings many moviegoers to tears at the conclusion of the movie. *Cinema Paradiso* is also about what the good and great movies of the silent movie era, and movies of the 1930s, 1940s, and 1950s—especially American movies—gave to the world, and how their sublime qualities have been progressively compromised, though not yet entirely lost, by the commercial energies that feed consumeritis. When the film director Salvatore—who shows he does not care too much about the "successful" late-twentieth-century films he is making—returns to the Sicilian town of his roots, he finds the Cinema Paradiso theater closed and abandoned. The town, Salvatore is told, has bought the land for a parking lot (possibly for a shopping mall). He encounters the man who built Cinema Paradiso for the town, and asks him why it has been closed. "People stopped coming to the theater," its owner tells Salvatore, and adds, "The old movie business is just a memory. The economy, TV, videos, you know." Going to a cinema complex in the local shopping mall, we might reflect, does not produce the same intimate experience and sense of occasion that going to a movie usually meant for most people at least until about the 1980s.

As Salvatore nostalgically strolls through the abandoned movie theater, he sees laying on the floor in the dust a plaster lion's head that reminds us of the MGM movie lion, through whose open mouth movies had formerly been projected at the Cinema Paradiso. On his walk through the village of his birth on this visit thirty years after he left it, where once he—and we—saw movie posters, we now see large commercial billboards; where once we saw an open town square in which people met, talked, quarreled, and gathered to go to the Cinema Paradiso, we now see a square so densely filled with parked automobiles that it can no longer be a community center. At the end of the movie, the tears ardent moviegoers are moved to shed may thus be not only for the poignancy of Alfredo's love for Toto and Salvatore's loss at the old man's death. The film has also borne witness to *our own* loss: the deeply human joys, sorrows, hopes, and elevated dreams and aspirations that classic good movies help us to experience—now all being sacrificed to the increasing commercialization of movies and to the focus of corporate media conglomerates on the bottom line. Hollywood's most distinguished producers during its great era of filmmaking were also businessmen who wanted to make money with their movies; but they insistently wanted to make great movies. Legendary producers of Hollywood's golden age, such as Samuel Goldwyn and Howard Hughes, not infrequently risked their personal fortunes in pursuit of their desire to make movies for which a profitable mass audience was not a certainty. Goldwyn did in fact lose his wealth at least once in his career, and, as Hughes's recent biopic, *The Aviator,* shows, Hughes nearly did before he became one of the super rich.

By massively popularizing the greatest new art form of the twentieth century, America's export of good movies, especially in the first half of the century, was the prime factor creating a world movie culture, and most of the world loved us for it. Hollywood's good movies showed America's good heart and connected the people of the United States to the universal joys, sorrows, struggles, dreams, and aspirations they shared with people around the world. That Hollywood did not often depict life as hard as it is, as Alfredo points out to Salvatore, does not lessen the significance of the fact that what it did show were usually moving depictions of the best and worst in people, with a decided tilt toward celebrating and elevating the best. If Hollywood tended often to glamorize America too much, it also helped to lighten our spirits in the worst of times, and give us enduring images of love and heroism in the face of hardship. It helped us to live on hope but also showed us, as Charlie Chaplin says in his last great movie, *Limelight,* that we should even "learn to live without hope" if we feel that hope is lost. The best American movies continue to embrace and celebrate the values of the old classics, while also sometimes dazzling audiences with advanced film technologies. As stated earlier, American movies remain overwhelmingly the most popular movies in the world (see fig. 8). Films like George Lucas's *Star Wars* series and Peter Jackson's *Lord of the Rings* trilogy exemplify the continued gifts to the world of good American movies, though on a grand scale. Within more human dimensions, so do films by directors like Steven Spielberg (such as *E.T.* and *Saving Private Ryan*), and other recent movies referred to in this book.

The surviving legacy of good movies, and their humanistic cultural expression, is not, however, what presently constitutes the dominant American cultural export to the rest of the world—to our great loss. Instead, we are pervasively exporting consumeritis, and its materialistic bias. To put the matter in poetic terms, for a long time the United States was recognized as the chief exporter of a cinema paradiso through the deeply human, elevated values its good movies expressed; now its exports more typically reflect baser human qualities—such as avarice, lust, and flattery—the kind punished in the almost cinematic depictions of Dante's *Inferno*. How people of other nations perceive and react to these manifestations of consumeritis, and how the change in the global reputation of the United States affects the security of Americans are the subjects of the remainder of this chapter.

U.S. Foreign Relations and Global Reputation

> *And the rockets' red glare, the bombs bursting in air,*
> *Gave proof through the night that our flag was still there.*
> *O say, does that star-spangled banner yet wave*
> *O'er the land of the free and the home of the brave?*
> —Francis Scott Key,
> *Star Spangled Banner* (1814)

For more than half its history the United States had a foreign policy that was largely isolationist, and the geography of the country helped protect it from foreign threats. In his 1798 Farewell Address, George Washington urged the American people to avoid "foreign entanglements." After its main troubles with England ended in 1815, the United States could afford to rely on the Atlantic and Pacific Oceans to insulate "Fortress America" from such entanglements. In the early nineteenth century, the United States reinforced its insulation by declaring in the Monroe Doctrine that America was "off limits" to further imperialist exploitation of the American continent by Europe. It was this isolationist policy that led the U.S. Congress to reject the Treaty of Versailles after World War I, excluding the United States from membership in the League of Nations despite President Woodrow Wilson's fervent promotion of the treaty. But by the end of the twentieth century, advanced communications and transportation technology and the increasing dependence of economies on international trade had transformed the world into a global community, making it no longer possible—even if it were desirable—for the United States to isolate itself from "foreign entanglements." In the twenty-first century, America's domestic policies are inextricably bound with its foreign relations.

Until the middle of the twentieth century, U.S. foreign policy centered almost entirely on Europe, principally England, France, and Spain: the first as the nation from which the United States declared its independence and with which it fought two wars (the Revolution and the War of 1812); the second because of the French Revolution and the rise of Napoleon Bonaparte (with whom the United States negotiated the Louisiana purchase); and the third because of Spain's American colonies and possession of part of Florida (acquired from Spain in 1821). During its early history, the United States also had significant foreign policy concerns with Mexico, with which it fought a war—resulting in U.S. acquisition in 1848 of its present southwestern states. American foreign policy continued to be engaged mainly with Europe during most of the twentieth century, during which it joined European allies in fighting the two World Wars. The events leading up to the Second World War and that cataclysmic event itself added

Asia—primarily Japan, China, and Korea—to the critical list of foreign nations with which U.S. foreign policy was concerned. During the period known as the Cold War, beginning in 1945 and ending in 1991 when the USSR collapsed, relations with the Soviet Union were the focus of America's international security concerns. The Cold War had successively engaged the United States in armed hostilities in Korea and Vietnam, and further extended its foreign entanglements. The American misadventure in Vietnam affected global opinion of the United States for the worse, but with the collapse of the Soviet system in the early 1990s, many felt that not only the United States but also the entire world had entered into a period of international security unprecedented in the modern era. The global reputation of U.S. power then rose to new heights.

The world's regard for American *power* may have reached its summit with the end of the Cold War, but *admiration* for the United States and its people was rooted in its revolutionary democratic history and was greatly heightened in the period following World War II. The United States has appropriately been called "a nation of immigrants." It had long been perceived globally as a unique land of opportunity whose doors were wide open to "huddled masses yearning to breathe free." In the 1950s, following the Allied victory against the Axis powers of Nazi Germany, Fascist Italy, and militarist Japan, the people of most nations—including the former enemies of the United States—saw the country and its people as an admirably generous nation. The benign occupation of Japan by the United States, and the recovery of Europe from devastation with the help of the U.S. Marshall Plan further confirmed the long-held opinion of people throughout the globe that the United States was a nation benevolently promoting democratic ideals and offering the privileges of its freedoms to immigrants. Between the post–World War II period and the end of the Cold War, the nations of Europe began a process of integration of their economic and political policies that created the European Union (EU). As a geopolitical entity, the EU represents the United States' first global rival for leadership of "the free world," as it was termed during the Cold War, and it has increasingly criticized U.S. unilateralism in international affairs.

On September 11, 2001, with the destruction of the Twin Towers in New York City and the attack on the Pentagon arranged by a native of Saudi Arabia, Osama bin-Laden, America's foreign policy decisively shifted its focus from Europe and Asia to its relations with Islamic countries and peoples, most notably Afghanistan, Iraq, Iran, and the Arab emirates and monarchies. Immediately after the events of 9/11, President George W. Bush declared that the attacks had "changed everything." The "everything" to which he referred was, in the main, U.S. foreign and domestic policy relating to American security. From the moment 9/11 legitimately heightened U.S. concerns about global terrorism, its foreign policy has been animated by a perceived level of threat to American security and a degree of international *insecurity* that is as least as great as any perceived by U.S. governments in the past. This perception of insecurity has resulted in federal domestic security acts and policies—embodied, for example, in the *Patriot Act*—even more invasive and at least as aggressive as those implemented during the height of the Cold War, when the perceived threat was from the USSR, a global power, not from Islamic terrorist bands. The U.S. invasion of Iraq, following the U.S. government's rejection of the widely held international view that there was an insufficient basis for military action, and that weapons inspections should be continued to better determine whether Iraq in fact posed a serious international security threat, has damaged the reputation of the United States in the community of nations. Perhaps the most scathing public denunciation of U.S. foreign policy in a prestigious forum has been the speech "Art, Truth, and Politics," made by the author Harold Pinter when he accepted the 2005 Nobel Prize for Literature at the Swedish Academy in Stockholm on December 7, 2005. In his speech, Pinter indicted the United States for its support of

> every right wing military dictatorship in the world after the end of the Second World War … [President George W. Bush and British Prime Minster Tony Blair should] be arraigned before the International Criminal Court of Justice [for the] invasion of Iraq [as] a bandit act, an act of blatant state terrorism, demonstrating absolute contempt for the concept of international law. The invasion was an arbitrary military action inspired by a series of lies upon lies and gross manipulation of the media and therefore the public … responsible for the death and mutilation of thousands and thousands of innocent people.

As a result of these acts and policies, at the time of this writing, the United States no longer enjoys, in Europe or in the Middle East or in parts of Asia, the same high esteem it enjoyed less than a decade ago. It is no longer universally perceived to be a power whose domestic and foreign policies exhibit a benevolent concern for the international community or even, in the words of the Declaration of Independence, "a decent respect for the opinions of mankind." This decline in esteem naturally further increases the extent to which American policymakers perceive an escalating insecurity in U.S. foreign relations.

The reasons for a marked decline in global opinion about the United States and an increase in its sense of insecurity are, of course, complex and many sided. The roots of international terrorism, for example, and the international insecurity it has created are grounded in large part (at least ostensibly) on the hostility of peoples and nations of the Middle East to U.S. foreign policy relating to the plight of the people of Palestine and to unwavering U.S. support for the State of Israel. This hostility, however, also has deep, historic, cultural roots independent of any particular grievances against the United States, as aggressive acts against the United States in the early nineteenth century by the Barbary Coast pirates attest. The shameful spectacle of U.S. maltreatment of Iraqi prisoners in Abu Ghraib, and the long U.S. presence as an occupying military power in Iraq have, however, greatly exacerbated this hostility. It is beyond the compass of this book to consider the extent to which the change in global regard for the United States is related specifically only to these and kindred U.S. policies and actions. But the reasons for a decline in the world's good opinion of the United States since the end of the Cold War also include the cultural materialism underlying consumeritis and pro-consumerist U.S. governmental policies, including particularly our excess oil consumption and disproportionately large contribution to environmental pollution. It is consideration of these causes of the decline in favorable world opinion of the United States, and the consequent perceived increase in American insecurity, to which we limit ourselves in the next section of this chapter.

International Reaction to American Materialism

The May 15, 2005, issue of *Newsweek* magazine reported that

> America has now unleashed history's greatest material binge. From 1995 to 1999 Americans have purchased (among other things) 77 million cars and light trucks, almost 8 million new homes, 57 million PC's and 64 million mobile phones. The number of millionaires in US and Canada rose 40% since 1997 to 2.5 million.

The preceding paragraph was quoted by a Muslim writer named Wael Nafee in an article titled "Cultural Imperialism: The Deadliest Export," which begins as follows:

Last week three Muslims were killed in Saudi Arabia. They did not die defending the land from colonial invaders. They did not die preparing for jihad. In the land where Prophet Muhammed shed his blood to raise the flag of Islam the highest, these people were killed because they wanted to get a good deal at IKEA. According to the BBC, a stampede at IKEA resulted in the death of three Muslims and caused sixteen to be injured. The stampede was a result of shoppers rushing into IKEA to claim a limited number of credit vouchers being offered to the public. The article also noted that "more than 8,000 people had gathered near the store for the $150 vouchers, some of them having camped overnight."

Reflecting on the BBC's story, Mr. Nafee details his hostility to American materialism and consumerism with the following observations:

It is truly a sad [day in] history when a Muslim's blood is shed not for defending Islam, but for the sake of accumulating material things. The Ummah of Islam that was put on Earth to be a witness upon humanity is now dying in the process of pursuing consumerism....

The Western way of life relies on a continual cycle of want. The people must always desire to own something new, regardless of whether they need it ... They work extra hard, in order to buy things they do not really need, in order to impress people they do not really care for. The objective is to have the newest and best ... For this "cult of the worship of newness" to prevail, the high priests of the (false) "god of consumerism" must work hard to preach their gospel. They are not just selling products, they are selling an ideology. They are promoting a value system that continuously bombards the public with messages of self-indulgence and instant gratification....

Some may feel that Muslims running in a stampede to buy furniture from IKEA is a trivial matter. However, we must understand the idea that motivates such a behavior ... and determine where it originates from. The

phenomenon of consumerism is noted to be a sickness
within the western society itself....

It is difficult to quarrel with Mr. Nafee's characterizations of
consumerism. They are tantamount to paraphrases of Thorsten
Veblen's account of "conspicuous consumption," and echo typical
descriptions of consumerism offered by contemporary Western
commentators quoted in this book. Nafee's condemnation of a
materialist culture of "More" expresses, for example, the views
of environmentally conscious westerners such as Tim Jackson,
whose article "Live Better by Consuming Less?" was quoted in
chapter 5:

> The eco-humanist view of consumption as a social pathol-
> ogy arises as a dialectical response to the conventional
> economic insatiability of *wants.* In place of insatiability,
> the eco-humanists place sufficiency in the satisfaction of
> *needs,* and they emphasize the social and psychological
> dangers of materialism.

We cannot say precisely how widely Mr. Nafee's views and the
similar views of others are disseminated and accepted by Islamic
peoples. That such views are being disseminated is beyond question, as is the fact that they are likely to find a receptive audience
among a significant and perhaps a growing portion of Islamic
peoples and nations, especially among those suffering from the
hardships of poverty and social inequality in their own countries.
Though some hostility against the United States may in part be
a form of scapegoating for internal inequities endemic to some
Islamic regimes, Mr. Nafee's indictment of consumerism is a particularly serious one in terms of how it is likely to be perceived by
Muslims. It asserts in effect that Western materialism and consumerism, and their roots in capitalism, are in deep opposition
to the sacred tenets of Islam; that they are *irreligious,* and an

insult to those who take their Islamic faith seriously. Others have pointed out that this view is not rare among Muslims:

> Capitalism is seen [by some Muslims] as a possible road to materialism, leading Muslims to abandon spirituality (become nihilistic), and to accumulate wealth without limits. For Dewan Dakwah, rich people, following the Islamic teaching, should share their wealth with the needy. Moreover, there is a fear that capitalism would simply accelerate the exploitation of the natural resources of the Muslim world. Dewan Dakwah preaches caution to the Muslims in that respect. Capitalism, in addition to materialism and nihilism, is seen as 'basically tyrannical and corrupted, and functions at the expense of people in the developing world, in particular in the Muslim world.' Thus, a Muslim has the right to reject them....

Such indictments of materialism should, however, come as no surprise to informed Westerners. Orthodox Christian teachings—including, for example, Jesus' Sermon on the Mount and the significance of his telling a rich man to give all he had to the poor if he wished to follow him—may be similarly understood to identify materialism as unfaithful to the spirit of holiness and, in Christian terms, to the Holy Spirit itself. Among the most radical segment of the Muslim population, consumerism and its materialist roots add a further justification for jihad—holy war—against the United States whether or not, as more conservative Muslims may argue, this would be an incorrect interpretation of the Koran. There can therefore be no doubt that at this point in the twenty-first century, hostility to consumeritis has added threats to American security and substance to otherwise spurious anti-American claims of Islamic terrorist organizations such as Osama bin-Laden's al-Qaeda. Moreover, as explained below, American consumeritis can understandably—even if mistakenly—be seen by the people of Islam to constitute a flagrant contradiction of the U.S. government's claim that it has invaded Iraq to help bring democracy to the nations of the Middle East.

The philosophical and spiritual bases for the democratic ideal articulated in the Declaration of Independence are asserted to be self-evident truths. These are "that all men are created equal, that they are endowed by their Creator with certain unalienable rights, that among these are life, liberty, and the pursuit of happiness." For those who believe that promotion of a democratic equality of *rights* throughout the world should also signify an economic and political order aspiring toward at least a roughly equal satisfaction of *needs* (not wants), the portion of the world's resources consumed by Americans represents a blatant violation of the democratic ideal. As Jeremy Rifkin, quoted earlier in chapter 5, has pointed out, despite the fact that the U.S. population is less than 5 percent of the world's, we consume a third or more of the world's energy and a disproportionate amount of the earth's other resources.

And as we have also pointed out in chapter 5:

> The average American consumer uses nearly 20 tons of raw materials each year, twice that of the average Japanese or European. One child born in the United States adds more to consumption and pollution over his or her lifetime than do thirty to fifty children born in developing countries. The food Americans throw away could, if transportable, alleviate much world famine. Americans throw away about 10 percent of the food they buy at the supermarket, dumping the equivalent of more than 21 million shopping bags full of food into landfills every year.... The largest component of American waste (40 percent) is paper and cardboard ... Much of this paper waste comes from junk mail ... If a million people stopped sending their junk mail, we'd save about 1.5 million trees a year.

To the extent that these and like facts are known—and they are fairly widely known and very widely suspected—and to the extent they are disseminated to people throughout the globe, they cannot fail to evoke hostility, and such hostility can only be exacerbated by envy.

Hostile reaction to U.S. consumerism by the people of other nations is far from limited to the people of Islam. It is expressed in anti-consumer movements, organizations, and writings produced, for example, in the United Kingdom, Europe, Asia, and Canada. We have previously pointed out European wonder at and hostility toward the preference of Americans for translating their productiveness into more consumer goods rather than enjoying increased leisure as Europeans do. A group based in the United Kingdom and calling itself ENOUGH! provides campaign materials "around a wide range of anti-consumerist initiatives." A bimonthly magazine called *Adbusters* is published by the Adbusters Media Foundation of Vancouver, Canada, which has also organized a global network of anti-consumerists who, among other projects, sponsor a "Buy Nothing Day" and a "No TV Week" as international protest events. Anti-consumerism has also found both domestic and international expression in a simplicity movement, which seeks to address many of the problems identified in this book as adverse consequences of consumeritis. Led by organizations such as Seeds of Simplicity, a nonprofit membership organization, the simplicity movement "fosters balance and fulfillment ... environmental stewardship, thoughtful consumption, financial responsibility, community involvement and simple, sustainable lifestyles."

Consumerism is also seen by the people of other nations to pose a serious cultural threat. In 2002, the Pew Research Center for People and the Press, headquartered in Washington, D.C., interviewed 2,189 Asian Indians on cultural issues. The interviewees had largely favorable views about foreign cultural exports such as movies and music; but 53 percent of these respondents "perceived consumerism and commercialism as threats to

Indian culture." France's Ministry of Culture is evidently even more fearful of American consumerism as a cultural threat. Unlike the surveyed Asian Indians who approve the import of American movies, a representative of the French Ministry of Culture has opined that

> Hollywood is a Trojan Horse bringing with it Disneyland Paris, fast-food chains and free advertising for American products from clothes to rock music. "America is not just interested in exporting its films," says Giles Jacob, the head of the Cannes Film Festival. "It is interested in exporting its way of life."

Consumerism itself as a U.S. cultural export is not the only major aspect of consumeritis from which the nation's global reputation has suffered. The *Exxon Valdez* incident may be seen as a symbol and metaphor for the ecological damage attributable in one way or another to American consumeritis. U.S. contribution to the causes of global warming is, like its consumption generally, disproportionate to its percentage of world population. As we have pointed out, in 1997 the United States emitted about one-fifth of total global greenhouse gases. Despite some efforts to mitigate the ecological damage attributable to the excesses of American consumption, our "ecological footprint" in the world continues to grow, fueling resentment against the United States by the worldwide Green movement in particular, but also by environmental authorities in the United States itself and throughout the world. As we have previously noted in chapter 5, authoritative institutions, including the U.S. National Academy of Sciences, the British Royal Society, the United Nations Environmental Program, and the U.S. President's Council on Sustainable Development, have identified unsustainable consumption and production as the root causes of ecological degradation.

The Kyoto Treaty is the first serious international effort to reach agreements and set goals to protect against further global warming. The United States has refused to sign the treaty on substantive grounds, asserting that the treaty is inadequate to accomplish its stated objectives and has been hypocritically subscribed to by some of its signatories. But its refusal has nevertheless aggravated the hostility of peoples and political leadership of other nations against the United States. Whether justly or unjustly, U.S. refusal to join the other Kyoto signatory nations has seriously injured the reputation of Americans among environmentalists throughout the world. Even the prime minister of Canada, Paul Martin, for example, has sharply criticized the United States for failing to join the Kyoto Treaty, and for its environmental policies generally.

In sum, much of the world now perceives Americans as gluttonous overconsumers who indulge themselves in more materialistic pursuits than is good for them—and at great expense to most of the rest of the world—while refusing to join the global community in its efforts to reduce environmental injuries and ecological dangers for which American consumeritis bears a disproportionately large responsibility. The export of consumeritis by the United States is also seen to pose subversive cultural threats, the kinds of threats that have (as the Nafee and BBC articles point out) led to the actual death and physical injury of people infected with it. Though it would be difficult to measure the extent to which hostile international opinion poses added dangers to American security, it clearly does not increase American security against foreign aggression. Rather, the critical way many peoples and nations around the globe presently perceive American materialism and consumeritis suggests that the decline in America's global reputation has substantially heightened our insecurity. This is a perilous respect in which consumeritis represents addictive habits of consumption that amount to too much for our own good.

American export of consumeritis is, however, a highly complex economic, political, and cultural matter that includes another side to the story. It is to this other side we now turn.

The Argument for Exporting Consumerism and Its Limitations

The preceding has described international hostility to American consumerism, pointing out how such hostility may contribute to the heightening of American insecurity. Mr. Nafee's article and the complaint of the head of the Cannes Film Festival, Giles Jacob, provide two examples among many others that could be cited showing how the contagion of American consumeritis has been spreading to other cultures, and how that contagion is resented and feared by some. But it is obvious that if consumeritis is a contagious malady, it is one whose victims—at least its adult victims—accept its addictive infection voluntarily, at least at first. Complaints by other nationals about Western consumerism in some respects parallel complaints by cultural conservatives in the United States about the corrupting influence of American entertainment. As Michael Medved, an American screenwriter turned cultural commentator, points out, "Tens of millions of Americans now see the entertainment industry as ... an alien force that assaults our most cherished values and corrupts our children." In response, the music critic Terry Teachout has said, "The 'enemy' at the gates is not free trade, or even Walt Disney; it is democracy." What Teachout seems to be saying is that it is the consumers of popular culture rather than the producers of its entertainments who are essentially to blame for any decay of values popular entertainments may exhibit. For those in other countries who may criticize an apparent decline in the quality of Hollywood's movies, another writer has similarly argued that it is less a matter of Hollywood corrupting the world than of the world corrupting Hollywood. The more Hollywood becomes preoccupied by the global market [which now accounts for more than half its revenue], the more it produces generic blockbusters made to play as well in Pisa and Peoria. Such films are driven by special effects that can be appreciated by people with minimal grasp of English rather than by dialogue and plot. They eschew fine-grained cultural observation for generic subjects that anybody can identify with, regardless of national origins. There is nothing particularly American about boats crashing into icebergs or asteroids that threaten to obliterate human life.

What these writers are discussing here is the "freedom" of the free market. It is a basic tenet of American conservatism, largely rooted in the capitalist manifesto of Adam Smith's *Wealth of Nations,* that free market capitalism is the best system for ensuring a society's civil liberties. It is with this rationale, for example, that conservatives argue that China's authoritarian state will eventually permit its people a greater degree of democratic freedom because it has now widely opened the door to the free market. The spread of America's consumerist culture can thus be seen not as a merely corrupting materialist force but as one that reflects the liberating spread of democracy. Consider, for example, the following observations in an article by Charles Paul Freund, "In Praise of Vulgarity: How commercial culture liberates Islam—and the West," published in the March 2002 edition of *Reason:*

> Who will ever forget the strangeness of the first images out of post-Taliban Afghanistan, when the streets ran with beards? As one city after another was abandoned by Taliban soldiers, crowds of happy men lined up to get their first legal shave in years, and barbers enjoyed the busiest days of their lives.

Only a few months earlier, in January 2001, dozens
of barbers in the capital city of Kabul had been rounded
up by the Taliban's hair-and-beard cops (the Ministry for
Promotion of Virtue and Prevention of Vice) because they
had been cutting men's hair in a style known locally as the
"Titanic." At the time, Kabul's cooler young men wanted
that Leonardo Di Caprio look, the one he sported in the
movie. It was an interesting moment in fashion, because
under the Taliban's moral regime movies were illegal,
Leonardo Di Caprio was illegal, and his hairdo, which
allowed strands of hair to fall forward over the face during prayer, was a ticket to jail. Yet thanks to enterprising
video smugglers who dragged cassettes over mountain
trails by mule, urban Afghans knew perfectly well who
Di Caprio was and what he looked like; not only did men
adopt his style, but couples were then celebrating their
weddings with Titanic-shaped cakes....

"I hated this beard," one happy Afghan told an
A. P. reporter. Being shaved was "like being free."

Although it's omitted from the monuments and rhetoric of liberation, brutal tyrannies have ended on exactly
this note before. When Paris was liberated from the Nazis,
for example, one Parisian cadged a Lucky Strike from an
American reporter, the first cigarette he'd had in a long,
long time. As he gratefully exhaled, the Frenchman smiled
and told the reporter, "It's the taste of freedom."

Afghan women, of course, removed their burqas, if
they chose to, and put on makeup again ...

Freund goes on in this article to argue that cultural concerns
amounting to near panic about a degeneration in public morals
stimulated by popular ("vulgar") entertainment, fashions, and
fads—the Beatles long hair, the obscenity of rap lyrics, the ubiquity
of pornography, to take a few examples—simply "run their course
in democratic societies until the media tire of them." (Freund,
evidently a libertarian, exempts the prohibition of drugs from this
analysis.) He points out, for example, that "the menacing hoods
of *Blackboard Jungle* [in the 1950s] became the lovable leads in

Grease" by the 1980s, then contrasts this cycle of concern and acceptance in democratic societies with places where the moral order is the legal order and ecstatic forms and assertive ways of being remain matters for police. In December, Cambodia's prime minister ordered tanks to raze the country's karaoke parlors. Last fall, Iran announced a new campaign against Western pop music and other "signs and symbols of depravity."

Freund's article offers further examples of suppression of popular culture in authoritarian societies.

The argument that consumerism exemplifies democratic freedom raises the question whether, if it is the free market that permits consumeritis, and if people choose conspicuous consumption or shallow entertainment even to the point of excess as a voluntary way of life, is it not elitist, paternalistic, and undemocratic to argue that they *ought* to do otherwise?

To this we reply that arguments equating the free market in either entertainment or consumer goods with the whole of freedom are seriously misplaced. Opposition to the export of consumeritis is not opposition to freedom of consumer choice; it is opposition to materialist *excess* and unhealthy self-indulgences. Insofar as foreign readers are concerned, these arguments are offered with the hope that others have the wisdom and good fortune not to suffer the same disabilities and costs of consumeritis to which so many Americans are now victim. The IKEA stampede reported by the BBC and lamented by Mr. Nafee is not an example of the consumeritis we are addressing; it is, rather, an example of the reaction of a relatively impoverished people to a scarce economic opportunity. It may far more exemplify the "More" of Oliver Twist than the "More" of Rocco in *Key Largo*.

The arguments favoring moderation and balance that are the gist of this book are not elitist, nor are they paternalistic or undemocratic. They constitute a call to those who are free to choose, to exercise their freedom in a way superior to materialist addictions, as a path toward discovery of more fulfilling pursuits of happiness. Chapter 2 points out the limitations of materialist pleasures in securing the quality of happiness for which most people yearn, and the documented fact that materialists are, as a group, unhappy people. Other chapters have described the damaging personal costs of consumeritis experienced by those who suffer from it in their personal, family, social, and economic lives, as well as the damaging effects it has on others. Consumeritis in the form and to the extent to which it has developed in the United States represents an economically and ecologically unsustainable social ill. As we have said, we do not argue that material pleasures are intrinsically wrong or that there is anything unhealthy in the desire to acquire things. The argument for exporting consumerism may indeed be understood as an argument for greater democratic freedom in impoverished societies particularly. True freedom, however, necessarily involves the liberty to make choices that enhance our own well-being rather than lessening it. Moderation and balance in our life choices enables us to enjoy our freedom with greater responsibility not only to our families and to our local, national, and world communities but even to ourselves. As previous chapters of this book clearly indicate, those who equate freedom entirely with access to material goods and their enjoyment to excess are at risk of either deceiving themselves or deceiving others. Among all the remedies for consumeritis we propose in the next (and concluding) chapter of this book, we regard as most necessary and potentially effective the salutary changes in consciousness and the voluntary choices Americans make about their consumption and life priorities in their individual pursuits of happiness.

In sum, this chapter and the six chapters preceding it have described the character and scope of American consumeritis; its diverting effect on our pursuits of happiness, including our moral and spiritual well-being; the damage it causes to American family, social, civic, and political life, and to the mental and physical health of our children; the threats it may pose to America's economic future; the harm it has done and continues to do to the environment and the ecological health of the planet; its contribution to the decline in the world's favorable opinion of the people and government of the United States; and how it may decrease American security and increase its insecurity in U.S. relationships to other peoples and nations. Along the way we have also shown how America's universally popular export—good movies—in contrast to America's export of consumeritis and a materialistic culture, continues to produce global good will toward the United States and its people. Having detailed the nature and scope of the problems created by consumeritis, it is incumbent on us to answer such questions as these: What, then, can and should we do about these problems? Are there practical solutions to them that will permit us to maintain American prosperity? The next chapter of this book reflects our best efforts to answer these and related questions with what the ancient Greeks called *phronesis*—practical wisdom.

Here's lookin' at you, kid.

Notes

217 *Humphrey Bogart as Rick to Ingrid Bergman as Ilse in Casablanca* The film *Casablanca* was directed by Michael Curtiz, written by Murray Burnett and Joan Alison, and released by Warner Brothers Films in 1942.

a picture is worth a thousand words Charlie Chaplin, comic master of the silent screen, put it this way: "The silent picture is a universal means of expression." "Biography," *Charlie Chaplin* (Roy Export Company Establishment), *www.charliechaplin.com/rubrique.php3?ed_ rubrique+22*.

218 Cinema Paradiso, *the first film by the Italian director Giuseppe Torna- tore* *Cinema Paradiso* (1989), directed by Giuseppe Tornatore, written by Giuseppe Tornatore and Vanna Paoli, produced by Franco Cristaldi (Cristaldifilm), Les Filmes Arianne, Radiotelevisione Italiana (RAJ), and TFI Film Productions.

to become, at least for a while, a little less of a foreigner The late San Francisco poet Thom Gunn pointed out that renting a movie video is a private matter, while going to a movie house to see a film is a commu- nity activity in which members of the audience share what is in fact an intimate experience under cover of the darkened theater. A conversa- tion with Thom Gunn reported to the authors by the photographer Jock McDonald, November 29, 2005.

219 *watching the British comedy* Clockwise *with John Cleese* *Clockwise,* produced by Verity Lambert, directed by Christopher Morahan, writ- ten by Michael Frayn (Moment Films and Thorn EMI, 1986).

first saw Federico Fellini's Satyricon *shortly after it opened* *Satyricon,* produced by Alberto Granaldi, written and directed by Federico Fellini (World Films, 1970).

Christ Church ("the most British city in the world outside of England"), where Joy and I went to see Head in the Clouds, Co-produced by Michael Cowan, Bertil Ohlsson, Jonathan Olsberg, Jason Piette, André Rouleau, and Maxime Rémil; written and directed by John Duigan (Sony Pictures Classic, 2004).

the first Western feature movie the Chinese government permitted to be filmed in China *The Last Emperor,* produced by Jeremy Thomas, directed by Bernardo Bertolucci, written by Mark Peploe (China Film Co-Production Corp., 1987).

The earliest feature movies George Méliès (1861–1938), Auguste Lumière (1862–1954), and Louis Lumière (1864–1948).

Charlie Chaplin and Douglas Fairbanks, though best known as American filmmakers See "Culture Wars," *The Economist.* September 10, 1998:

"Some of the great figures of Hollywood—Chaplin, Murnau, Stroheim, Hitchcock—were imports." Those great figures included Mary Pickford (1892–1979), Charlie Chaplin (1889–1977), and Douglas Fairbanks (1883–1939).

220 Alfred Hitchcock: *Psycho*, produced by Alfred Hitchcock, screenplay by Joseph Stefano, based on the novel by Robert Bloch (Shamley Productions, 1960); *The Birds*, produced by Alfred Hitchcock, screenplay by Evan Hunter, based on the story by Daphne du Maurier (Alfred J. Hitchcock Productions and Universal Pictures, 1963); *Dial M for Murder*, produced by Alfred Hitchcock, written by Frederick Knott (Warner Brothers Films, 1954); *The Lady Vanishes*, produced by Edward Black, written by Sidney Gilliat and Frank Launder (Gainsborough Pictures, 1938).

David Lean: *Lawrence of Arabia*, produced by Sam Spiegel and Robert Harris, written by Robert Bolt and Michael Wilson (Horizon Pictures, 1962); *A Passage to India*, produced by John Heyman and Edward Sands, written by David Lean (EMI Films, Ltd., HBO, Thorn EMI Screen Entertainment, 1984); *The Bridge on the River Kwai*, produced by Sam Spiegel, written by Pierre Boulle, starring Alec Guinness (Columbia Pictures and Horizon Pictures, 1957).

Ingmar Bergman: *The Seventh Seal*, produced by Allan Ekelund, written by Ingmar Bergman (Svensk Filmindustri, 1957); *Wild Strawberries*, produced by Allan Ekelund, written by Ingmar Bergman (Svensk Filmindustri, 1957); *Fanny and Alexander*, produced by Jorn Donner, written by Ingmar Bergman (Cinematograph AB, 1982).

Akira Kurosawa (1910–1998):   *Seven Samurai*, produced by Sojiro Motoki, written by Akira Kurosawa and Shinobu Hashimoto (Toho Company, Ltd., 1954); *Ran*, produced by Katsumi Furukawa, written by Akiro Kurosawa, Hideo Oguni, and Masato Ide (Greenwich Film Productions, Herald Ace Inc., Nippon Herald Films, 1985).

Luis Buñuel: *The Discreet Charm of the Bourgeoisie*, produced by Serge Silberman, written by Jean-Claude Carriere and Luis Buñuel (Dean Film, 1972); *Obscure Object of Desire*, produced by Serge Silberman, written by Jean-Claude Carriere and Luis Buñuel (Greenwich Film Productions, 1977); *Tristana*, produced by Robert Dorfmann and Luis Buñuel, written by Julio Alejandro and Luis Buñuel, based on a novel by Benito Perez Galtos (Les Films Corona, 1970).

Fritz Lang: *Metropolis*, produced by Erich Pommer, written by Thea von Harbou (Universum Film, 1927); *M*, produced by Seymour Nebenzal, written by Thea von Harou and Fritz Lang (Nero Film AG, 1931); *The Woman in the Window*, produced and written by Nunnally Johnson, based on a novel by J. H. Wallis (International Pictures, Inc., 1945).

Jean Renoir: *The Grand Illusion*, produced by Albert Pinkovitch and Frank Rollmer, written by Jean Renoir and Charles Speak (R.A.C., 1937);

The Crime of Monsieur Lang   Produced by Andre Halley des Fontaines and Jean Renoir, written by Jean Castanyer and Jacques Prevert (Oberon, 1936).

Satyajit Ray: *Pather Panchali,* written by Bibhutibhushan Bandyopadhyay and Satyajit Ray (Government of West Bengal, 1955).

D. W. Griffith (1875–1948):   *Broken Blossoms* or *The Yellow Man and the Girl,* produced and written by D. W. Griffith, based on a story by Thomas Burke (D. W. Griffith Productions, Paramount Pictures, 1919); *The Birth of a Nation,* produced by D. W. Griffith and David Sheppard, written by Thomas F. Dixon Jr. (David W. Griffith Corp., 1915).

Bicycle Thief   Produced by Guiseppe Amato and Vittorio De Sica, directed by Vittorio De Sica, written by Luigi Bartolini and Cesare Zavattini (Produzioni De Sica, 1948).

Amarcord   Produced by Franco Cristaldi, directed by Frederico Fellini, written by Tonino Guerra and Frederico Fellini (F.C. Produzioni and PECF, 1973).

Life Is Beautiful   Produced by Gianluigi Braschi, John M. Davis, and Elda Ferri; directed by Roberto Benigni, written by Vincenzo Cerami (Cecchi Gori Group Tiger Cinematographica and Melampo Cinematographico, 1997).

221   *Stagecoach*   Produced by Walter Wanger, directed by John Ford, written by Ernest Haycox and Dudley Nichols (Walter Wanger Productions, Inc., 1939).

Shepherd of the Hills   Produced by Jack Moss, directed by Henry Hathaway, written by Stuart Anthony, Grover Jones, and Harold Bell Wright (Paramount Pictures, 1941).

Dr. Jekyll and Mr. Hyde   Produced by Victor Saville, directed by Victor Fleming, written by John Lee Mahin, Percy Heath, and Samuel Hoffenstein based on the novel by Robert Louis Stevenson (Loew's Inc., MGM, 1941).

Ulysses   Produced by Dino De Laurentiis and Carlo Ponte, directed by Mario Camerini and Mario Bava, written by Franco Brusati, Mario Camerini, Ben Hecht, Irwin Shaw, and others, based on the poem by Homer (Lux Film, S.p.a., 1955).

223   *the increasing commercialization of movies*   See the source cited in the second note to page 1, "Movies and The Selling of Desire."

224   Samuel Goldwyn (1882–1974):   Producer of *Porgy and Bess* and *Guys and Dolls.*

Howard Hughes (1905–1976):   Uncredited producer of *Hells Angels, Scarface,* and *Front Page.*

Hughes's recent biopic, The Aviator, *shows* The Aviator (2004), Warner Brothers and Miramax Films, produced and directed by Martin Scorsese, written by John Logan, starring Leonardo Di Caprio as Howard Hughes, with a cameo appearance by the English actor Jude Law as the British-born Hollywood actor Errol Flynn. The film for which Hughes risked his fortune without obtaining proportionate box office returns was *Hell's Angels* (1930). *Hells Angels* was favorably compared in technical originality and filmmaking daring to George Lucas's *Star Wars* by Stephen Hunter in *The Washington Post* (December 19, 2004) in a story captioned "Howard Hughes, Spreading His Wings: In 1930, the Legendary Eccentric Created a Roaring Yet Rickety Vehicle for His Aviation Interest."

Limelight Produced, directed and written by Charles Chaplin (Celebrated Productions, 1952).

American movies remain overwhelmingly the most popular movies in the world "A strong case can be made out that America dominates world cinema. It may not make most feature films. But American films are the only ones that reach every market in the world ... In major markets around the world, lists of the biggest grossing films are essentially lists of Hollywood blockbusters in slightly differing orders with one or two local films for variety. In the European Union the United States claimed 70% overall of the film market in 1996, up from 56% in 1987; even in Japan, America now accounts for more than half the film market ... Between 1995 and 1996 Europe's trade deficit with the United States in films and television grew from $4.8 billion to $5.65 billion." "Culture Wars," *The Economist,* September 10, 1998. "Hollywood's foreign box-office revenues now make up over one half of its total, compared with a quarter ten years ago." "The Polygram Test," *The Economist,* August 13, 1998. "In France, American films now account for 60% of box-office revenues; in Britain, for an astonishing 95%.... 'The majority of European films have virtually zero box-office appeal,' says Mr. [Martin] Dale [a media consultant] bluntly. Whereas a typical Hollywood film is eventually seen, one way or another, by 220 million people, a European film is lucky to be seen by 1% of that number." "Home Alone in Europe," *The Economist,* March 20, 1997.

Star Wars Produced, directed, and written by George Lucas (Lucasfilm Ltd., 1977).

Lord of the Rings Produced by Peter Jackson and others, directed by Peter Jackson, written by Fran Walsh, Filippa Boyens, and Peter Jackson, based on the novels by J. R. R. Tolkien (New Line Cinema, 2001–2003).

225 *E.T.* Produced by Steven Spielberg and Kathleen Kennedy, directed by Steven Spielberg, written by Melissa Mathison (Amblin Entertainment and Universal Pictures, 1982).

Saving Private Ryan   Produced by Steven Spielberg, Gary Levinsohn, Mark Gordon, and Ian Bryce, directed by Steven Spielberg, written by Robert Rodat (Paramount Pictures, Dreamworks, Amblin Entertainment, Mark Gordon Productions, Mutual Film Corporation, 1998).

almost cinematic depictions of Dante's Inferno   Dante, *Dante's Inferno* (Vancouver, B.C., Canada: Chronicle Books, LLC, 2004). As to Avarice, see Canto 7; as to Lust, Canto 5; Flattery, Canto 17.

In his 1798 Farewell Address   The relevant portion of Washington's address asks, "Why, by interweaving our destiny with that of any part of Europe, entangle our peace and prosperity in the toils of European ambition, rivalship interest, humor, or caprice?" See *The People Shall Judge*, vol. 2 (hereafter, *The People*) (Chicago: University of Chicago Press, 1949), 494, edited by The Staff, Social Sciences 1, The College of the University of Chicago.

226 *the Monroe Doctrine*   The doctrine was announced by President Monroe in his annual message to Congress in 1823: "We owe it, therefore, to candor and to the amicable relations existing between the United States and [European] powers to declare that we should consider any attempt on their part to extend their system to any portion of this hemisphere as dangerous to our peace and safety." *The People*, 513.

the Treaty of Versailles   The treaty was presented to the U.S. Senate on July 10, 1919, and was rejected on March 19, 1920.

the Louisiana purchase   Thomas Jefferson doubled the territory of the United States with a treaty signed on April 30, 1803. The land acquired by the Louisiana Purchase was approximately 800,000 square miles; it was bought for $15 million or less than $20 per square mile.

Florida (acquired from Spain in 1821)   The Adams-Onis Treaty of 1819 went into effect on February 22, 1821. Under this treaty Spain agreed to renounce any claims to the territories of east and west Florida. See Article 2 of the Treaty of Amity, Settlement and Limits between the United States of America, and his Catholic Majesty in "Adams-Onis Treaty of 1819," *www.tamu.edu/ccbn/dewitt/adamonis.htm*, accessed on February 13, 2006.

foreign policy concerns with Mexico   The U.S.-Mexican War (1846–1848) led to Mexico losing half of its territory to the United States, covering the present-day southwest from California to Texas. See "The U.S.-Mexican War (1846–1848)," *www.pbs.org/kera/usmexicanwar/* (accessed February 13, 2006).

227 *when the USSR collapsed*   The USSR was officially dissolved on December 31, 1991, six days after Boris Yeltsin replaced Mikhail Gorbachev as president of the Soviet Union.

Korea and Vietnam   The Korean conflict, termed a "police action," began in June of 1950 and continued through July of 1953. In reference to the Korean conflict as a "police action," see, for example, the following: "Thus began the so-called Forgotten War, a three-year 'police action,' a sideshow to the Cold War in Europe, a bloody conflict that surged up and down the Korean peninsula, killing and wounding more than 2-million soldiers and civilians. President Harry Truman used the term 'police action' to avoid making the American public deal with the more uncomfortable term—war." David Ballingrud, "Korea, the forgotten war," *St. Petersburg Times Online* (Tampa Bay, FL: July 20, 2003), *www. sptimes.com/2003/07/20/news_pf/Korea/Korea_the_forgotten_.shtml.* The Vietnam conflict (1964–1974) escalated with passage by the U.S. Congress of the Gulf of Tonkin Resolution on August 7, 1964, in response to an incident in the Gulf of Tonkin in which the North Vietnamese army allegedly attacked two American military ships.

a nation of immigrants   See John Kennedy and Robert Kennedy, *A Nation of Immigrants* (New York: HarperCollins, 1986).

huddled masses yearning to breathe free   The complete inscription on the Statue of Liberty reads as follows: "Not like the brazen giant of Greek fame, With conquering limbs astride from land to land; Here at our sea-washed, sunset gates shall stand A mighty woman with a torch, whose flame Is the imprisoned lightning, and her name Mother of Exiles. From her beacon-hand Glows world-wide welcome; her mild eyes command The air-bridged harbor that twin cities frame. 'Keep ancient lands, your storied pomp!' cries she with silent lips. 'Give me your tired, your poor, Your huddled masses yearning to breathe free, The wretched refuse of your teeming shore. Send these, the homeless, tempest-tost to me, I lift my lamp beside the golden door!'" Emma Lazarus (1849–1887), *The New Colossus*, 1883, engraved on the Statue of Liberty.

228   *the attacks had "changed everything"*   See, for example, Harrison Sheppard, "The War on Terrorism: The Conflict between Liberty and Security," A Talk to the Hellenic Law Society of San Francisco, October 14, 2004, published in an edited version in *The Hellenic Journal*, November, 2004: "It has been just over three years since the Twin Towers in New York City were destroyed in what may be considered the single most horrifying and destructive act of foreign aggression on the territory of the United States in its history. That day, according to the President of the United States and others, 'has changed everything.' 'Everything' is a lot, surely too much, and I presume it is wise not to take this declaration too literally. One thing it appears to have changed, however, is the degree of the U.S. government's willingness to engage in 'preemptive' war as part of the 'war on terrorism' declared by the President following the Twin Towers (and Pentagon) disaster. Citing the war on terrorism as part of his justification, and as a preemptive strike against possible use of weapons of mass destruction against the United States, the President ordered the invasion of Iraq."

Four years after 9/11, reports continue that President Bush and his advisors "are concerned that the threat of terrorism is unspeakably high, with nightmare scenarios such as a nuclear attack on Washington, D.C., disturbingly real to them." *San Francisco Chronicle,* "Experts ponder Bush's rationale" [for ordering wiretaps on U.S. citizens without judicial authorization], December 20, 2005, A11.

The Patriot Act   The USA PATRIOT Act, Public Law 57, 107th Cong., 2d sess. (October 10/11, 2001). Throughout its history, in times of war or the threat of war, the United States has enacted legislation designed to increase American security, commonly giving such enactments patriotic nomenclature. In the 1950s, for example, during the McCarthy period of the Cold War era, the U.S. government required that individuals sign loyalty oaths before they could be employed by federal-funded organizations. Truman Loyalty Oath, 1947, "Prescribing the Procedures for the Administration of an Employees Loyalty Program in the Executive Branch of the Government," 3 CFR, 1943–1948 Comp. Provisions of the Patriot Act compromising the civil liberties of Americans, such as their freedom from invasions of privacy and judicially unauthorized wiretaps, were strongly opposed by members of the U.S. Congress when the act came up for renewal in December 2005; see, for example, the front page story of the *San Francisco Chronicle* of December 20, 2005, headlined "Bush plays hardball on spying, Patriot Act."

The U.S. invasion of Iraq, following the U.S. government's rejection of the widely held international view   See for example the published remarks of the International Atomic Energy Agency's (IAEA) director general, Mohamed ElBaradei: "I hope the U.S. does not know anything we do not know. If they do, they should tell us. If they are talking about indigenous capability, Iraq is far away from that. If Iraq has imported material hidden, then you're talking about six months or a year. But that's a big if.... I think it's difficult for Iraq to hide a complete nuclear-weapons program. They might be hiding some computer studies or [research and development] on one single centrifuge. These are not enough to make weapons." Marge Michaels, "Q&A With the Top Sleuth: Chief Weapons Inspector ElBaradei Searches for Substance from the Iraqis," *Time Magazine* (January 20, 2003) as referenced from Dr. Glen Rangwala's "Middle East Reference: Claims and Evaluations from Iraq's Proscribed Weapons" (February 6, 2003), *middleeastreference.org.uk/iraqweapons.html#about.*

229 *the United States no longer enjoys, in Europe or in the Middle East or in parts of Asia*   "The 18 months since the launch of the Iraq war has left the country's hard-earned respect and credibility in tatters. In going to war without a legal basis or the backing of traditional U.S. allies, the Bush administration brazenly undermined Washington's long-held commitment to international law, its acceptance of consensual decision-making, its reputation for moderation, and its identification with

the preservation of peace. The road back will be a long and hard one."
Robert W. Tucker and David C. Hendrickson, "The Sources of American Legitimacy," *Foreign Affairs* (November/December, 2004). *www.
foreignaffairs.org/20041101faessay83603/robert-w-tucker-david-c-hen-
drickson/the-sources-of-american-legitimacy.html?mode=print.*

230 *as aggressive acts against the United States in the early nineteenth century by the Barbary Coast pirates attest* See Christopher Hitchens,
Thomas Jefferson: Author of America (New York: HarperCollins, 2005),
128, recounting the Barbary pirates' justification of their aggression
against the United States as a nation of non-Muslim sinners as follows:
"The Ambassador answered us that it was founded on the Laws of the
Prophet, that it was written in their Koran, that all nations who should
not have answered their authority were sinners, that it was their right
and duty to make war upon them wherever they could be found, and
to make slaves of all they could take as prisoners."

Abu Ghraib A summary of one early report of the Abu Ghraib
incident is the following by James Risen, "The Struggle for Iraq: The
Treatment of Prisoners; G.I.'s Are Accused of Abusing Iraqi Captives," *New York Times* (April 29, 2004): "American soldiers at a
prison outside Baghdad have been accused of forcing Iraqi prisoners into acts of sexual humiliation and other abuses in order to make
them talk, according to officials and others familiar with the charges.
The charges, first announced by the military in March, were documented by photographs taken by guards inside the prison, but were
not described in detail until some of the pictures were made public.
Some of the photographs, and descriptions of others, were broadcast
Wednesday night by the CBS News program '60 Minutes II' and were
verified by military officials. Of the six people reported in March to be
facing preliminary charges, three have been recommended for court
martial trials ..."

America has now unleashed history's greatest material binge Wael
Nafee, "Cultural Imperialism: The Deadliest Export" (July 18, 2005),
www.msuj.org/article.php?id=29 (accessed February 13, 2006).

233 *Capitalism is seen [by some Muslims]* "Communication and Dakwah,"
by Andi Faisal Bakti in *Terrorism and Human Security: From Critical
Pedagogy to Peacebuilding?* Wayne Nelles, ed. (New York: Palgrave
Macmillan, 2003), 114–115.

*Orthodox Christian teachings—including, for example, Jesus' Sermon
on the Mount* Jesus' Sermon on the Mount admonishes those who
would follow him to "Lay not up for yourselves treasures upon earth ...
But lay up for yourselves treasures in heaven ... For where your treasure is, there will your heart be also" (Matthew 6:19–21); see also Matthew 6:24–32. Jesus' admonition to the rich man in Mark 10:21 is likewise "Go and sell all you have and give the money to the poor, and you

will have riches in heaven; then come and follow me." The rejection of materialism continues to be a proselytizing tenet of many Christian Evangelicals; see, for example, the story reported on the front page of the December 24, 2005, edition of the *San Francisco Chronicle*, "Gift rift: Evangelicals split over plan to ban presents," reporting a debate among Evangelicals stimulated by a proposal of the American Family Association that adults not exchange Christmas gifts but "funnel their consumer cash to a charity that helps the poor."

more conservative Muslims may argue   See, for example, "Saudi Arabia's highest religious authority urged Muslims yesterday to shun extremism and avoid waging unjustified jihad as the Kingdom cracks down on militants." "Don't Abuse the Concept of Jihad: Grand Mufti," *Allaahuakbar.net* (Riyadh, Saudi Arabia: August 22, 2003), *www.allaahuakbar. net/JIHAAD/dont_abuse_the_concept_of_jihad.htm.*

234   *we consume a third or more of the world's energy*   See Jeremy Rifkin's *The European Dream* (New York: Jeremy Tarcher/Penguin, 2005), 133.

235   *A group based in the United Kingdom and calling itself ENOUGH! provides campaign materials*   Enough, One World Centre, 6 Mount Street, Manchester UK. E-Mail: ethicon@mcr1.poptel.org.uk. Web site: *www. enough.org.uk/* (accessed February 14, 2006).

    A bimonthly magazine called Adbusters   Adbusters Media Foundation is located at 1243 W 7th Ave., Vancouver, BC. E-Mail: info@adbusters. org. web site: *www.adbusters.org.*

    Seeds of Simplicity   This is a national, nonprofit membership organization for the general public centered on voluntary simplicity. It is a Los Angeles-based program of the Center for Religion, Ethics & Social Policy at Cornell University. As of this writing, it announced plans to host a web site at *www.simplelivingamerica.org.*

    Pew Research Center for People and the Press   "Indians Wary of Consumerism," *Asia Africa Intelligence Wire* (*Financial Times*, June 5, 2003).

236   *Hollywood is a Trojan Horse bringing with it Disneyland Paris*   "Culture Wars," *The Economist*, September 10, 1998.

    The Kyoto Treaty   Kyoto Protocol to the United Nations Framework Convention on Climate Change, *English Conference of the Parties*, Third Session, Kyoto, Japan, December 1–10, 1997.

237   *The United States has refused to sign the treaty on substantive grounds*   Supporters of U.S. rejection of the Kyoto Treaty claim that the United States is being more honest in its rejection of the treaty than some nations who have signed it are in their acceptance, arguing than many signatories do not sincerely intend to carry out their obligations under the treaty. They also point out that exemption from the treaty of

large developing nations such as China, whose industries are major polluters, and provisions of the treaty relating to the allocation and trading of environmental debits and credits, practically nullify the treaty's effectiveness; see, for example, Robert J. Samuelson, "The Kyoto Delusion," *Washington Post* (June 21, 2005), A25; and Debra Saunders, "Blair Takes Heat for Global-Warming Remarks," *San Francisco Chronicle* (October 2, 2005), C5. In response to these claims, supporters of the treaty argue that, despite the treaty's admitted shortcomings, the United States owes it to the rest of the world to join in this first significant international effort to address the problem, first, because the United States bears a large responsibility in light of its disproportionately great greenhouse emissions; and, second, because of the unique global position of the United States, it is obligated to show leadership on environmental issues.

Even the prime minister of Canada, Paul Martin   "Canada's Prime Minister has urged the U.S. to 'listen to its conscience' and take further steps to reduce emissions linked to global warming." Tim Hirsch, "BBC News: Canada Turns Climate Focus on U.S." (December 8, 2005), *news.bbc.co.uk/1/hi/sci/tech/4508928.stm.*

238 *the contagion of American consumeritis has been spreading to other cultures*   For example, I received the following note from an Italian artist and anthropologist, Giovanni Caselli, after he had read part of this book in manuscript form: "A few days ago I sent an anthropological essay to Columbia University, for consideration for publication. I think it has a lot in common with your forthcoming book. Mine is a history of Italian society during the 20th century, seen through the eyes of my family: my grandfather, my father and then myself. Italy seems to have become more American than America itself." E-mail from Giovanni Casselli to Harrison Sheppard, February 9, 2006.

The 'enemy' at the gates is not free trade   Terry Teachout, "Culture Wars," *The Economist* (September 10, 1998).

239 *that it is less a matter of Hollywood corrupting the world than of the world corrupting Hollywood*   "Culture Wars," *The Economist* (September 10, 1998).

240 *Blackboard Jungle*   Produced by Pandro S. Berman, directed and written by Richard Brooks (MGM, 1955).

241 *Grease*   Produced by Allan Carr and Robert Stigwood, directed by Randal Kleiser, written by Jim Jacobs and Warren Casey (Paramount Pictures, 1978).

Brad Pitt as Tyler Durden (left) and Edward Norton as the Narrator in *Fight Club* (20th Century Fox, 1999)

8

What Is to Be Done: Cures for Consumeritis

It is the first duty of every individual to develop all his faculties of body, mind and spirit as completely and harmoniously as possible; but it is a still higher duty for each of us to develop our special faculty to the uttermost consistent with health; for only by doing so shall we attain to the highest self-consciousness or be able to repay our debt to humanity.... Nine men and women out of ten go through life without realizing their own special nature: they cannot lose their souls, for they have never found them.
—Frank Harris, *My Life And Loves* (1922)

IN THE MOVIE *The Wild One*, the leader of a motorcycle pack, Johnny Strabler (played by Marlon Brando), is asked what he is rebelling against, to which he replies, "What've you got?" Motorcycle gangs may appear to be antisocial in their lifestyles, but they also tend to adopt rules to which they strictly conform among themselves. Similarly, the materialistic lifestyles many Americans have adopted may appear to be expressions of individuality, but they also commonly involve bondage to the addictions of materialism, including especially keeping up with the Joneses.

It is a cultural paradox that in societies in which people are highly socialized, they subordinate their individuality to the good of the community in public, but *in private* they cultivate their individuality vigorously; in highly individualist societies such as our own, however, people openly exhibit the individualistic social lifestyle they have chosen to adopt, but then strictly conform to the dictates of their chosen subculture in private. Which kind of culture is more likely to promote an individual's happiness in harmony with his or her community may be an open question; but it is at least clear that keeping up with the Joneses is not a formula for individual self-fulfillment.

The ambivalence of many Americans about their culture is exploited in a movie metaphor dramatizing it: *Fight Club*. The antihero of this Luddite film, Tyler Durden (played by Brad Pitt), exhorts his fellow club members to "reject the basic assumption of civilization, especially the importance of material possessions," but the members conform to the club rules with military rigor. In a central speech in the film, Durden states the reasons he has assembled a private army dedicated to violence, mayhem, and destruction of our credit-card culture:

> Advertising has us chasing cars and buying clothes, working at jobs we hate so we can buy shit we don't need. We're the middle children of history, man, no purpose or place. We have no Great War, no Great Depression. Our Great War is a spiritual war; our Great Depression is our lives. We've all been raised on television to believe that one day we'll all be millionaires and movie gods and rock stars, but we won't. We're slowly learning that fact. We're very, very pissed off.

Later, in a coda to this speech, the movie god Brad Pitt, in the persona of Tyler Durden, adds:

You're not your job, you're not how much money you have
in the bank, you're not the car you drive, you're not the
contents of your wallet. You're not your fucking khakis.

The movie ends—in an eerie and ominous scene that may
remind us of the events of 9/11—with explosive destruction of
the city's skyscrapers: the buildings that house the city's major
banks, commercial corporations, and credit-reporting agencies.
This final scene depicts the fantasy of Tyler Durden's alienated,
conformist alter ego (played by Edward Norton).

The private army assembled by Durden to destroy the city's
centers of commercial power consists of some of its low-income
servants: waiters, blue-collar workers, ambulance drivers, security guards, and so forth. *Fight Club* thus plays out the violent
fantasies of alienated Americans who recognize a gulf in their
lives between "the stuff that dreams are made of," typical of the
appeals of commercial advertising, and the reality of their cul-
turally impoverished and subordinate condition. It is an angry
movie; so angry, it is sometimes hard to watch.

We may ask ourselves, is *Fight Club* "only a movie"?

The attitudes of the club members depicted in the film are
not pure fiction. We see on television news from time to time,
or read in newspapers, stories of people—including some highly
educated people—who have exploded into homicidal violence in
frustrated reaction to America's consumer culture and financial
or other pressures they have experienced in pursuit of materialistic goals. Tyler Durden expresses the anger and frustration
people feel when they realize they are not going to become "millionaires and movie gods and rock stars," feelings that may exist
more commonly than we are inclined to think. If you can't keep
up with the Joneses, but are, in effect, told at least forty thousand

times a year that this is what you should be doing, isn't mounting frustration predictable? It is a basic rule of psychology that great frustration may lead to violence. Even among affluent Americans who have either a keen sense of the shallowness of materialism or who are alienated from the corporate culture of buying and selling and its increasing impersonality, frustration and anger are foreseeable emotional responses.

Despite its grittiness and determined depiction of some of life's coarser realities, there is a crucial sense in which *Fight Club* (though a gripping work of cinematic art) is only a movie. There are no good guys in *Fight Club,* and no depiction of a middle way. The film offers to the angry and frustrated the fantasy of destroying materialism's superstructures, but it offers no hope. Fortunately, this is not the reality in which we Americans live. There are more practical nonconforming choices and remedies available to each of us other than Tyler Durden's radical choices and his alter ego's fantasized violence. In fact, the greatest choice available to adults in opposition to materialist conformity is chiefly a matter of inner, not outer, revolution. It is not the superstructure of American materialism that needs to be destroyed: it is our own bondage to its seductions and dictates. Any one of us who is not entirely clueless about the limitations we impose on ourselves by excessively indulging our materialist addictions may choose to liberate ourselves from bondage—if we recognize it as such. The purpose of this chapter is to identify the core problems of consumeritis in need of cure, and to set out the remedies we propose. Because we believe that the chief problems at the root of consumeritis are temptations leading us away from a mature, healthy, and self-respecting consciousness, we first directly address readers who are relatively young in years, heart, or spirit; that is, those who have the capacity to enjoy greater—and more enduring—happiness by considering changes in their choices that will help them realize their own capacity for personal success and happiness.

Self-knowledge as a Remedy for Consumeritis
We are generally guided in what we do by what we think about ourselves, the world we live in, and the choices available to us. Our actions generally follow from our thoughts. ("Thought and action" is the motto of this book's publisher.) We all want to be happy. What we do to achieve that goal through conscious effort therefore depends on what we believe "happiness" to be. What we do to achieve our life goals also depends on how we define "success," the idea that commonly guides ambition.

Whatever ideas we may have about success or happiness, the first thing we require to put ourselves on a path toward them is to secure satisfaction of our basic *needs*. We are not likely to become either successful or happy without having the nourishment and bodily protection and shelter we must have to survive. These are our most basic physical needs. As human beings, we also have other basic needs. Erik Erikson, the great humanist psychologist, found that the first basic psychological need that must be satisfied if we are to develop as healthy human beings is *trust*. If, Erikson said, an infant is not given what it needs to learn to trust that the world is a more or less safe place, and that the infant's basic physical needs will be more or less regularly met, it is not likely to develop its human capacities very well; instead, it will live in a chaos of insecurity, doubt, and fear. Basic trust is, in fact, indispensable to fulfillment of one of our other most basic human needs: the need for *love*. Loving and showing love to others are acts of trust, and the ability to love and accept love in return is indispensable to human happiness.

If you have enough trust to get along in the world, enough trust to learn how to satisfy your basic physical needs, enough trust to be able to work toward realization of your capacities, and enough trust to love others and accept love in return, you have just about all you *need* to achieve success and find happiness. We have other human needs as basic as the need for trust: a need for knowledge, for example, and for the society of others. ("All men by nature desire to know," wrote Aristotle, who also observed that human beings are by nature social animals.)

If satisfaction of our basic needs was our only human challenge, life would be much simpler than it is. In addition to our needs, we find at an early stage in life—at least if we are as privileged as most Americans are—that we also have *wants*. Wants are desires for things that are not essential to our survival; things that are not required to satisfy our basic needs but that give us pleasure of one kind or another. Here is where our difficulties begin. For if we come to be guided in our quest for success and happiness by a constant pursuit of things we want, we are likely to find that we have deprived ourselves of the possibility of satisfying our more basic—and at the same time higher—human needs: the need to love and to be loved by others, for example, and our need for self-knowledge. This seems to be an inescapable implication of research findings about why materialists are unhappy, as discussed in chapter 2. To define "success" in terms of material rewards only is therefore not merely risky but self-defeating. Recognition of this fact requires us to take a long-term rather than a short-term view of what we mean by "success." In the short term, it is tempting to follow our desire for instant gratification, to yield to an impulse to take whatever may be available to us at the moment to satisfy our wants—for more money, for a more prestigious or flashier car, for advancement in the hierarchy we happen to be part of—and the future be damned. Carpe diem. Seize the day, and live for it.

Advice to "seize the day" is good advice—provided we have grown wise enough to understand whether we can do so in a way that will help to satisfy our basic needs—needs we will surely have tomorrow.

The problem is that when we acquire the habit of seizing the day for the material pleasures it offers, our lives tend to become more and more complicated and out of balance. There are *so many* pleasures to be had, *so many* things we can want. And the more and more things we have, the more and more time it takes to manage them and continue to acquire them, and the less and less time we have for enjoying experiences other than our pleasure in *things*. This is also a finding of psychological research into the unhappiness of materialists: their materialism progressively interferes with other life goals. If we are human, we have other wants and—more importantly—other needs in addition to materialist satisfactions that must be fulfilled if we are to be happy. Especially our need for the friendly society of others, and love.

In my talks to lawyers and members of bar associations throughout the United States, in which I advocate the advantages of a peacemaking rather than a war-making model of legal education and practice, I have been told by "successful" attorneys, well-off enough to be wearing $2000 suits and expensive jewelry, that they were making more money than they ever thought they would make but were also unhappier than they ever thought they would be. They had, in other words, lost sight of their needs in the sea of their wants: for more cases won as trial lawyers; for more billable hours generated by their law firms; for more good and costly suits—of both kinds. At a certain point, losing sight of our needs because we have become lost in the sea of our wants results in our being bound by what other "successful" but unhappy people have called gold chains. Like Midas, they find they do not really need all that gold, but they also find themselves unable to stop making it long enough to get what they do need.

This is the tragedy of a false definition of "success"; and by their acceptance of this definition, so many affluent Americans have been captured and felled. Avoiding this kind of tragedy, which is far too common in the United States, requires that we keep in the front of our minds a longer-term view of what success really is—defining success as something that will help us realize our potential for happiness without binding us so completely in gold chains that we can no longer move toward it.

If we are wise, or cherish the hope of becoming so one day, then we must not lose what we already have that can help us to enjoy success and realize our capacity for happiness. This turns out to be real wisdom, a truth expressed by the fictional Wizard of Oz.

What most of us already have—if we have not recklessly lost it by prolonged short-term thinking—is awareness of our higher basic need for the society of others, and for giving and receiving love. For most of us (though not all), this usually includes the need for a life partner, marriage, and family. For all of us, it means the companionship and love of friends; a place in and with a community; and the satisfactions of living in the society of others in ways that provide opportunities for loving and being loved, including pursuing common goals with others. The word "society" is derived, in fact, from the Latin word for "friend," while old Aristotle defined "friendship" as "companionship in common pursuit of human excellence."

If this book is to make any contribution toward remedying the problems it identifies, it will have to compete with an overwhelming media onslaught promoting consumeritis. To even begin to achieve its purposes, *Too Much for Our Own Good* therefore requires that you, the reader, take its teachings seriously enough to consider the choices detailed in this book that will help you remedy those problems you can personally relate to. We most effectively and certainly change the world for the better when we change ourselves for the better. If the preceding paragraphs on the remedy for consumeritis in self-knowledge help you recognize what you most fundamentally need for success and enjoyment of your own unique pursuit of happiness, then thinking about and choosing to act on this recognition is the main remedy we propose to help you avoid infection by consumeritis and to cure it if you are already stricken.

We now consider the other core problems at the root of consumeritis—in addition to a failure to know ourselves—and the practical remedies we propose to cure these core problems.

Problems and Possible Remedies

> *It is not until one [travels abroad] that he can appreciate his own government, that he realizes the fearful responsibility of the American people to the nations of the whole earth, to carry successfully through the experiment that men are capable of self-government.*
> —William H. Seward (Abraham Lincoln's secretary of state) *An Autobiography* (1891)

From the beginning of our history, Americans have cherished great dreams. The seminal "American dream" is the dream of equality before the law securing human rights to life, liberty, and the pursuit of happiness. The United States gave that dream to the modern world in the words of its Declaration of Independence, and advanced it with the establishment of the Constitution. Thus conceived, Abraham Lincoln called the United States "the last, best hope of earth." The founders of the United States and Abraham Lincoln (its great re-founder) referred to the translation of that dream into our particular form of government as an "experiment," an experiment intended to shape the dream progressively into reality: "the experiment that men are capable of self-government." This experiment has so far, after more than two hundred years, proven to be remarkably successful if measured by the power the U.S. government has achieved in the world and the relative affluence of most Americans. But the experiment is a continuing one, and it could still fail. If we are in true crisis, this is doubtlessly its nature: that the experiment is in danger of failing in the foreseeable future, as other aged imperialistic regimes have failed after achieving the height of their power.

The complex of problems documented in this book indicates that the American experiment is in danger of failing in crucial respects. Our transformation into a dominating culture of buying and selling is seriously misleading many of us about what the pursuit of happiness really is, and is thus diverting us from fully enjoying our right to it. The American experiment is also in danger of failing because Americans are showing less interest in acting as informed, responsible citizens than in being well-served consumers, and have progressively lost their sense of community with one another. We may, in reality, hardly be governing ourselves at all. We may be at the greatest risk of failing in the American experiment because our political life, rather than being characterized by appeals to reason and the persuasions of sound argument, is now mainly characterized by the use of sophisticated commercial advertising techniques designed to manipulate rather than to prudently inform public opinion.

The causes of possible failure of the American experiment in the foreseeable future thus happen to parallel the chief causes of consumeritis. As the first seven chapters of this book have described them, the six core problems causing the ills of consumeritis and threatening to end the success of our American experiment are (1) commercial advertising, (2) human temptation and ignorance, (3) easy credit, (4) overreliance on oil and gas-fueled transportation, (5) corruption of the political process, and (6) U.S. government policies that promote and protect consumeritis. For each of these six problems, remedies are proposed and explained in detail below. (For a summary of the remedies, see table 8.1.)

(1) Commercial Advertising: When Less Is More

The extraordinary volume of commercial advertising and its pervasive intrusion into our lives has elevated its harm beyond that of a merely wearying nuisance. It has become far too much of a presence in our lives for our own good. It wastefully clogs our minds and mailboxes, and surrounds us with its messages everywhere we turn; it appropriates use of our fax machines for its own purposes without prior authorization and at our expense; it ubiquitously invades our enjoyment of electronic media news, sports, and entertainment, though the airwaves are supposed to be public property; and, most crucially, it has habituated us by its persistence to patiently accept the culture of buying and selling as our own. The culture of buying and selling insistently promoted by commercial advertising deceptively equates the pursuit of happiness with an endless acquisition of things and enjoyment of materialist satisfactions. It promotes credit in ways that encourage excessive debt. It seriously harms our children by appeals to them to consume products harmful to their physical and mental health and well-being, helping to increase childhood obesity, diabetes, alcoholism, depression, and teenage violence. Its successful transformation of American culture into one of voracious consumerism has resulted in the wholesale import of its insidious techniques into the conduct of American politics at the highest levels. So far as the quality of our lives is concerned, with commercial advertising, less is more. We therefore need to consider adoption of the following remedies to combat its excesses:

(a) *Self-Awareness.* The most basic remedy available to us to combat the pernicious and insidious effects of commercial advertising on us personally may be to cultivate an habitual, conscious awareness of, and resistance to, its demands and seductions. The following paragraph appears in chapter 2. We think it bears repeating.

Rather than allowing the tidal wave of commercial advertising simply to sweep over us, pretending to ourselves that we can ignore what it is doing or that we can screen it out by only half hearing or seeing the commercials affecting our consciousness, we need to resensitize ourselves to the manipulations of advertising. If, as soon as we are conscious of any commercial advertising assaulting us, we are able to keep in the front of our minds the fact that we are individual persons and citizens, not objects to be enlisted in a culture of buying and selling, we are far more likely to begin to recover from the addictions of consumeritis and, to that extent, combat its infection. Try this for only a day or two, and see what difference it may make in the extent you are able to perceive the true stature of your own humanity, and thereby resist manipulation by the culture of buying and selling. To this extent, at least, you may find that "facts are better than dreams."

(b) *Commercial Advertising Filters.* The annoyance many Americans already feel at the constant interruption of their radio listening and television viewing has led the market to develop products that can help us filter or eliminate commercial advertising from our enjoyment of broadcasts. With or without such filtering—which includes devices enabling us to fast forward through commercial interruptions of the TV programs we choose to watch—we can reduce our exposure to commercial advertising by tuning in to commercial television and radio much less often, and for shorter periods, than many of us now do. In fact, entirely eliminating TV as a regular, passive family activity can help bring families closer through more interactive entertainments—play, games, and sports, for example. More generally, reduction of our commercial radio and TV time increases the opportunity for more gratifying leisure activities and enjoyment of other pursuits—which may include the company of family and friends—that *actively* engage our interest and help us realize our own creative potential. Satellite communications have also made available a variety of commercial-free radio stations and television channels offering music, news, education, and entertainment without interruption, although access to these stations is not free. Some of these are even available via cell phone.

(c) *Remedial Regulation and Legislation.* A variety of regulatory and legislative actions by government agencies could help remedy the damage caused by the excesses of commercial advertising, and especially its harmful effects on children. The possibilities of governmental correction of the problems at the base of consumeritis are too numerous to catalogue exhaustively. Here we will summarize the three that we believe deserve the most immediate and serious consideration.

(i) The Federal Communications Commission (FCC). The FCC regulates and licenses use of the airwaves. It should consider rolling back its permissive allocations of the amount of time licensees may devote to commercial advertising, and also propose regulations isolating permissible commercial advertising to the beginning and end of broadcasts so audiences may enjoy their offerings without commercial interruption.

The FCC issued regulations, implementing the Junk Fax Protection Act, to be effective "around August 2006." The act was signed into law by President Bush on July 9, 2005. Transmission of unsolicited commercial faxes to homes and businesses is an especially obnoxious example of abusive advertising excess. It is intrusive and wasteful. It is done at the direct expense of the recipient and in effect confiscates private property for the advertiser's benefit. As of this writing, it remains to be seen how effectively the FCC will regulate and enforce the Junk Fax Prevention Act, but effective implementation will help remedy a commercial advertising practice that clearly goes beyond the bounds of decency and directly injures members of the public.

(ii) The Federal Trade Commission. For reasons discussed in chapter 3, the commercial advertising that is most in need of remedy is television advertising aimed at children. On February 20, 2004, an American Psychological Association Task Force on Advertising and Children issued its report. Because of the currency of the issue of regulating advertising aimed at children, the report deserves to be quoted at length (with citations omitted):

> In 1874, the English Parliament passed the Infants' Relief Act to protect children "from their own lack of experience and from the wiles of pushing tradesmen and moneylenders." The act ... is one of the earliest governmental policies to address children's unique vulnerability to commercial

exploitation. This law was produced in an era long before major corporations earned huge profits by marketing products such as toys, snacks, sugared cereals, and fast food products directly to children, and also before the advent of television provided marketers of such products with unprecedented access to the minds of young people. The issues underlying this 19th century policy remain much the same today, more than 100 years later....

Over the past several decades, a broad collection of academic research has addressed developmental differences in how children recognize and defend against commercial persuasion. That knowledge ... has been the basis for many policies involving both governmental laws and industry self-regulation that are intended to protect young children from excessive or inappropriate advertising tactics ... Our focus is devoted primarily to the examination of television advertising for three reasons. First, marketers who seek child audiences for commercial purposes rely primarily on television because it is the easiest and most effective vehicle for reaching large numbers of children nationwide. Second, television affords marketers access to children at much earlier ages than print media can accomplish, largely because textual literacy does not develop until many years after children have become regular television viewers. And third, much is known about how children understand and are influenced by television advertising, while almost no evidence is yet available in the public domain regarding how children respond to advertising in new media environments such as the World Wide Web.

In 1978, the Federal Trade Commission (FTC) promulgated a Trade Regulation Rule proposing to ban all commercial television advertising directed to very young children. It was never adopted as a result of strong pressures exerted on members of the U.S. Congress by industry lobbyists. Awareness of the harm done to children by commercial advertising has significantly increased during the past quarter century. Interest in prohibiting or regulating advertising aimed at children has therefore recently revived. Our increased knowledge of the harmful effects of advertising on children may now make the time ripe—that is, politically feasible—for the FTC and the FCC to promulgate and adopt regulations completely banning advertising directed at very young children, requiring disclosures of the harmful effects of certain products marketed to children, and other remedies to combat the baneful effects of children's advertising as the evidence may justify. The federal regulatory agencies and Congress should also consider restrictive remedies protecting children from commercial advertising on the Internet. The FTC has already taken some initiatives in this area.

(iii) Federal Tax Enactments. The excesses of commercial advertising have imposed on the public a variety of social costs, and have operated to injure the physical and mental health of our children. Commercial speech is not as fully protected by the guarantees of our First Amendment rights to freedom as is noncommercial speech. The adverse effects of television advertising on American society may be mitigated and partially remedied by the imposition of substantial federal taxation on it. Revenue earned from such taxation could be allocated to federal programs relating, for example, to public education. To the extent that taxation would further reduce televised commercial advertising, it may contribute to mitigating the ills it causes.

(2) Human Temptation and Ignorance: Redefining "Success"

> *Then the Spirit led Jesus into the desert to be*
> *tempted. After spending forty days and nights*
> *without food, Jesus was hungry. The Devil came*
> *to him and said, "If you are God's Son, order*
> *these stones to turn to bread." Jesus answered,*
> *"The scripture says, 'Man cannot live on bread*
> *alone, but on every word that God speaks.'"*
> —Matthew 4:1–4

At least six of the classic seven deadly sins to which human beings are inclined by nature are contributing causes of consumeritis in the ways suggested below:

1. Avarice ("More")
2. Envy ("Keeping up with the Joneses")
3. Lust ("Sell them their dreams")
4. Gluttony ("More")
5. False Pride ("Keeping up with the Joneses")
6. Sloth (easy addiction and lack of self-discipline)

The acting out of these human frailties inherently leads to excess. As one of antiquity's greatest philosophers, Plato, maintained, human vice is most often—perhaps invariably—the product of ignorance or forgetfulness, a lack of adequate knowledge or understanding, or willful ignoring of what is required to achieve our own good. We are certainly not free to make choices we do not know exist. As a cause of consumeritis, such ignorance conspicuously includes lack of adequate knowledge of the adverse effects of materialist excess on both our community life and our natural environment, and insensitivity to the critical need for moderation and balance to avoid these adverse effects. Ignorance also makes us vulnerable to political deception and diversion from pursuits of true happiness, including in particular the healthy cultivation of our own better natures and capacities independent of what the Joneses might think. Here are some specific down-to-earth measures to help us combat our vulnerability to the temptations of consumeritis.

(a) *Seeing Things as They Are.* Whatever our religious views may be, the story of the temptation of Jesus suggests a profound truth we may easily forget. When we hunger for something, our desire can be parent to a belief that we have obtained it, or can obtain it, despite the relevant facts. If we fall passionately in love, to take a vivid example we may all relate to, we are naturally eager and tempted to find signs that our love is returned. ("She loves me, she loves me not.") Perhaps the person we love is kind to us, even attentive. But his or her regard for us is not the same as ours for him or her. If we want to avoid unnecessary suffering from this situation, we need to recognize that fact. We need to recognize, in other words, that despite our hunger, a stone is not bread; it is a stone, with its own proper and indispensable place in the cosmos. "If you ask a man for a fish," Kahlil Gibran's *Prophet* said, "and he gives you a stone, you must remember that a stone may be all that he has to give." In other words, we must resist the temptation to believe that he really has a fish he is hiding from us, understand what it is he has to give—and *see it* for what it is. Stones have their use, but they are not bread.

The temptation the Devil offers when he demands Jesus to satisfy his hunger by turning stones into bread is a temptation human beings often succumb to. When we deeply want something to be so, it can be difficult to resist the temptation to believe that it *is* so. Having more things, or more costly, fashionable things, we may say to ourselves, will bring us what we really crave: the flashy car *will* get the right girl: the precious perfume, the right guy. We ignore the reality and act as if the facts are as we wish

them to be. In psychological jargon, this is called denial. Jesus'
reply to this temptation is that we cannot live by bread alone, "but
on every word that God speaks." What his response signifies is
that we must satisfy ourselves through things as they actually
are, without permitting our desire to distort the reality. This
insight is precisely what Winston Churchill meant when he said
that "facts are better than dreams." If we are to achieve real happiness rather than live in fantasy, we must satisfy our longings
with things as they really are.

To use biblical allusions to stones in another way: Who among
us can cast the first stone against those who yield to temptation
without also condemning himself? The chief sources of the ills
of consumeritis lie within ourselves: our desire for material satisfactions that become excessive; an habitual impulse to acquire
"More." Envy of others is also a temptation we may yield to. This
is part of the impulse to keep up with the Joneses. In a society as
competitive as ours, these impulses follow from the conventional
idea of success. In chapter 2 we quoted the following psychological definition of a materialist:

> A materialist is a person whose psychic energy is dis-
> proportionately invested in things and their symbolic
> derivatives—wealth, status, and power based on pos-
> sessions—and therefore whose life consists mainly
> of experiences with the material dimension of life.

For all of us, but especially for the ambitious young, our idea
of success largely determines where we place our psychic energies. This is the meaning of the biblical admonition

> Lay not up for yourselves treasures upon earth, where
> moth and rust doth corrupt, and where thieves break
> through and steal. (Matthew 6:19)

We are easily—and in fact now *constantly*—tempted to believe
that the path to happiness is the same as the road to material

satisfaction. But this belief is turning stones into bread, because it is not the reality. Having more than enough is never enough by itself to secure our happiness. For that, we need what all of creation provides for us to satisfy our spiritual as well as our material needs.

(b) *Redefining Success; Self-education.* In more conventional and secular terms, for those who wish to remedy their own consumeritis and free themselves from its burdens, and for those who may be ignorant of the full range of life choices available to them, it may be necessary to educate themselves or be educated by others to *redefine success.* This is nearly identical to arriving at a better understanding of what the phrase "pursuit of happiness" really signifies. As studies of materialism and materialists indicate, materialistic goals tend constantly to expand beyond reach, so that their attainment is perpetually frustrated. Goals related to achievement in the occupations (or pursuits) we choose or loving human relationships or service to others or public-spirited activity in community with others—nonmaterial success of these kinds—these goals are less likely to be inherently unattainable. They are also more likely to bring enduring and multiplying satisfactions.

A key remedy to the problem of human temptation and ignorance of a kind that helps fuel consumeritis may thus simply be *redefining success* for ourselves, and better educating our children—at the earliest possible age—about what "success" can mean. The redefinition of success we refer to would mean ordering our lives to avoid the constant temptation to turn stones into bread; living our lives with greater simplicity; consciously distinguishing our needs from our wants; shifting the emphasis of our attention from isolated individualism to more active involvement with our families and friends; experiencing a larger sense of community with others—perhaps even considering changes in our living arrangements for the economies they will bring; and, in general, living our lives with a better appreciation of when enough is enough and more is too much. If we can, in other words, do more to surround and occupy ourselves with a broader range of those gifts of creation—metaphorically, the "words of God"—that can satisfy our spiritual needs, we will to that extent be far less tempted to turn stones into bread.

(c) *Becoming Citizens Again.* Curing the acquired habit of thinking of ourselves as consumers by remembering ourselves more often as citizens is difficult. It is not easy, in twenty-first-century America, to consistently behave as conscientious citizens. It has become so much more work to be a good citizen than it was, for example, when Benjamin Franklin simply proposed an ordinance requiring that houses be built farther apart to lessen the danger of fire in residential areas. Now, with literally millions of laws on the books, it is probably almost impossible to keep up with all the demands that civil society places on us, and all the political, social, and economic issues of the day. We are now often compelled to obtain the professional advice of experts to help us discharge our civic duties—like filing our income tax returns, or complying with zoning regulations for home or business improvements. The psychic energy we have available to spend is limited, and our lives have become very complicated by the overheated, technological culture of buying and selling. But finding ways to remove ourselves progressively from the frenzied habits of this culture is precisely what may enable us to recover enough energy to discover our nonmaterialist satisfactions, and also rediscover what it means to be active, aware, and responsible members of a community.

(d) *Enacting a Federal Consumption Tax.* There is one other significant possible remedy to mitigate the human temptations and ignorance that are at the root of so much consumeritis. It is an institutional, governmental remedy, not an individual one. Replacing the income tax with a consumption tax on the purchase of all consumer goods and services other than food and medicine would reduce consumption more directly than any other public policy measure. This proposed remedy is likely to be rejected by many people as too radical a change in the American system of taxation. But imposition of such a national tax is not unprecedented. It evidently works well, for example, in Chile. In addition to directly remedying much excess consumption, it would have the advantage (as would a progressive flat tax) of sharply reducing opportunities for lobbyists to promote amendments to the tax code that would serve private interests contrary to the public interest. Perhaps the chief objection to such a system of taxation—apart from those bound to be raised by the many special interests relying on our complex income tax system for their livelihood (such as lawyers, bookkeepers, and CPAs)—is that it would work unfairly against the poor, especially those who are already unable to afford consumer goods of near necessity to maintain a decent standard of living. Ardent advocates of a consumption tax meet this objection by proposing that the system include direct income transfers to the poor. We propose consideration of this remedy at least as a provocation to stimulate more creative thought about the necessity for strong remedies to help mitigate consumeritis. We recognize, however, that adoption of any such system would require careful study, debate, and public education before it could become politically feasible or be found to be socially desirable.

(3) Easy Credit: Saving Ourselves from Trouble

In Shakespeare's *Hamlet,* as the elderly Polonius sends his son Laertes off to a foreign university, he distills the lessons of his own life experience and gives Laertes advice about how to conduct himself in the world. His loving speech concludes as follows:

> Neither a borrower nor a lender be,
> For loan oft loses both itself and friend,
> And borrowing dulls the edge of husbandry.
> This above all—to thine own self be true,
> And it must follow, as the night the day,
> Thou canst not then be false to any man.
> Farewell, my blessing season this in thee.

Polonius is a figure of fun for Hamlet, but each thread in this cloak of wisdom with which Polonius intends to wrap his son maintains its worldly and spiritual truth. As we pointed out in chapter 1, the number of personal bankruptcies filed in the United States each year since 1996 has exceeded the number of students graduating from college, and some students are dropping out of college because of their inability to handle their credit-card debt. Consumeritis is thus contributing to impairment of an important national resource: educated youth. With the college drop-out phenomenon particularly in mind, but also considering the bankruptcy statistics and the escalating levels of American debt (both private and public) described in chapter 1, we propose the following remedies relating to how easy credit has helped fuel consumeritis:

(a) *Public Education.* Public schools should include in their curricula, beginning at the primary school level, basic instruction in responsible financial management, the practical adverse consequences of excessive indebtedness, and the advantages of habitual saving.

(b) *Federal Regulation.*

(i) Credit Cards and Junk-Mail Solicitations: The solicitation or offering of credit cards to students of any age at their educational institutions should be prohibited. The issuance of credit cards to minors should also be prohibited, or at least limited to a modest credit line of no more than $500.00. Minors under 18 should be immune from liability for debt incurred as the result of non-fraudulent acceptance of an unsolicited credit-card offering. Junk-mail solicitations for credit-card issuance to the same adult addressees should at least be limited to no more than one a year, or altogether prohibited. Prohibition would be a highly preferable remedy because unsolicited credit-card offerings facilitate identity theft and fraud.

(ii) Limitations on Home-Equity Loans: In light of the economic risks described in chapter 4, and the increasing use of second-mortgage financing to fund consumer spending, banks and other financial institutions should be restricted or prohibited from advertising—especially through junk-mail solicitations—private equity (second mortgage) lines of credit; and the permissible amounts of such lines of credit should be limited, for example, so that they do not exceed the percentage of homeowner equity that would remain after the combined first- and second-mortgage financing. Thus, for example, if the amount of first-mortgage debt equals fifty percent of the appraised value of the home, no equity line of credit or loan greater than half the remaining appraised value of the property should be permitted. This would inherently limit the portion of home equity that can be used to finance consumer spending, and in effect preserve some "savings" of homeowner assets.

(iii) Tax Policy: Consideration should be given to tax deductions or credits for amounts of personal savings held in savings accounts for more than one year (or a greater period) in addition to permissible deductions for retirement accounts, and consideration should be given to raising the limits of annual tax-deductible IRA and SEP contributions. This remedy would be consistent with the recommendation of FRB Chairman Bernanke (quoted in chapter 4) that the government should "increase household saving in the U.S., for example by creating tax-favored savings vehicles." The simplest way to reduce easy credit of course would be for the Federal Reserve to raise interest rates substantially. But the rate at which this should be done to avoid unnecessary economic trauma is a policy question implicit in the entire discussion in chapter 4 of the risks and opportunities we face as a result of consumeritis. We do not presume here to calibrate the rate of FRB increases that most economists foresee as inevitable.

(iv) Public Service Advertising: The U.S. Department of the Treasury or other appropriate federal agencies should fund televised public-service announcements educating the general public to the advantages of savings as well as the economic risks of not devoting a portion of disposable income to personal savings.

(4) Oil and Gas-fueled Transportation: Winged Migration

Of all the problems at the root of consumeritis with threatening implications for the future of democracy and our national security (in terms of both environmental safety and international relations), the complex of problems related to our excessive use of and dependence on oil and private gas-fueled automobile transportation may be the most difficult to solve. This is particularly ominous because failure to solve this complex of problems may have the most disastrous consequences for Americans, both domestically and internationally. The movie *Syriana*, released in 2006, intensely portrays an alliance of plutocratic interests, antidemocratic Middle Eastern regimes, and powerful government agencies committed to maintaining the status quo, and ruthlessly defending it. Whether or not you accept *Syriana's* conspiracy theory as depicting the truth, or at least a large part of it, there is no doubt that powerful interests actively oppose diminution of American dependence on, and high consumption of, oil and gas and gas-fueled transportation, or what we have termed "car consumeritis." This complex of problems is also particularly difficult because of the anxieties summarized in chapter 5 about potential adverse effects on employment from increased conservation. While no studies have as yet settled this issue, we believe that the proposed remedies listed below are, in combination, likely to result in economic gains, not losses; and they will also help to avert potential economic disaster on a scale that would dwarf the magnitude of any potential economic loss attributable to conservation. Fears about the adverse effects of conservation measures on employment are chiefly related to the short term. In the medium to long term, as most economists will point out, markets adjust to higher prices with little or no effect on employment. Moreover, technological developments and product innovations designed to meet the challenges required by shrinking (and eventually depleted) oil and gas reserves will add new industries and employment opportunities to the economy.

In any case, remedying the complex of problems related to excessive fuel consumption, as with remedying all the core problems at the root of consumeritis, will largely depend on voluntary changes in public habits (in addition to the virtual coercion of higher prices), including the ever-increasing reliance on solo auto travel. As individuals, we all need help to effect a winged migration above our own auto addiction and the powerful private and governmental interests that oppose change. We believe the following remedies may help us most.

(a) *Public Education.* To help effect voluntary change, education is, again, a key remedy. In some parts of the country, young people are already enlisted in the Green movement, and are far more environmentally conscious than most of their elders. But greater environmental awareness should be even more widely promoted in our public schools, especially with respect to the potentially disastrous effects of global warming and the disproportionately high contribution of the United States to carbon-dioxide emissions through gas-fueled transportation. Higher gas prices have been helping to stimulate the market to produce hybrid vehicles whose wider public acceptance may significantly help remedy the problem, and this is an instance in which competitive commercial advertising may play a positive educational role.

(b) *Private Voluntary Associations: Community Activity.* Alexis de Tocqueville identified "private voluntary associations" as one of the key safeguards against the excesses of democracy. This is an area in which such associations, especially those that are part of or related to the Green and Simplicity movements, may be especially effective in helping remedy the problem through their educational efforts and community activities. Greater public awareness of alternatives to conventional gas-fueled transportation, and the serious adverse effects of SUVs and other luxury gas-guzzlers, could help persuade some Americans to fuel down their private transportation choices. More generally, a renaissance of interest in community activity, with some cooling down of our feverish American individualism, would be likely to produce a variety of serendipitous benefits (including economic efficiencies) to individuals, families, and communities alike. A wider sense of community among us could help not only by promoting carpooling, but also by the effects it might have in stimulating other shared activities and business and living conditions that would reduce excessive or redundant American oil and gas consumption, thereby promoting greater heating-fuel efficiency and lower fuel costs.

(c) *Green Architecture.* As suggested above, great fuel savings may be realized by green architecture; that is, more intelligent, environmentally conscious planning in the material construction and use of office buildings. Other countries, especially the United Kingdom, but also Japan, are already following this model, and realizing fuel efficiencies that help increase their competitive edge in global business competition.

(d) *Governmental Remedies.*

(i) The Kyoto Treaty: Recent events suggest that U.S. skepticism about the commitment of EU countries to meet the goals of the Kyoto Treaty may be less justified than it appears to be. The EU is evidently making serious efforts toward further implementation of the treaty's purpose to reduce carbon-dioxide emissions. For the reasons indicated in chapters 5 and 7, we strongly favor the United States joining the Kyoto Treaty as an act of exemplary global leadership, despite the treaty's shortcomings, and in recognition of the seriousness of the problem of global warming and the disproportionately high per capita contribution of the United States to it. U.S. commitment to the principles of the Kyoto Treaty would be a salutary act helping both to educate the public to the importance of the issues the treaty addresses, and to mitigate foreign antipathy toward U.S. environmental policies.

(ii) Gasoline Taxation, Administration of Revenue, and Special Allocation: Americans become highly exercised each time there is a significant increase in fuel prices. But the fact is that the cost of automobile fuel in the United States remains significantly less than in the EU. To further discourage excessive oil and gas dependence and consumption, and to encourage more fuel-efficient alternatives, especially carpooling and use of hybrid and other alternative fuel systems, substantially higher federal taxation should be imposed on gasoline. The revenue received from such increased taxation should, ideally, be administered by a specially created, independent agency with the authority to fund remedial conservation projects and programs.

(iii) Setting Auto Fuel-Efficiency Standards and Requirements: The *necessity* for reducing our inefficient use of fuel is already apparent, and will become inescapably clear to all but the most ignorant in the near future. Enactment by the U.S. government of the strictest possible fuel-efficiency requirements for automobile manufacturers consistent with available technology would increasingly reduce our fuel consumption. Japan long ago outpaced Detroit in recognizing the economy and appeal of more fuel-efficient automobiles, and the time is overdue for the American automobile industry to catch up and even use American entrepreneurial ingenuity to excel in this technology. The market has been pressing the American automobile industry to move in this direction and the government should set fuel-efficiency requirements that will compel industry to travel along this road as speedily as applied technology and industrial change will permit. In fact, we would endorse a sufficiently high increase in gasoline taxation to fund a major effort to improve our public transportation systems nationwide as recommended below.

(iv) Improved Public Transportation and Urban Private-Auto Restriction: Perhaps the single most effective remedy for American dependence on, and excess consumption of, oil and gas resulting from private automobile usage would be development of a superlative public transportation system throughout the United States, and particularly in and around our cities. This would give victims of car consumeritis strong incentives to prefer public transportation for daily travel. Creation of the federal highway system under the leadership of President Eisenhower in the 1950s, though very costly, was a productive contribution to American commerce, personal mobility, and even our national security at the time. But present realities, as described in chapter 5, including the anticipated shortfall in oil production in the near future, indicate that the public interest warrants a similar major effort in the improvement and streamlining of our urban public transportation systems, coupled with greater restrictions (beyond metered parking) on use of private automobiles in central or commercial urban areas. Achieving substantial national improvement of our public transportation systems would require energetic, courageous, and committed political leadership, and it would be costly. But it would be a program in which allocation of revenues from increased taxation of automobile fuel would be especially appropriate. The public education recommended above would probably be indispensable to obtain the breadth of public support needed for congressional authorization and funding of such a program. As Lincoln said, "With public sentiment, nothing can fail; without it, nothing can succeed."

(v) Raising the Age of Auto Licensing: Some states have already raised the age at which an unrestricted driver's license may be obtained from 16 to 18. This is an appropriate remedial measure both for fuel economy and public safety, even for teenagers themselves. To avoid special hardships this may impose on teenagers in isolated rural areas with little or no public transportation, restricted licenses for younger drivers could be issued to meet necessities, especially in states whose major cities are few and far between.

(5) Corruption of the Political Process: Return to a Decent Respect

The power of mass media to influence public opinion was illustrated in the movie *Citizen Kane* with this exchange between the media mogul Kane and a woman, previously quoted in chapter 6:

Woman: "Really, Charles, people will think—"
Kane: "—what I tell them to think."

Kane's remark indicates contempt for public opinion. It expresses the view that most people don't really think for themselves but will be guided by whatever they see published in the newspapers, despite the old maxim "Don't believe everything you read." While the founders of the American republic were also skeptical of public opinion, some of them—especially Thomas Jefferson—placed great faith in the power of public education to develop an informed citizenry and nurture a "natural aristocracy of virtue and talent" to assume the country's political leadership. From the very first public utterance of the founders in the Declaration of Independence, they indicated that a "decent respect for the opinions of mankind" required them to state sound reasons for pledging their "lives, fortunes, and sacred honor" to effect political separation from England. The Declaration takes great pains to persuade those who read it, including particularly the signers' (former) British compatriots, that justice and reason supported American determination to form a free and independent United States. And while the composition of the Declaration by Thomas Jefferson contained eloquent rhetorical flourishes, the document may be read as one intending to persuade with logic, reason, practical wisdom, high political principle, and a concern for human rights within the limitations of contemporary mores—and, for some signers, even beyond.

Political discourse by candidates for high public office and elected leaders of American democracy—which is now much more inclusive in its citizenry than it was at the time of the founding—no longer exhibits the same degree of decent respect for the opinion of mankind, for politicians' own constituents, or for the "Laws of Nature and of Nature's God." American political rhetoric, thoroughly schooled by commercial advertising, is overwhelmingly dominated by hollow, manipulative appeals to public passions and prejudices. Its sound-bite technique admits little room for the kind of discourse that logic, reason, practical wisdom, and high political principle require—including respect for the natural rights asserted in our Declaration of Independence. Abraham Lincoln's speeches, writings, and political debate were most eloquent in their dedication to these characteristics of authentic political discourse; they survive today as models of political communication expressing a decent respect for the opinions of mankind and the American public—including even those who, at the time Lincoln spoke and wrote, supported secession from the Union. Born in poverty, Lincoln was a self-educated man who had barely any formal schooling. His character and political standards are paradigms of the kind of virtue and talent Jefferson hoped the United States (and each state) would produce for its democratic leadership. We urgently need to help restore among our political leadership greater regard for public opinion and capability. Some remedies that might help mitigate the present corruption of contemporary American politics follow.

(a) *Elevating Public Consciousness: Adult Education.* Most adults in the United States are at least vaguely aware of the intended manipulation and common deceptions—both implicit and explicit—typical of political campaign advertising. Action by private voluntary associations, and a greater degree of vigilance and candor by the news media, could substantially help to raise this consciousness to a level that would broaden public demand for change and stimulate higher standards of political discourse by political candidates and incumbents. A broader segment of the public needs to demonstrate its awareness of the implicit contempt politicians have for the public's evident incapacity to distinguish between hollow rhetoric and authentic, reasoned political discourse. If more Americans demonstrated an awareness of this contempt in their political activities, candidates and government officials would be pressed to raise their standards and exhibit greater respect for the intelligence and opinions of American voters.

(b) *Help from the Internet.* As the survey of political reporting summarized in chapter 6 showed, television provides little help and a great deal of harm to Americans in their efforts to become well-informed citizens equipped to see through the fog of dream-making in political ad bites and to determine the facts behind the candidates' political campaign rhetoric. The Internet has, however, become a powerful piece of equipment in this respect. The accuracy of political bloggers' assertions may also require evaluation, but the Internet now gives the public a host of sources that not only enable us to check facts but also to acquire information and additional relevant facts that competing political candidates may, in their own interest, fail to disclose or discuss in their campaigns. For many concerned citizens, the Internet therefore presents a promising source of hope for elevation of political discourse and the expansion of democracy to government of, by, and for the people. Increased use of the Internet as a political forum may greatly assist us (and voluntary private associations across the spectrum of opinion) to evaluate the integrity of political speech and, through the pressures it creates, elevate the factual accuracy, materiality, and level of political communication in the United States. (We can anticipate, however, that as use of the Internet becomes an increasingly important factor in forming political opinion and influencing voters, the politicians will find creative ways to use it for the most effective soap-flake political advertising possible in that medium.)

(c) *Restricting Political Advertising on Television.* The enormous growth in the volume of political advertising and its cost, especially on television, has been documented in chapter 6. Thoughtful observers have proposed the complete prohibition of political advertising on television in light of its inherently misleading character and the intrinsically inadequate opportunity it provides for significant political discourse. The prevailing condition of contemporary American politics gives merit to such proposals. There is now an urgent need to couple the right of free speech by political candidates in critical venues with politically significant, nondeceptive discourse. This fact, and the authority of the federal government to regulate use of the airwaves, may justify limitations on political advertising on television if carefully formulated to comply with constitutional rules.

(d) *Allocating Broadcast Time to Important Issues.* A positive measure to help elevate the quality of American political discourse on radio and television has been recommended by Edward G. Rendell, the governor of Pennsylvania. Rendell shares the views expressed in this book about the general decline in standards of political discourse attributable to prevalent use of ad bites in political campaign rhetoric. To help remedy the situation, he recommends that the FCC use its authority to require major broadcast networks to allocate free broadcasting time during campaign periods to major political candidates in fifteen-minute segments, on the condition that each segment be devoted exclusively to one subject, such as education, health care, or tax policy. By this means, Rendell persuasively argues, competing candidates would be compelled to present detailed and reasoned arguments for their positions on particular issues, thereby elevating the substance of political discourse.

(e) *Campaign Financing and Lobbying Reform.* John McCain, the Republican senator, and other public-spirited political incumbents have been trying for years to keep the issue of the corrupting influence of campaign financing practices before the American public in efforts to enact remedial legislation. Far more needs to be done to achieve effective reform. First Amendment protections, designed especially to secure our right to freedom of speech and the press—which has been held by the U.S. Supreme Court to include electronic media—complicate the problem and narrow the range of permissible solutions. But the pernicious influence of special interest lobbyists may be further reduced by greater strictures on campaign financing and other measures limiting the opportunities for improper or undue influence of legislators. Arguments for adoption of a progressive flat tax, radically simplifying our Byzantine federal tax code, include the salutary effect that such taxation would have on limiting the undue political influence of special interests by removing much of the incentive and the opportunity to lobby Congress for special treatment under the tax code. Public support must be encouraged to foster stricter and more effective campaign financing laws and other measures limiting the opportunities for undue influence by special interest lobbyists.

(f) *Establishing Standards for Presidential Debates.* There is some truth to the proposition that all politics is local, but the most important elections affecting Americans are the presidential elections. Major presidential candidates have sufficiently respected public opinion to have now made it virtually mandatory for the candidates to agree to televised debates during presidential campaigns. But the rules for these debates are ad hoc. They are chiefly negotiated between the major candidates' representatives. This process enables presidential candidates to evade certain kinds of issues, disguise their real views on some matters, and avoid disclosure of their political vulnerabilities. Creation by Congress of a special, independent, multipartisan commission to recommend standards for the conduct of televised presidential debates, and enforcement of the procedures and standards such a commission would recommend, could pass constitutional muster. Moreover, presidential candidates would be hard-pressed to oppose or avoid implementation of the recommendations of such a commission if its membership was sufficiently distinguished by the public's respect for it and trust in its public-spirited objectives and intentions.

(6) Pro-Consumeritis Government Policies: A Community of Nations

> *For an empire to be born, a republic first has to die ... No country can expect to behave imperially abroad while preserving republican values at home. ... Hard as it may be for Americans to grasp, much of the world no longer sees the U.S. as a force for good.... The world is losing faith in America.*
> —Tony Judt, "The New World Order," *The New York Review of Books,* July 14, 2005

Anthony Grafton teaches the history of Renaissance Europe at Princeton University. He has a rigorous scholar's understanding of the spiritual, intellectual, and general cultural influences that formed the thought and shaped the political principles of our American founders. It would be easy to be distressed and dismayed (as I was) on reading the following report by Grafton that exposed the views of one of President George W. Bush's advisers who, as you will see, frankly rejected the principles underlying the formation of the United States and its Constitution:

> We Americans trace our origins, spiritual and intellectual, largely to the heralds of the Newtonian movement: writers and doers like Benjamin Franklin. The creators of the United States couched their arguments for its independence and their visions of its constitution in the Newtonian language of reason, nature's laws, and factual evidence. Nowadays, powerful leaders around the world defy these forms of intellectual self-discipline. In the summer of 2002, one of President Bush's advisers explained to the writer Ron Suskind "that guys like me were 'in what we call the reality-based community,' which he defined as people who 'believe that solutions emerge from your judicious study of discernible reality.' I nodded and murmured something about enlightenment principles and empiricism. He cut me off. 'That's not the way the world really works anymore,' he continued. 'We're an empire now, and when we act, *we create our own reality.*'"
> (emphasis added)

As Grafton suggests, George Washington, James Madison, and Thomas Jefferson would each have recoiled from such arrogance in his own way, and regarded it as absolutely antithetical to the spirit in which they conceived the American republic. So, more than 150 years later, would President Truman, who affirmed that Americans

> all have to recognize—no matter how great our strength— that we must deny ourselves the license to do always as we please.

The contrary attitude expressed by the White House adviser has led not only to distrust of the United States by many nations and their people but to the profound concern of highly patriotic, conservative Americans. It is an attitude that may have been at work in the U.S. government's increasing unilateralism, as evidenced by its failure to join the Kyoto Treaty, and its disregard of the larger portion of the community of nations who counseled a more patient strategy regarding possible threats to international security posed by Iraq. As Tony Judt has written, reviewing a book by Andrew J. Bacevich titled *The New American Militarism: How Americans Are Seduced by War:*

> President George W. Bush most decidedly does not share the interests and objectives of the international community. Many in that community would say that this is because the United States itself has changed in unprecedented and quite frightening ways. Andrew Bacevich would agree with them.
>
> Bacevich is a graduate of West Point, a Vietnam veteran, and a conservative Catholic who now directs the study of international relations at Boston University. He has thus earned the right to a hearing even in circles typically immune to criticism ... The United States, he writes, is becoming not just a militarized state but a military society: a country where armed power is the measure of national greatness, and war, or planning for war, is the exemplary (and only) common project ...
>
> As a former soldier, Bacevich is much troubled by the consequent militarization of American foreign relations, and by the debauching of his country's traditional martial values in wars of conquest and occupation....
>
> No nation, as Madison wrote in 1795 and Bacevich recalls approvingly, can "preserve its freedom in the midst of continual warfare."

We may also recall that it was a Republican president and former five-star general, Dwight D. Eisenhower, who warned in his farewell address against the dangers to the republic of a "military-industrial complex," echoing the words of another general and conservative president, George Washington, who said that "overgrown military establishments are inauspicious to liberty ... and are to be regarded as particularly hostile to republican liberty."

Bacevich's concerns, amplifying Eisenhower's, focus on the preoccupation of American policy with the might of our military establishment, and a consequent disregard of the opinions of lesser nations about our policies and actions. Our disregard of the opinions of others—such as in our refusal to sign the Kyoto Treaty—has inevitably had negative effects on their regard for us. That refusal may, however, be a relatively trivial instance of the nation's refusal to feel itself obligated to act with "a decent respect for the opinions of mankind." Continued failure to do so, particularly on the basis of a belief that America's imperial military power enables it to "create its own reality," is likely to lead to disastrous results sooner or later, considering in particular the progressive rise in global economic power of the European Union, China, and India. Here too the ancient Greeks had a word for the character of those who, defying the dictates of prudence, choose to act as though their fate is entirely in their own hands because they create their own reality; that word is *hubris,* overweening pride of a kind likely to precede a fall.

If such hubris is habitual and common among those who administer the unprecedented, unique scope and force of American power, it is clearly too much for our own good. It may, in fact, be partly responsible for reckless perpetuation of the deficit policies that encourage Americans to increase their own borrowing and consuming and forget about the prudence of saving to guard against reverses of fortune. The reality is that in all of human history, the wheel of fortune has never ceased to turn, and what goes up sooner or later comes down. The chief remedy for this problem has become obvious: the need for a return to perceptions of reality uncorrupted by the arrogance of power or polluted by solipsism. Our global interdependence is a new reality whether we like it or not. We, the authors of this book, are inclined to like it, despite its dangers, because of our shared belief in the better angels of human nature and our continued faith in their historic ascendancy—assuming enough thought and action among people of good will, and at least a little bit of luck.

The need for the people and government of the United States to change their behavior in ways that will help achieve a return to higher standing in the opinion of the people of other nations has been pointed out by those who respect and admire this country's contributions to global civilization. In a passage comparing America's past role in the world to Pericles' pride in ancient Athens as a model of civilization for the whole of Greece, Chris Patten observes in the final paragraph of his book *Cousins and Strangers: America, Britain, and Europe in a New Century*:

> For so much of my lifetime America has been an education to the world—to every nation, every continent, and every civilization. It has been a living lesson, a paradigm to which others could aspire, an example for others to follow. I hope that Europe can help America to be that again. When it is, it will not be America that triumphs, but the ideas that America has traditionally represented. So the century ahead will not be America's, as was the last one. It will belong to mankind. It will be a century dominated by the values that American history enshrines and that American leadership at its best embodies and defends without bragging or blustering: democracy, idealism, pluralism, enterprise, and the rule of law.

(a) *World Citizenship: The Need for Political Change.* No populated corner of the world is now more than seconds away from any other in communication; or more than minutes away from exposure to devastating destruction; or more than hours away from departure from one corner to arrival at the other. Baghdad, Moscow, and Paris are now closer in time to New York, Chicago, and Los Angeles than Boston was to Philadelphia when the Declaration of Independence was drafted. We can no longer afford to follow George Washington's advice to avoid foreign entanglements as much as we may nostalgically wish we could. The people of the United States must therefore now become more vigilant, active, and prudent citizens of their democracy and again elevate their citizenry above their status as consumers. We Americans—and particularly our political leadership—need to acquire the knowledge, wisdom, and will to resume a decent respect for the opinions of mankind in our international relations. We will not deserve to be admired as an ethical member of the community of nations unless we also recognize our duty to respect the laws of nature and of nature's God—just as our founders did. Woe to us if we do not find that will, preferring to live as the subjects of local kings rather than cosmopolitan citizens of a pluralistic democracy able to distinguish needs from wants, think about when enough is enough, and take political actions appropriate to our thought.

Considering the Cures for Consumeritis

> *It is part of the cure to wish to be cured.*
> —Seneca, *Phaedra* (c. AD 80)

> *A human being lives out not only his*
> *personal life as an individual, but also,*
> *consciously or subconsciously, the lives*
> *of his epoch and his contemporaries.*
> —Thomas Mann, *The Magic Mountain* (1924)

If we are correct in asserting that American culture has become so thoroughly a culture of buying and selling that it is now too much for our own good; if the maxim that "the business of America is business" and its corollary, "What's good for General Motors is good for the country," no longer serve us as the best principles to promote our pursuits of happiness, then we have before us a very difficult agenda to correct this situation. The agenda for change of the kind this book advocates is one that, to succeed, must lead to a paradigm shift in American consciousness: a change from self-seeking materialism, philosophically grounded in part on faith in the invisible hand of self-interest, to a higher faith. It will also require a shift, especially for young adults, in personal definitions of success and happiness. There may be some hope for achieving such shifts because of the fierce spirit of American individualism. The greater faith that is needed is in the unique value of our own selves, which includes an understanding that, to be true to ourselves, we must also recognize ourselves as social beings with natural connections and obligations to others. This is not an impossible hope precisely because human beings are in their very nature social animals.

With this book we invite you to consider the possibility of achieving greater scope and depth in your pursuits of happiness than American materialism and the culture of buying and selling invites you to consider, and then to act on what your own reflections and self-examination may lead you to conclude. We are not alone in extending this invitation to cultivate sounder pursuits of happiness. There is a growing literature on the subject in the writings of psychologists, sociologists, journalists, and economists, including Richard Layard, author of *Happiness,* cited and quoted in the introduction to this book. An article by Andrew Oswald titled "The hippies were right all along about happiness" (*Financial Times,* January 19, 2006) describes economists' growing recognition that a developed country's continued economic growth does not increase personal well-being, and describes increasing public and professional awareness that "more" in terms of affluence and material possessions does not equal greater happiness.

> Surveys show that the industrialized nations have not become happier over time. Random samples of UK citizens today report the same degree of psychological well-being and satisfaction with their lives as did their poorer parents and grandparents. In the U.S., happiness has fallen over time.... American females are markedly less happy than were their mothers. Second, using more formal measures of mental health, rates of depression in countries such as the UK have increased. Third, measured levels of stress at work have gone up. Fourth, suicide statistics paint a picture that is often consistent with such patterns. In the U.S., even though real income levels have risen sixfold, the per capita suicide rate is the same as the year 1900...
>
> Yet surely, it might be argued, what about power showers, televised football, titanium wristwatches, car travel for all—are these not compelling evidence for the long arm of [economic] growth? Yes they are, but we need these because Mr. and Mrs. Jones have them, not because they make an intrinsic difference.
>
> Economists' faith in the value of growth is diminishing. That is a good thing and will slowly make its way into the minds of tomorrow's politicians. Led by the distinguished psychologist Edward Diener of the University of Illinois, a practical intellectual manifesto signed by many of the world's researchers entitled *Guidelines for National Indicators of Subjective Well-Being and Ill-Being* has just begun to circulate on the Internet. The document calls for national measures of separate facets of well-being and ill-being, including moods and emotions, perceived mental and physical health, satisfactions with particular activities and domains, and the subjective experience of time allocation and pressures.
>
> Happiness, not economic growth, ought to be the next and more sensible target for the next and more sensible generation.

This book has sought to demonstrate that failure to recognize that an habitual, addictive quest for "more" not only diverts us from more effective pursuits of happiness but may actually be dangerous to our health and continued physical survival to a natural old age. We need to consider carefully what we may do to remedy the problems that promote our tendencies toward consumeritis, or our actual infection by it; and we need to promote public policies that will reverse its harms.

The Greeks have a phrase for it: *Pan metron ariston*—moderation and balance in all things is the best way.

Here's lookin' at you, kid.

Notes

255 *The Wild One* Directed by Laszlo Benedek, produced by Stanley Kramer, written by John Paxton (Columbia Pictures 1953).

256 *a cultural paradox that in societies in which people are highly socialized* See, for example, Triandis et. al., "Individualism and Collectivism: Cross Cultural Perspectives on Self-Ingroup Relationships," *Journal of Personality and Social Psychology,* 54:2 (1988).

Fight Club Directed by David Fincher, produced by Art Linso, screenplay by Jim Uhls, based on the novel by Chuck Palahniuk (Twentieth Century Fox 1999). In a speech from the film quoted in the text, the written script says, "We've all been raised on television to believe that one day we'll all be millionaires and movie gods and rock stars, but we won't. We're slowly learning that fact." In the film, Brad Pitt renders the latter sentence as "We're *already* learning that fact."

257 *stories of people—including some highly educated people—who have exploded into murderous violence* The most notorious case of a well-educated twentieth century Luddite may be the Unabomber, eventually identified as Ted Kaczynski, a Harvard-educated academic whose letter bombs were linked to the deaths of three persons and injuries to nearly two dozen. He eluded capture for seventeen years and was the most wanted man in the United States in 1995. His manifesto, titled "Industrial Society and Its Future," condemned "the industrial technological system" and advocated revolution against it. Kaczynski's manifesto was published by the *New York Times* and the *Washington Post* on September 19, 1995, at the recommendation of Attorney General Janet Reno and FBI Director Louis Freeh "for public safety reasons" as a response to threats by Kaczynski of further violence unless his manifesto was published. Kaczynski was apprehended in April 1996, and indicted on June 18, 1996. He is serving four life sentences without parole at a federal prison in Colorado. Edward Abbey, in *The Monkey Wrench Gang* (New York: Avon Books, 1975), also recounts in novelistic form the real-life escapades of a group of professionals who systematically vandalized commercial installations such as advertising billboards and other property, scrupulously avoiding causing human injury. Anthony Burgess's novel *A Clockwork Orange* (New York: Norton, 1986), made into a movie of the same name by Stanley Kubrick (*A Clockwork Orange,* produced, directed, and written by Stanley Kubrick, Warner Brothers Films, 1971), depicted a future in which random acts of violence by rebellious youth would become a common reaction to social conformity, requiring the authorities to remedy such violence through dehumanizing psychological conditioning. The Christian Longo case, in which a small-businessman operating a construction cleaning business and described as

"winsome and mature" murdered his wife and three children in the wake of financial troubles, provides another notorious example of violent explosion. Longo had no prior history or record of violence. His father-in-law was quoted as saying, "You hear about stories like this and you know they're out there, but when it hits home ... it's so devastating to our family ... There was no history of him beating on her, being abusive verbally or physically. And then to turn around and kill his family ... I think he had a nervous breakdown. Something snapped." John Flesher, "Wife's father recounts downfall of slain Oregon family," Associated Press, as reported in *The Olympian*, Olympia Washington, January 15, 2002. For further actual examples of murderous and suicidal violence related to the pressures of consumer society, see the notes to pages 65 and 111.

259 *Erik Erikson, the great humanist psychologist* In his book *Identity and the Life Cycle* (New York: Norton, 1980), 64–65, Erik Erikson (1902–1994) writes, "It is against the combination of these impressions of having been deprived, of having been divided, and of having been abandoned, all of which leave a residue of basic mistrust, that basic trust must be established and maintained."

264 *Abraham Lincoln called the United States "the last, best hope of earth"* In his annual message to Congress on December 1, 1862, speaking of what is at stake in the conduct of the Civil War, Lincoln concludes, "We shall nobly save, or meanly lose, the last best hope of earth."

Abraham Lincoln (its great re-founder) See, for example, Garry Wills, *Lincoln at Gettysburg: The Words That Remade America* (New York: Simon & Schuster, 1992); and James M. McPherson, *Abraham Lincoln and the Second American Revolution* (New York: Oxford University Press, 1991).

267 *Commercial Advertising Filters* TiVo is a digital video recorder (DVR) service and product that allows its subscribers to use a hard drive to record television programs for future viewing so that instead of being forced to conform to network television schedules, viewers may watch programs at their leisure. Its recording option allows viewers to "blast past commercials if [they] wish to" by fast-forwarding through them. Potential buyers of this device should be cautioned, however, that TiVo and other DVR producers might be planning to insert their own brief ads into the fast-forwarding time span. Satellite Radio, a recent technological innovation, now rivals traditional radio with an ever-expanding customer base. Listeners are offered ad-free radio while given the choice of hundreds of music genres. Both TiVo and Satellite Radio services are provided under monthly payment conditions.

268 *The FCC is required to implement the Junk Fax Prevention Act* The following summary of the act's provisions is taken from an FCC press release issued on December 9, 2005. The Junk Fax Prevention Act (1)

codifies an established business relationship exemption to the prohibition on sending unsolicited facsimile advertisements; (2) provides a definition of an established business relationship to be used in the context of unsolicited facsimile advertisements; (3) requires the sender of a facsimile advertisement to provide specified notice and contact information on the facsimile that allows recipients to "opt-out" of any future facsimile transmissions from the sender; and (4) specifies the circumstances under which a request to "opt-out" complies with the act. The act also authorizes the FCC, after a period of three months from the date of enactment of the act, to consider limits on the duration of an established business relationship.

270 *The FTC has already taken some initiatives in this area*   See, for example, "Web Sites Warned to Comply With Children's Online Privacy Law; FTC Also Works to Educate Children's Sites About Law's Privacy," an FTC press release dated July 17, 2000.

279 *Syriana*   Produced by Jennifer Fox, Michael Nozik, and Georgia Kacanzes; directed and written by Stephen Gaghan; starring George Clooney and Matt Damon (Warner Brothers Pictures, 2005).

281 *Alexis de Tocqueville identified "private voluntary associations" as one of the key safeguards*   See Harrison Sheppard, "The Hazardous Future of Democracy in America: Tocqueville and Lawyers in America," a lecture given at St. John's College, Santa Fe, New Mexico, on November 5, 2004, soon to be published by Paul Dry Books, Philadelphia, PA, as one of the essays in a Festschrift honoring Eva Brann, former dean of St. John's College in Annapolis, Maryland.

282 *Other countries, especially the United Kingdom*   For a lengthy list of environmental conferences, held in the United Kingdom and elsewhere, relating to the topic of environmental and sustainable architecture, see *www.conferencealerts.com/environment.htm.*

The EU is evidently making serious efforts   See, for example, a story in the *Financial Times* on January 10, 2006, headlined "EU sets industry target of reducing carbon dioxide emissions by 6%."

the cost of automobile fuel in the United States remains significantly less than in the EU   The average cost of automobile gasoline in EU countries is nearly twice the price of gasoline in the United States; see the graph at *www.eia.doe.gov/emeu/international/prices.html#Motor.*

284 *Some states have already raised the age at which an unrestricted driver's license may be obtained*   California has recently raised the minimum age to obtain an unrestricted license to 18. See *www.dmv.ca.gov/pubs/hdbk/pgs12thru16.htm* and *www.dmv.ca.gov/dl/dl_info.htm#PERMINOR.*

288 *Thoughtful observers have proposed the complete prohibition of political advertising on television*   See the note citing George Anastaplo's *The American Moralist* on page 211.

Edward G. Rendell, the governor of Pennsylvania   The views and recommendations of Governor Rendell summarized in this paragraph were expressed by him in a television interview on PBS's Charlie Rose broadcast on February 16, 2006.

290   *Pro-Consumeritis Government Policies: A Community of Nations*   Unless otherwise noted, all quotations in this subsection are taken from the article by Tony Judt quoted in its epigraph, or from a review by Anthony Grafton of an exhibition at the New York Public Library from October 8, 2004 through February 5, 2005: the exhibition was called "The Newtonian Moment: Science and the Making of Modern Culture." The quotations in the text from Grafton's review, "The Ways of Genius," appeared on pages 38–39 of the *New York Review of Books* on December 2, 2004.

294   *For so much of my lifetime America has been an education to the world*   Quoted from Chris Patten, *Cousins and Strangers: American, Britain, and Europe in a New Century.* (New York: Henry Holt, 2006), 293.

Epilogue

It's a Wonderful Life

JOHN ALONE SITS and hears the whirring of his fax as he
arranges for the electronic payment of his computer-gen-
erated bills and listens to the recorded option menu on the
number he has dialed. No one really talks to him except on TV,
and he rarely talks to anyone. He has more or less accepted his
lot as part of a larger machine by which he is employed to earn
the money he needs so he will know no real want and be able to
buy enough things to help the larger machine continue to whir.
He lives a dream of perpetual motion, going nowhere faster and
faster.

This technological nightmare has in fact been predicted for
more than a century by writers such as George Gurdjieff, who
foresaw industrial technology transforming the mass of human
beings into parts of a machine ("Is there life before death?"). But
we cherish the hope that we are not yet so far gone that we are
unable to wake up.

In a letter to the editor published in the *San Francisco Chronicle* on September 6, 1998, I wrote:

> Woodrow Wilson, accused of being an idealist, pleaded
> guilty: "Americans are the most idealistic people in the
> world." The American tradition of looking upward while
> keeping one's feet on the ground was reflected in Robert

Kennedy's saying "Some men see things as they are and say
why. I dream things that never were and say, why not."
   Aspiring toward the best is at the heart of the American dream. It is a flame that often flickers against the
winds of misfortune and malice; but it will never die. It
will remain so long as there are people with vision, heart,
and mind, true bearers of the American spirit.
   Those who bear this flame may sometimes sink in the
mire of their own personalities or partisan politics, but its
spirit is an unquenchable part of the best in all of us.

American idealism is, however, not abstract. It is pragmatic.
Tocqueville thought Americans were among the least philosophic
people on earth, but among the most practical. If something does
not work, we want to fix it. Excessive materialism and misplaced
individualism in a technological society are not working well for
us as unique human beings, and we need to fix them. The paradox
is that we need to learn how to fix them for ourselves if we are
going to help fix them for others. This may require us to find more
leisure time so we can creatively use our imagination in pursuits
of greater happiness. To paraphrase Wendell Berry, in his playful
poem "Manifesto: The Mad Farmer Liberation Front": "As soon as
the advertising agencies and the politicos can predict the motions
of your mind, lose it." Berry also exhorted us to follow this advice:

> So, friends, every day do something
> that won't compute. Love the Lord.
> Love the world. Work for nothing.
> Take all that you have and be poor.
> Love someone who does not deserve it.
> Denounce the government and embrace
> the flag. Hope to live in that free
> republic for which it stands.
>
> ⁓
>
> Put your faith in the two inches of humus
> that will build under the trees
> every thousand years.

~

Be joyful though you have considered all the facts.

Imagine that all your material needs have been met. What would you do with your time? If you first think of going shopping for something you might want to buy, you have not yet imagined that all your material needs have been met. When you think of something you would like to do that you have not done, or have not done enough, you are on the path to curing consumeritis. Imagine this: Traveling to other places—not only to another country but maybe even just down the block, across town, or to a nearby city—to meet new people and maybe find a new friend. Learning a foreign language. Reading the books you've never gotten around to reading. Volunteering to help others. Serving as a mentor to a younger person. Learning a new skill. Furthering your education. Taking better care of your health by losing weight with long walks in the park, to the beach, up a mountain. Looking for a better job, even though it may pay less, if you will be happier doing it. Trying your hand at writing prose or poetry. Catching up with old friends by writing them letters. Playing more sports. Learning how to draw, paint, or fix things—your car, or a broken door or fence, or your children's toys. Thinking more and learning how to get along with less so you can better manage what you have. Turning off the TV to spend more time playing with your children and really enjoying the company of your family and friends. Bicycling with your grandchildren. Reading the voter information pamphlets you usually discard for lack of time. Thinking about what the political ads are really saying to and about you. Considering what you yourself can do to help clean up the mess in Washington, on your streets, in your parks, on the beach near you, or in our relations to people in other countries. Finding a pen pal. Having a picnic. Rediscovering love and

306 Too Much for Our Own Good

your youthful love of life. Going with your family or friends to a good movie, and then talking to them about it.

This book has invited you to follow the better angels of your own nature; to become habitually more aware of your own higher good as, for example, we may from time to time be made more aware of it in elevated states experienced in the drama of good movies: like Frank McCloud's victory over the gangster Rocco's "MORE" in *Key Largo;* or Cher's discovery of a new path to happiness through love and respect for others in *Clueless;* or Peter's rediscovery of a healthy use of imagination in *Finding Neverland;* or *Auntie Mame's* resolution to feast at the banquet life offers; and even Scarlett O'Hara's determination not to be defeated by circumstances in *Gone with the Wind.* As each of these illuminating dramas suggests, we are free to remedy the problems diverting us from finding and succeeding in our own pursuit of happiness—if we have the will to do so.

> *Of Life immense in passion, pulse, and power,*
> *Cheerful, for freest action form'd*
> *under the laws divine,*
> *The Modern Man I sing.*
> —Walt Whitman, *Leaves of Grass*

It's a wonderful life.

Figures

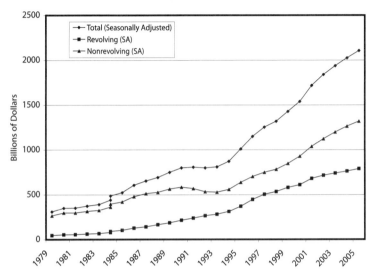

Fig. 1.1. Seasonally adjusted consumer credit (January 1979–July 2005)
Source: The Federal Reserve Bank, G.19, Consumer Credit, December 7, 2005

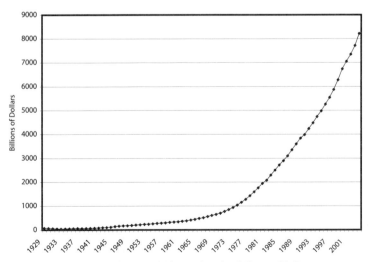

Fig. 1.2. U.S. personal consumer expenditures (PCE) in billions of dollars, 1929–2003
Source: The Bureau of Economic Analysis

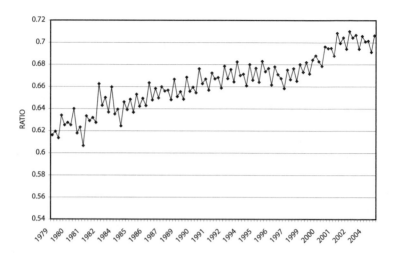

Fig. 1.3. U.S. personal consumer expenditures as a percentage of GDP, by quarter of year, 1979–2004
Source: The Bureau of Economic Analysis

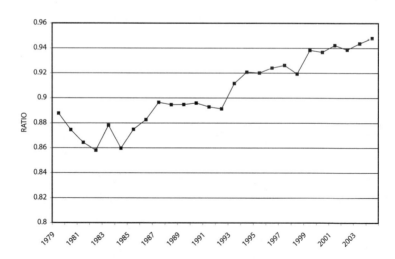

Fig. 1.4. U.S. personal consumer expenditures (PCE) as a percentage of disposable personal income, 1979–2004
Source: The Bureau of Economic Analysis

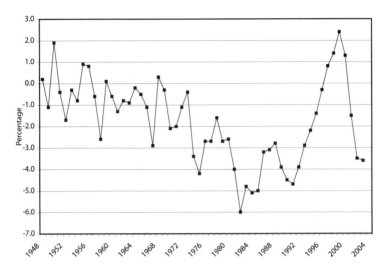

Fig. 4.1. Federal government surplus or deficit as a percentage of GDP, 1948–2004
Source: Historic Tables, Budget of the United States Government–Fiscal 2006,
Office of Management and Budget, December 21, 2005

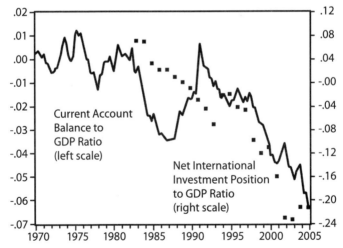

Fig. 4.2. Current account balance and net international investment position
expressed as a proportion of GDP 1948–2004
Source: Menzie D. Chinn, "Getting Serious About the Twin Deficits," *Council on
Foreign Relations,* CRS No. 10, September 2005, data derived from *The Bureau of
Economic Analysis*

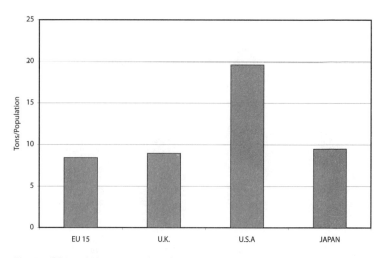

Fig. 5.1. CO2 emissions per capita, 2002
Source: OECD Factbook and World Bank Development Indicators, epp.eurostat.
cec.eu.int

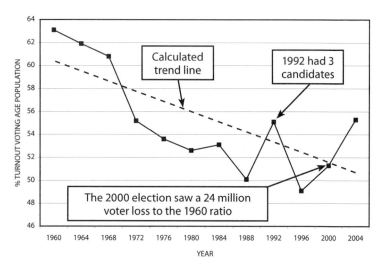

Fig. 6.1. Presidential elections % turnout, 1960–2004
Source: Federal Elections Commission

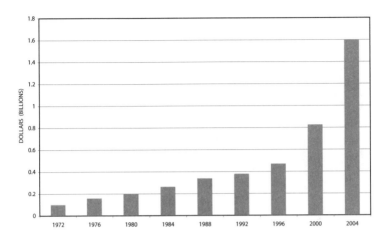

Fig. 6.2. Political advertising expenditures, 1972–2004
Source: The Political Standard, December 2004; TNSMI/Campaign Media Analysis Group, Television Bureau of Advertising

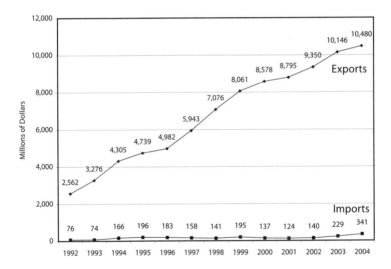

Fig. 7.1. Exports and imports of film and television rentals (1992–2004)
Source: The Bureau of Economic Analysis, International Economic Accounts

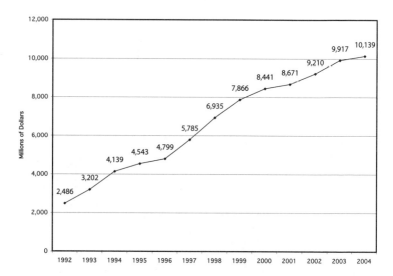

Fig. 7.2. Film and television rentals trade balance as a percentage of the total private services trade balance, 1992–2004
Source: The Bureau of Economic Analysis, International Economic Accounts

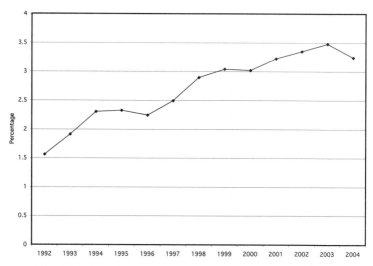

Fig. 7.3. Film and television tape rentals as a percentage of total private service exports, 1992–2004
Source: The Bureau of Economic Analysis, International Economic Accounts

Tables

Table 1.1. Advertising: Estimated expenditures by medium, 1990 and 1995–2003 in millions of nominal dollars

Medium	1990	1995	1997	1998	1999	2000	2001	2002	2003[1]
Total	129,968	165,147	191,307	206,697	222,308	247,472	231,287	236,875	249,156
National	73,638	96,933	112,809	122,271	132,170	151,664	141,797	145,429	154,882
Local	56,330	68,214	78,498	84,426	90,138	95,808	89,490	91,446	94,274
Newspapers	32,281	36,317	41,670	44,292	46,648	49,050	44,255	44,031	45,438
National	3,867	3,996	5,016	5,402	6,358	7,229	6,615	6,806	7,282
Local	28,414	32,321	36,654	38,890	40,290	41,821	37,640	37,225	38,156
Magazines	6,803	8,580	9,821	10,518	11,433	12,370	11,095	10,995	11,765
Broadcast TV	26,616	32,720	36,893	39,173	40,011	44,802	38,881	42,068	43,247
Four TV networks	9,863	11,600	13,020	13,736	13,961	15,888	14,300	15,000	15,525
Syndication	1,109	2,016	2,438	2,609	2,870	3,108	3,102	3,034	3,489
Spot (National)	7,788	9,119	9,999	10,659	10,500	12,264	9,223	10,920	10,647
Spot (Local)	7,856	9,985	11,436	12,169	12,680	13,542	12,256	13,114	13,586
Cable TV	2,631	6,166	8,750	10,340	12,570	15,455	15,536	16,297	18,983
Cable TV networks	2,000	4,500	6,450	7,640	9,405	11,765	11,883	12,071	14,123
Spot (Local)	631	1,666	2,300	2,700	3,165	3,690	3,653	4,226	4,860
Radio	8,726	11,338	13,491	15,073	17,215	19,295	17,861	18,877	19,493
Network	482	480	560	622	684	780	711	775	822
Spot (National)	1,635	1,959	2,455	2,823	3,275	3,668	2,956	3,340	3,540
Spot (Local)	6,609	8,899	10,476	11,628	13,256	14,847	14,194	14,762	15,131
Yellow Pages	8,926	10,236	11,423	11,990	12,652	13,228	13,592	13,776	13,914
National	1,132	1,410	1,711	1,870	1,986	2,093	2,087	2,087	2,108
Local	7,794	8,826	9,712	10,120	10,666	11,135	11,505	11,689	11,806
Direct Mail	23,370	32,866	36,890	39,620	41,403	44,591	44,725	46,067	49,061
Business papers	2,875	3,559	4,109	4,232	4,274	4,915	4,468	3,976	3,857
Out of home[2]	1,084	1,263	1,455	1,576	1,725	5,176	5,134	5,175	5,304
National	640	701	795	845	925	2,068	2,051	2,061	2,112
Local	444	562	660	731	800	3,108	3,083	3,114	3,192
Internet	(NA)	(NA)	800	1,383	2,832	6,507	5,752	4,883	5,615
Miscellaneous[3]	16,656	22,102	26,005	28,500	31,545	32,083	29,988	30,730	32,479
National	12,074	16,147	18,745	20,312	22,264	24,418	22,829	23,414	24,936
Local	4,582	5,955	7,260	8,188	9,281	7,665	7,159	7,316	7,543

NA Not available. [1] Preliminary data. [2] Prior to 2000, represents only "outdoor" billboards. Beginning 2000 includes other forms of outdoor advertising (i.e. transportation vehicles, bus shelters, telephone kiosks, etc.) previously covered under "Miscellaneous." [3] Beginning 2000, part of miscellaneous not included under "out of home" advertisng. See footnote 2.
Source: U.S. Statistical Abstracts 2005 (Table No. 1275)

Table 1.2. Computer and Internet usage by 5- to 12-year-olds (in thousands)

Age	Total population	Use computers		Use the Internet	
		#	%	#	%
5	3,992	2,930	73.40	998	25.00
6	3,989	3,267	81.90	1,201	30.10
7	4,009	3,452	86.10	1,564	39.00
8	3,905	3,460	88.60	1,742	44.60
9	4,201	3,840	91.40	2,315	55.10
10	4,350	3,972	91.30	2,601	59.80
11	4,263	3,909	91.70	2,702	63.40
12	4,179	3,866	92.50	2,808	67.20
Total	32,888	28,696	87.30	15,931	48.40

Source: National Center for Education Statistics, "Computer and Internet Use by Children and Adolescents in 2001," October 2003

Table 1.3. Children ages 5–12 using computers at home and in school (in thousands)

Age group	Total population	Use of computer at home		Use of computer at school	
		#	%	#	%
5–7	11,990	6,762	56.40	8,177	68.20
8–10	12,455	7,709	62.70	10,350	83.10
11–14	16,493	11,314	68.60	14,052	85.20
Total	40,938	25,785	63.00	32,579	79.60

Source: National Center for Education Statistics, "Computer and Internet Use by Children and Adolescents in 2001," October 2003

Table 5.1. U.S. registered motor vehicles, 2003

	Private and commercial	Publicly owned†	Privately and publicly owned†
Automobiles	134,336,851	1,333,046	135,669,897
Motorcycles	5,328,300	41,735	5,370,035
Buses	324,694	451,856	776,550
Trucks*	92,814,454	2,129,097	94,943,551
Total including motorcycles	232,809,952	3,961,387	236,765,686
Total without motorcycles	227,481,652	3,919,652	231,395,651

Sources: Bureau of Transportation Statistics and U.S. Department of Transportation

Note: In 2003, out of a population of 290,809,777, there were 196,165,666 licensed drivers or 67.5 percent of the population. The driving-age population (above 16) was 225,953,387. Thus, the licensed drivers made up almost 87 percent of the eligible population.

The United States has 231,395,651 vehicles (excluding motorcycles and military vehicles) and 196,165,666 licensed drivers. Thus, there are almost 18 percent more vehicles than licensed drivers. This was not always the case. In 1971, the number of licensed drivers and vehicles was equal. After that year, the number of cars steadily and progressively outpaced the number of drivers. Prior to 1971, the number of drivers exceeded the number of vehicles. For example, in 1965 there were 9 cars for every 10 drivers.

*Includes pickups, vans, sport utility vehicles, and other light trucks as well as medium and large trucks.

†Does not include military vehicles.

Table 8.1. Remedies discussed in chapter 8

1. Commercial Advertising	2. Temptation and Ignorance
a. Self-Awareness	a. Seeing Things as They Are
b. Commercial Advertising Filters	b. Redefining Success
c. Government Regulation	c. Becoming Citizens Again
(i) FCC Regulation, TV, Junk Mail	d. Enacting a Federal Consumption Tax
(ii) FTC Children's Advertising, TV and Internet	
(iii) Taxation on TV Advertising	

3. Easy Credit	4. Oil and Gas-Fueled Transportation
a. Public Education	a. Public Education
b. Government Regulation	b. Private Voluntary Associations and Community Activities
(i) Restricting Credit Card and Junk Mail Solicitations Especially to Students and Young People	c. Green Architecture
	d. Governmental Remedies
(ii) Placing Limitations on Home Equity Loans Solicitations to Adults	(i) Kyoto Treaty
	(ii) Higher Gas Taxation with Revenue Allocation
(iii) Enacting Tax Policies Favoring Savings	(iii) Fuel Efficiency Standards
(iv) Funding Educational Public Service Advertising	(iv) Major National Improvement in Public Transportation Systems
	(v) Raising the Age of Auto Licensing

5. Corruption of Political Process	6. Pro-Consumeritis Government Policies
a. Elevating Public Consciousness through Education	a. Growth toward World Citizenship and Respect for the Opinions of Mankind
b. Getting Help from the Internet	
c. Restricting Political Advertising on TV	
d. Allocating Broadcast Time to Important Issues	
e. Reforming Campaign Financing and Lobbying	
f. Establishing Standards for Presidential Debates	

Acknowledgments

A
S THE CONTENT of this book and the volume of its chapter notes indicate, many schooled and thoughtful minds contributed extensive labor to its composition and production. In particular, the diligent efforts of Andres Centeno (Economics Department, University of San Francisco) and Timothy Crawley (assistant editor-in-chief of Aristotle and Alexander Press) were essential to completion of the work, and the fruits of their labors appear throughout. Andres Centeno's researches and syntheses constitute the backbone and heart of the economic data and analyses presented. He created most of the graphs and tables that appear in the back of the book (using some of the data provided by Kostas Dimoyannis, who is further identified below). But we are most indebted to him for his extraordinary ability to locate on short notice, and then promptly and cogently analyze, sources containing the most current available quantitative data and authoritative writings germane to the main subjects of each chapter.

Timothy Crawley's contributions include editorial and substantive review of every page of the text, finalizing the graphs and tables, preparing the bibliography, and the titanically tedious task of coordinating the text and notes in each successive manuscript draft. His meticulous collection of documentation to support the authors' assertions; his imaginative use of research tools; and his fresh, creative suggestions for amplification or improvement of the authors' arguments make him one of this book's critical cocreators, in both senses of the word "critical."

Kostas Dimoyannis is an Hellenic economist and scholar who now lives in the San Francisco Bay Area. We greatly appreciate his expertise, which he used to gather the economic data and conduct the original research needed to summarize factors justifying identification of consumeritis as a pathology, and documenting its direct economic costs.

Even before this book was conceived, the authors were inspired by George Anastaplo's expositions of the history, interpretation, uses, and abuses of the U.S. Constitution and its first ten amendments; the Declaration of Independence; and Abraham Lincoln's thought and writings. Anastaplo's writings enable us to appreciate the intentions of the founders of the United States in creating, and Lincoln in preserving, our democratic republic. His review of the introduction and parts of the manuscript relating to political life in the United States led to salutary amendments, corrections, and additions.

Peter deSwart and Richard Freis, Ph.D., are, in our judgment, the best literary craftsmen—the finest writers—we know personally among a wide acquaintance of writers over many years. A review and critique of the manuscript by Peter deSwart removed a host of defects, enhanced the depth and scope of its analyses, elevated the quality of its composition, and refined the precision of its prose. And it was he who brought the movie *Clueless* to our attention for its relevance to our theme. Richard Freis, a classmate of Harrison Sheppard at St. John's College, was "present" at the inception of this book. In addition to his cogent critiques and consequent improvement of every part of the text submitted to him for review, his mentorship energetically stimulated its creation.

Edward Quattrocchi, a highly successful man of business and a scholarly bibliophile, knows Renaissance and English literature and rare books at least as well as he knows the world of commerce, commodities, and futures. He vetted all chapters of the manuscript, most particularly to assess their practicality and to temper their idealistic bent with good pragmatic sense. We have sought to follow his prudent advice to acknowledge appropriately the positive merits of some of the market phenomena we subject to adverse criticism, such as commercial advertising and consumer credit.

Thomas E. Woodhouse, Esq., is also a man of practical affairs and a rare book connoisseur, a careful reader well schooled in good and great literature. We express our gratitude to him because, in his review of every chapter, he provided a punctilious editorial eye and identified many solecisms, giving us an opportunity to correct the manuscript.

Paul Addison, Ph.D., of the University of Edinburgh Center for the Study of World War II, first came to our attention through his biographies of Winston Churchill and his books relating to the post–World War II period. We were honored by his willingness to write a prepublication review of the completed manuscript, and we gratefully acknowledge our debt to him for his critical praise of the work and the historical perspectives his review provided to us.

We are also indebted to the photographer Jock McDonald, who deserves thanks for his creative critical comments and what his artist's eye has added to visual presentations; Dennis Jaffe, Ph.D., a member of the faculty of Saybrook Graduate School of Psychology in San Francisco, for pointing the way toward the most relevant, current, and comprehensive psychological research into materialism and consumerism; Ralph Lieberman, Ph.D., at Williams College in Williamstown, Massachusetts, whose highly disciplined eye as an art historian and architectural photographer helped correct and improve transcriptions of recorded movie dialogue; The Hon. James Warren, San Francisco, California, for his encouragement of the authors and his thoughtful counseling at critical moments of decision; Kevin Hughes, Esq., a former Californian now residing and teaching English in China, whose impassioned criticisms and laments about the contemporary political landscape in the United States and its relations to other countries stimulated our own thought about the issues he raised; Robert Powsner, Esq., of Inverness, California, for reviewing the book's structure and helping to eliminate redundancies, both real and apparent; Andrew Kokesh, for noticing the difference between references and quotations and bringing the difference to our attention; Erika Wodinsksy, Esq. of the San Francisco Regional Office of the Federal Trade Commission, for helping to keep the authors current on FTC initiatives in the field of unfair and deceptive commercial advertising, especially television advertising aimed at children; and the late David Weetman, whose review of the introduction and early chapters resulted in their refinement and expansion, and whose assistance in the final stages of production facilitated completion of the manuscript on schedule.

The authors also gratefully acknowledge Mike MacMillan, of Into Video, San Francisco, for use of the movie DVDs and VHSs that permitted us to verify the summaries and quotations for the films whose scenarios provided themes for the introduction and each chapter. His friendship and benevolence are gifts of the spirit, of the kind that enable us to say "It's a Wonderful Life."

Completion of a manuscript is the beginning of a rigorous process designed to make it suitable for publication. Chief among those who helped perfect the manuscript for this purpose is its copy editor, Lisa A. Smith. The thoroughness with which she removed errors in the manuscript and conformed it to high editorial standards and publishing conventions humbled and awed us, and her discovery of ambiguities or deficiencies in expositions have improved the text throughout. Our gratitude to her for these contributions is immeasurably great. Pete Masterson designed the book's interior and cover. We gratefully acknowledge his steady and invaluable advice and counsel from an early date in the progress of production, and his brilliantly creative sense of design.

We also acknowledge those whose support and encouragement made creation of this book possible, and a labor of love. First among these is the founding president of Aristotle and Alexander Press, Dimitri Magganas, who gave us the privilege of writing its first book. He is as much the originator of *Too Much for Our Own Good* as any Hollywood executive can claim to be the producer of a good movie. He has been unfailingly generous in his support and encouragement, enthusiastically facilitating production every time we asked for his help. We also specially acknowledge with heartfelt thanks the personal contributions to this project made by our life partners. In addition to inspiring and encouraging her partner's endeavors for more than forty years, Joy Sheppard (both a Beatrice and Penelope) made seminal contributions to the composition of this book, including her imaginative suggestion to expand the reference to a good movie, made in an early draft of the Introduction, to its continuous use as a thematic vehicle throughout. Mrs. Alex Aris, whose identity will be kept as anonymous as her husband's, has been an equally inspiring, unremittingly encouraging and supportive partner in this and every one of his projects, both personal and professional.

In addition to those whose contributions we have specifically acknowledged, in the course of writing this book we have benefited from the thought, concern, and helpful comments of others along the way; we apologize if necessary limitations of these pages have led us unintentionally to omit mention of others we would also want to thank.

Each person named above may be regarded to some extent as

a coauthor of this book. But the named authors accept complete responsibility for any defects that may remain in the work, and we close with our sincere expression of gratitude to each person named here, and to others who might have been named.

Bibliography

Listings are divided into three sections: books, articles and papers, and movies.
Entries marked with an asterisk (*) are quoted or cited in the text.

Books

*Anastaplo, George. *The Amendments to the Constitution: A Commentary.* Baltimore: The Johns Hopkins University Press, 1995.

*———. *The American Moralist: On Law, Ethics, and Government.* Athens: Ohio University Press, 1992.

*———. *The Constitutionalist: Notes on the First Amendment.* Dallas, TX: Southern Methodist University Press, 1971.

*Angle, Paul M., and Earle Schenck Miers. *The Living Lincoln: The Man and His Times in His Own Words.* New York: Barnes and Noble Books, 1992.

*Appiah, Kwame Anthony. *The Ethics of Identity.* Princeton, NJ: Princeton University Press, 2005.

*Augustine. *Confessions.* New York: Oxford University Press, Inc., 1992.

*Austen, Jane. *Emma.* 1816. London: Collins Clear-Type Press, 3rd ed., 1953.

Bagozzi, Richard, Zynep Gurhan-Canli, and Joseph R. Priester. *The Social Psychology of Consumer Behaviour.* Buckingham, UK: Open University Press, 2002.

*Bakti, Andi Faisal. *Terrorism and Human Security: From Critical Pedagogy to Peacebuilding?* New York: Palgrave Macmillan, 2003.

*Barrie, J. M. *Peter Pan.* New York: Henry Holt, 1987.

*Baum, Frank. *The Wonderful Wizard of Oz.* 1900. New York: Tor Classics, 1993.

Bauman, Zygmunt. Work, *Consumerism, and the New Poor.* New York: Open University Press, 2005.

*Beck, Aaron. *Depression: Causes and Treatment.* Philadelphia: University of Pennsylvania Press, 1967.

*Bentham, Jeremy. *Introduction to the Principles of Morals and Legislation.* 1789. New York: Oxford University Press, 1996.

Bloom, Paul N. "Competing in the Consumerism Industry: Strategies for Success." In *The Future of Consumerism,* edited by P. N. Bloom and R. B. Smith. Lexington, MA: Lexington Books, 1986.

Bloom, Paul N., and Ruth Belk Smith, eds. *The Future of Consumerism*. Lexington, MA: Lexington Books, 1986.

*Brodie, Richard. *Virus of the Mind*. Seattle, WA: Integral Press, 1996.

Brooks, David. *Bobos in Paradise: The New Upper Class and How They Got There*. New York: Simon & Shuster, 2000.

Brubaker, Pamela K. *Globalization at What Price? Economic Change and Daily Life*. Cleveland, OH: The Pilgrim Press, 2001.

*Burgess, Anthony. *A Clockwork Orange*. New York: W.W. Norton, 1962.

Campbell, Colin. *The Romantic Ethic and the Spirit of Modern Consumerism*. Oxford: Blackwell, 1987.

Cate, Curtis. *George Sand: A Biography*. New York: Houghton Mifflin, 1975.

*Carson, Rachel. *Silent Spring*. New York: Houghton Mifflin, 1962.

*Chernow, Ron. *Alexander Hamilton*. New York: Penguin Press, 2004.

*Churchill, Winston. *The Second World War*. vol. 1, *The Gathering Storm*. Boston: Houghton Mifflin, 1948.

*Chicago, College of the University of. The Staff, Social Sciences I, eds. *The People Shall Judge*. Chicago: The University of Chicago Press, 1949.

Cohen, Lizabeth. *A Consumer's Republic: The Politics of Mass Consumption in Postwar America*. New York: Alfred A. Knopf, 2003.

Critzer, Greg. *Fat Land: How Americans Became the Fattest People in the World*. New York: Houghton Mifflin, 2003.

Cross, Gary. *An All-Consuming Century: Why Commercialism Won in Modern America*. New York: Columbia University Press, 2000.

*Dale, Martin. *The Movie Game: The Film Business in Britain, Europe and America*. London: Cassell, 1997.

*Danziger, Pamela N. *Why People Buy Things They Don't Need*. Ithaca, NY: Paramount Market Publishing, 2002.

Davis, Melinda. *The New Culture of Desire: 5 Radical New Strategies That Will Change Your Business and Your Life*. New York: The Free Press, 2002.

*De Graff, John, David Wann, and Thomas Naylor. With a foreword by Scott Simon. *Affluenza: The All-Consuming Epidemic*. San Francisco: Berrett-Koehler Publishers, 2001.

De Grazia, Victoria. *Irresistible Empire: America's Advance through Twentieth-Century Europe*. Cambridge, MA: Belknap Press of Harvard University Press, 2005.

DeChant, Dell. *The Sacred Santa: Religious Dimensions of Consumer Culture*. Cleveland, OH: The Pilgrim Press, 2002.

*Diamond, Jared. *Guns, Germs, and Steel*. New York: W. W. Norton, 1997.

*Dickens, Charles. *David Copperfield*. 1850. New York: Random House, 2000.

*Dickens, Charles. *Oliver Twist*. New York: Tom Doherty Associates, 1998.

Drake, John. *Downshifting: How to Work Less and Enjoy Life More*. San Francisco: Berrett-Koehler Publishers, 2000.

*Durning, Alan. *How Much is Enough? The Consumer Society and the Future of the Earth*. New York: W. W. Norton, 1992.

*Ehrensaft, Diane. *Spoiling Childhood: How Well-Meaning Parents Are Giving Children Too Much But Not What They Need*. New York: The Gilford Press, 1997.

Enis, Ben M., and Dean L. Yarwood. "Consumer Protection in Public Sector Marketing: A Neglected Area of Consumerism." In *The Future of Consumerism*, edited by P. N. Bloom and R. B. Smith. Lexington, MA: Lexington Books, 1986.

Fernstrom, Meredith M. "Corporate Public Responsibility: A Marketing Opportunity?" In *The Future of Consumerism*, edited by P. N. Bloom and R. B. Smith. Lexington, MA: Lexington Books, 1986.

Foxall, Gordon R., and Ronald E. Goldsmith. *Consumer Psychology for Marketing*. London: Routledge, 1994.

*Frankl, Victor. *Man's Search for Meaning*. Boston: Beacon Press, 1959.

*Freud, Sigmund. *The Standard Edition of the Complete Psychological Works of Sigmund Freud*. London: Hogarth Press, 1968.

Frey, Bruno S., and Alois Stutzer. *Happiness and Economics: How the Economy and Institutions Affect Human Well-Being*. Princeton, NJ: Princeton University Press, 2002.

*Galbraith, John Kenneth. *The Affluent Society*. New York: Houghton Mifflin, 1998.

*———. *The New Industrial State*. New York: Houghton Mifflin, 1967.

Gaski, John F., and Michael J. Etzel. "Evolution of Consumer Attitude toward Business: 1971–1984; A Replication." In *The Future of Consumerism*, edited by P. N. Bloom and R. B. Smith. Lexington, MA: Lexington Books, 1986.

*Gelpi, Rosa-Maria, and Francois Julien-Labruyere. *The History of Consumer Credit*. New York: St. Martin's Press, 2000.

*Gibran, Kahlil. *The Prophet*. New York: Alfred A. Knopf, 1923.

Goodman, Douglas J., and Mirelle Cohen. *Consumer Culture: A Reference Handbook*. Santa Barbara, CA: ABC-CLIO, Inc., 2004.

*Goodwin, Doris Kearns. *Team of Rivals: The Political Genius of Abraham Lincoln*. New York: Simon & Schuster, 2005.

Goodwin, Neva R., Frank Ackerman, and David Kiron, eds. *Frontier Issues in Economic Thought*, vol. 2. Washington, D.C.: Island Press, 1997.

Gottdiener, Mark, ed. *New Forms of Consumption: Consumers, Culture, and Commodification.* Lanham, MD: Rowman and Littlefield, 2000.

*Govier, Trudy. *A Delicate Balance: What Philosophy Can Tell Us About Terrorism.* Boulder, CO: Westview Press, 2002.

Greider, William. "One World of Consumers." In *Consuming Desires: Consumption, Culture, and the Pursuit of Happiness,* edited by R. Rosenblatt. Washington, D.C.: Island Press, 1999.

*Hammett, Dashiell. *The Maltese Falcon.* New York: Alfred A. Knopf, 1929.

*Hammond, J. L., and B. Hammond. *The Rise of Modern Industry.* New York: Harcourt, Brace, 1926.

Harding, Philip A. "The New Technologies: Some Implications for Consumer Policy." In *The Future of Consumerism,* edited by P. N. Bloom and R. B. Smith. Lexington, MA: Lexington Books, 1986.

Harris, Daniel. *Cute, Quaint, Hungry, and Romantic: The Aesthetics of Consumerism,* 1ˢᵗ ed. New York: Basic Books, 2000.

Haskell, Molly. "Movies and the Selling of Desire." In *Consuming Desires: Consumption, Culture, and the Pursuit of Happiness,* edited by R. Rosenblatt. Washington, D.C.: Island Press, 1999.

*Herodotus. *The Histories.* London: Penguin Books, 1954.

*Holmes, Richard. *In the Footsteps of Churchill.* New York: Basic Books, 2005.

Horowitz, Daniel. *The Morality of Spending: Attitudes toward the Consumer Society in America, 1875–1940.* Baltimore: The John Hopkins University Press, 1985.

*Huizinga, Johan. *Homo Ludens.* Boston: Beacon Press, 1955.

*Hunnicutt, Benjamin. *Work without End.* Philadelphia: Temple University Press, 1988.

*James, Simon, and Robert Parker. *A Dictionary of Business Quotations.* New York: Simon & Schuster, 1990.

*Jefferson, Thomas. *Thomas Jefferson: Writings.* New York: Library Classics of the United States, The Library of America, 1984.

Jones, Mary Gardiner. "Wanted: Consumer Perspectives on the New Technologies." In *The Future of Consumerism,* edited by P. N. Bloom and R. B. Smith. Lexington, MA: Lexington Books, 1986.

*Kasser, Tim. *The High Price of Materialism.* Boston: MIT Press, 2002.

*Kasser, Tim, and Allen D. Kanner, eds. *Psychology and Consumer Culture: The Struggle for a Good Life in a Materialistic Culture.* Washington, D.C.: APA Books, 2003.

*Kazantzakis, Nikos. *The Odyssey: A Modern Sequel.* New York: Simon & Schuster, 1958.

*Kennedy, John F., and Robert F. Kennedy. *A Nation of Immigrants*. New York: HarperCollins, 1986.

Kotlowitz, Alex. "False Connection." In *Consuming Desires: Consumption, Culture, and the Pursuit of Happiness*, edited by R. Rosenblatt. Washington, D.C.: Island Press, 1999.

*Kubizek, August. *Young Hitler I Knew*. Westport, CT: Greenwood Publishing Group, 1976. Originally published as *Young Hitler: The Story of Our Friendship*. London: A. Wingate, 1954.

*LaChance, Albert J. *Cultural Addiction: The Greenspirit Guide to Recovery*. Berkeley, CA: North Atlantic Books, 2006.

*La Rouchefoucauld, François de. *Maxims*. New York: Penguin Books, 1959.

*Lakoff, George. *Don't Think of an Elephant: Know Your Values and Frame the Debate*. White River Junction, VT: Chelsea Green Publishing, 2004.

*Layard, Richard. *Happiness: Lessons from a New Science*. London: The Penguin Press, 2005.

Levine, Suzanne Braun. "A News Consumer's Bill of Rights." In *Consuming Desires: Consumption, Culture, and the Pursuit of Happiness*, edited by R. Rosenblatt. Washington, D.C.: Island Press, 1999.

*Lincoln, Abraham. *The Living Lincoln: The Man, His Mind, His Times, and the War He Fought, Reconstructed from His Own Writings*, edited by Paul M. Angle and Earl Schenck Miers. Rutgers, NJ: Barnes & Noble Books, 1992.

*Linn, Susan E. *Consuming Kids: The Hostile Takeover of Childhood*. New York: The New Press, 2004.

*Locke, John. "Second Essay on Civil Government." In *The English Philosophers from Bacon to Mill*, edited by Edwin A. Burtt. New York: Random House, 1939.

*Lucretius Caros, Titus. *De Rerum Natura*. Cambridge, MA: Harvard University Press, 1924.

*Luttwak, Edward N. "Consuming for Love." In *Consuming Desires: Consumption, Culture, and the Pursuit of Happiness*, edited by R. Rosenblatt. Washington, D.C.: Island Press, 1999.

*MacMillan, Margaret. *Paris 1919*. New York: Random House, 2003.

*Manning, Robert. *Credit Card Nation: The Consequences of America's Addiction to Credit*. New York: Basic Books, 2000.

Marty, Martin E. "Equipoise." In *Consuming Desires: Consumption, Culture, and the Pursuit of Happiness*, edited by R. Rosenblatt. Washington, D.C.: Island Press, 1999.

*Marx, Karl. *Das Kapital*. New York: Charles H. Kerr, 1906.

Mason, Roger S. *The Economics of Conspicuous Consumption: Theory and*

Thought Since 1700. Northampton, MA: Edward Elgar, 1998.

*May, Rollo. *The Discovery of Being: Writings in Existential Psychology.* New York: W. W. Norton, 1983.

*———. *Psychology and the Human Dilemma.* Princeton, NJ: Van Nostrand, 1967.

McDaniel, Jay. *Living from the Center: Spirituality in an Age of Consumerism.* St. Louis, MO: Chalice Press, 2000.

*McKeon, Richard, ed. *The Basic Works of Aristotle.* New York: Random House, 1941.

McKibben, Bill. "Consuming Nature." In *Consuming Desires: Consumption, Culture, and the Pursuit of Happiness,* edited by R. Rosenblatt. Washington, D.C.: Island Press, 1999.

*McPherson, James M. *Abraham Lincoln and the Second American Revolution.* New York: Oxford University Press, 1991.

*Mencken, H. L., ed. *A New Dictionary of Quotations on Historical Principles from Ancient and Modern Sources.* New York: Alfred A. Knopf, 1966.

*Merriam-Webster. *Webster's Biographical Dictionary: A Dictionary of Names of Noteworthy Persons with Pronunciations and Concise Biographies.* Springfield, MA: G and C Merriam, 1971.

Metzen, Edward J. "Consumerism in the Evolving Future." In *The Future of Consumerism,* edited by P. N. Bloom and R. B. Smith. Lexington, MA: Lexington Books, 1986.

Meyers, David G. *The American Paradox: Spirituality in an Age of Plenty.* New Haven, CT: Yale University Press, 2000.

Mick, David Glen, Cynthia Huffman, and S. Ratneshwar. *The Why of Consumption: Contemporary Perspectives on Consumer Motives, Goals and Desires.* New York: Routledge, 2000.

Miles, Steven. *Consumerism as a Way of Life.* Thousand Oaks, CA: Sage Publications, 1998.

Mills, Stephanie. "Can't Get That Extinction Crisis Out of My Mind." In *Consuming Desires: Consumption, Culture, and the Pursuit of Happiness,* edited by R. Rosenblatt. Washington, D.C.: Island Press, 1999.

Milner Jr., Murray. *Freaks, Geeks, and Cool Kids: American Teenagers, Schools, and the Culture of Consumption.* London, UK: Routledge, 2004.

*Mitchell, Margaret. *Gone with the Wind.* New York: The Macmillan Company, 1936.

Mitchell, Robert Cameron. "Consumerism and Environmentalism in the 1980s: Competitive or Companionable Social Movements?" In *The Future of Consumerism,* edited by P. N. Bloom and R. B. Smith. Lexington, MA: Lexington Books, 1986.

*Morison, Samuel Eliot. *The Oxford History of the American People*. New York: Oxford University Press, 1965.

Mukherjee, Bharati. "Oh, Isaac, Oh, Bernard, Oh, Mohan." In *Consuming Desires: Consumption, Culture, and the Pursuit of Happiness*, edited by R. Rosenblatt. Washington, D.C.: Island Press, 1999.

Orr, David W. "The Ecology of Giving and Consuming." In *Consuming Desires: Consumption, Culture, and the Pursuit of Happiness*, edited by R. Rosenblatt. Washington, D.C.: Island Press, 1999.

Packard, Vance Oakley. *The Hidden Persuaders*. New York: Pocket Books, 1957.

———. *The Waste Makers*. New York: David McKay, 1960.

*Pascal, Blaise. *Pensees*. 1663. New York: Random House, 1941.

*Patten, Chris. *Cousins and Strangers: America, Britain, and Europe in a New Century*. New York: Henry Holt, 2006.

Peterson, Esther. "Consumerism and International Markets." In *The Future of Consumerism*, edited by P. N. Bloom and R. B. Smith. Lexington, MA: Lexington Books, 1986.

Post, James E. "International Consumerism in the Aftermath of the Infant Formula Controversy." In *The Future of Consumerism*, edited by P. N. Bloom and R. B. Smith. Lexington, MA: Lexington Books, 1986.

Preston, Lee E., and Paul N. Bloom. "The Concerns of the Rich/Poor Consumer." In *The Future of Consumerism*, edited by P. N. Bloom and R. B. Smith. Lexington, MA: Lexington Books, 1986.

*Rauschning, Hermann. *Voice of Destruction*. 1939. Gretna, LA: Pelican Publishing, 2003. Published in London as *Hitler Speaks*.

Richardson, Stewart Lee, Jr. "The Evolving Consumer Movement: Predictions for the 1990s." In *The Future of Consumerism*, edited by P. N. Bloom and R. B. Smith. Lexington, MA: Lexington Books, 1986.

*Rilke, Rainer Maria. *Letters to a Young Poet*. 1908. San Rafael, CA: New World Library, 1992.

*Rosenblatt, Roger, ed. *Consuming Desires: Consumption, Culture, and the Pursuit of Happiness*. Washington, D.C.: Island Press, 1999.

Schiffrin, André. "When We Devoured Books." In *Consuming Desires: Consumption, Culture, and the Pursuit of Happiness*, edited by R. Rosenblatt. Washington, D.C.: Island Press, 1999.

Schor, Juliet. *Born to Buy: The Commercialized Child and the New Consumer Culture*. New York: Scribner, 2004.

———. *The Overspent American: Why We Want What We Don't Need*. New York: Basic Books, 1999.

*———. "What's Wrong with Consumer Society? Competitive Spending and the 'New Consumerism.'" In *Consuming Desires: Consumption, Culture, and the Pursuit of Happiness*, edited by R. Rosenblatt. Washington, D.C.: Island Press, 1999.

Schor, Juliet, and Douglas B. Holt, eds. *The Consumer Society Reader.* New York: The New Press, 2000.

*Schor, Juliet, et al. *Do Americans Shop Too Much?* Boston: Beacon Press, 2000.

*Schwartz, Barry. *The Paradox of Choice: Why More is Less.* New York: HarperCollins, 2004.

Settle, Robert B., and Pamela L. Alreck. *Why They Buy: American Consumerism Inside and Out.* New York: John Wiley and Sons, 1986.

*Shakespeare, William. *Hamlet.* Oxford: Oxford University Press, 1987.

*———. *The Sonnets of William Shakespeare.* 1609. New York: Crown Publishers, 1961.

*———. *The Tempest.* Oxford: Oxford University Press, 1987.

*Singer, Dorothy, and Jerome Singer, eds. *Handbook of Children and the Media.* Thousand Oaks, CA: Sage Publications, 2001.

Smiley, Jane. "It All Begins with Housework." In *Consuming Desires: Consumption, Culture, and the Pursuit of Happiness*, edited by R. Rosenblatt. Washington, D.C.: Island Press, 1999.

*Smith, Adam. *Wealth of Nations.* New York: Random House, 1937.

Smith, Darlene Brannigan, and Paul N. Bloom. "Is Consumerism Dead or Alive? Some Empirical Evidence." In *The Future of Consumerism*, edited by P. N. Bloom and R. B. Smith. Lexington, MA: Lexington Books, 1986.

Smith, N. Craig. *Morality and the Market: Consumer Pressure for Corporate Accountability.* London: Routledge, 1990.

Smith, Ruth Belk, and George T. Baker. "The Elderly Consumer: A Perspective on Present and Potential Sources of Consumerism Activity." In *The Future of Consumerism*, edited by P. N. Bloom and R. B. Smith. Lexington, MA: Lexington Books, 1986.

Stearns, Peter. *Consumerism in World History: The Global Transformation of Desire.* London: Routledge, 2001.

*Stein, Gertrude. *What Are Masterpieces?* New York: Pitman Publishing, 1970.

Sullivan, Teresa A., Elizabeth Warren, and Jay Lawrence Westbrook. *The Fragile Middle Class: Americans in Debt.* New Haven, CT: Yale University Press, 2000.

*Tocqueville, Alexis de. *Democracy in America*. New York: Alfred A. Knopf, 1972.

Twitchell, James B. *Lead Us Into Temptation: The Triumph of American Materialism*. New York: Columbia University Press, 1999.

————. *Living It Up*. New York: Columbia University Press, 2002.

*Veblen, Thorsten. *The Theory of the Leisure Class*. New York: Dover Publications, 1994.

Warland, Rex H., Robert O. Herrmann, and Dan E. Moore. "Consumer Activism, Community Activism, and the Consumer Movement." In *The Future of Consumerism*, edited by P. N. Bloom and R. B. Smith. Lexington, MA: Lexington Books, 1986.

Warren, Elizabeth, and Amelia Warren Tyagi. *The Two-Income Trap: Why Middle Class Mothers and Fathers Are Going Broke*. New York: Basic Books, 2003.

————. *All Your Worth: The Ultimate Lifetime Money Plan*. New York: Free Press, 2005.

Weems, Robert E., Jr. *Desegregating the Dollar: African American Consumerism in the Twentieth Century*. New York: New York University Press, 1998.

*Whybrow, Peter. *American Mania: When More Is Not Enough*. New York: W. W. Norton, 2005.

*Wills, Garry. *Lincoln at Gettysburg: The Words That Remade America*. New York: Simon & Schuster, 1992.

Articles and Papers

All-Consuming Passion: Waking Up from the American Dream. The New Road Map Foundation. *www.ecofuture.org/pk/pkar9506.html* (accessed September 22, 2005).

Allaahuakbar.net. "Don't Abuse the Concept of Jihad: Grand Mufti." Riyadh, Saudi Arabia: August 22, 2003. *www.allaahuakbar.net/JIHAAD/dont_abuse_the_concept_of_jihad.htm*.

*"Anatomy of Thrift: What Causes People to Save and Invest?" *The Economist*, September 22, 2005.

*Andrews, Edmund L. "Snow Urges Consumerism on China Trip." *New York Times*, October 13, 2005.

Asia Africa Intelligence Wire. "Indians Wary of Consumerism." *Financial Times*, June 5, 2003.

*Ballingrud, David. "Korea, the Forgotten War." *St. Petersburg Times*, July 20, 2003. *www.sptimes.com*.

*Baker, Russell. "The Entertainer." *The New York Review of Books,* November 3, 2005

*Barbalace, Roberta Crowell. "Protecting Wildlife from Trash." *Environmental, Chemistry & Hazardous Materials News, Information & Resources. environmentalchemistry.com/yogi/hazmat/articles/trash.html.*

*Baltake, Joe. "'Winged' Is a Soaring Achievement in Filmmaking." *The Sacramento Bee,* June 13, 2003.

*Barefoot, Darek. *A Response to Nicholas Tattersalls: A Critique of Miracles by C. S. Lewis. www.infidels.org/library/modern/nicholas_tattersall/miracles.html.*

*Bartkis, Kate, Kristin Cahayla, and Christi Ulrich. "Do Break-Ups Cause Break-Ins?" Muhlenberg College Study, supervised by Dr. Arthur Raymond, Issues in Political Economy: Undergraduate Student Research in Economics, vol. 9. Elon University and Mary Washington College. Allentown, PA: Mary Washington College Press, July 2000.

*Beddoes, Zanny Minton. "The Great Thrift Shift." *The Economist,* September 22, 2005.

*Bernanke, Ben S. "The Global Savings Glut and the U.S. Current Account Deficit." Federal Reserve Board Publication, April 14, 2005.

*Blendon and Benson. Working Paper, "How Americans View Their Lives: An Annual Survey." *Challenge,* vol. 47:3. Cambridge, MA: Harvard University, May–June 2004.

*Branigin, William. "Consumer Debt Grows at Alarming Pace: Debt Burden Will Intensify When Interest Rates Rise." *Washington Post,* January 12, 2004.

*Brown, Robert, and Ruth Washton. *The U.S. Teens Market: Understanding the Changing Lifestyles and Trends of 12- to 19-Year Olds.* Packaged Facts, A division of MarketResearch.com, 5th ed. August 2002. *www.marketresearch.com.*

*———. *The U.S. Kids Market: Understanding the Trends and Lifestyles Affecting 3- to 12-Year-Olds.* Packaged Facts, A division of MarketResearch.com, 6th ed. April 2004. *www.PackagedFacts.com.*

*Chang, Won Ho, Jae-Jin Park, and Sung Wook Shim. *Effectiveness of Negative Political Advertising.* WJMCR 2:1. December 1998. *www.scripps.ohiou.edu/wjmcr/vol02/2-1a-B.htm.*

*"Culture Wars." *The Economist,* September 10, 1998.

*DeAngelis, Tori. "Consumerism and Its Discontents." *Monitor on Psychology* 35, no. 6 (2004). *www.apa.org/monitor/jun04/consumetoc.html.*

———. "Too Many Choices?" *Monitor on Psychology* 35, no. 6 (2004). *www.apa.org/monitor/jun04/consumetoc.html.*

*DeLong, J. Bradford. *Cornucopia: The Pace of Economic Growth in the Twentieth Century.* Working Paper 7602. Cambridge, MA: National Bureau of Economic Research, March 2000. *www.nber.org/papers/w7602.*

*Durning, Alan. *Save the Forest: What Will It Take?* Worldwatch Paper #117. Worldwatch Institute, 1993.

*Dittmann, Melissa. "Protecting Children from Advertising." *Monitor on Psychology* 35, no. 6 (2004). *www.apa.org/monitor/juno4/consumetoc.html.*

*Eisenhower, Dwight D. "Military Industrial Complex Speech." *Public Papers of the Presidents.* Washington, D.C.: Office of the Federal Register, 1960. *coursesa.matrix.msu.edu/~hst306/documents/indust.html.*

*Epstein, Edward. "Bush Plays Hardball on Spying, Patriot Act: President calls wiretap revelation 'shameful,' says public hearings would help enemies." *San Francisco Chronicle,* December 20, 2005.

*Flesher, John. "Wife's Father Recounts Downfall of Slain Oregon Family." *The Associated Press,* January 15, 2002.

*Flora, Carlin. "Consumerism: One Choice Too Many." *Psychology Today,* January 16, 2004, Document ID 3227. *cms.psychologytoday.com/articles/pto-20040116-000001.html.*

*Freund, Charles Paul. "In Praise of Vulgarity: How Commercial Culture Liberates Islam—and the West." *Reason Online,* March, 2002.

*Gathright, Alan. "Suicide Note Says Family Deep in Debt." *San Francisco Chronicle,* August 20, 2005, sec. B1.

*Grafton, Anthony. "The Ways of Genius." *The New York Review of Books,* December 2, 2004.

*Gribble, Paul. "Political Television Advertisements." *Teletimes,* February, 1994.

*Hagerty, Michael. "Was Life Better in the Good Old Days?" *Journal of Happiness Studies,* 4, no. 2 (2003).

Hertwich, Edgar. "Consumption and Industrial Ecology." *Journal of Industrial Ecology,* 9:1–2, 2005. *mitpress.mit.edu/journals/JIEC/v9n1_2/jiec_9_1-2_001_0.pdf* (accessed March 2, 2006).

Holloway, Jennifer Daw. "The Value of Money." *Monitor on Psychology,* 35, no. 6 (2004). *www.apa.org/monitor/juno4/consumetoc.html.*

*Hodges, Michael. "Voter Participation Report." *Grandfather Economic Reports,* November 2002 (updated). *mwhodges.home.att.net/voting.htm.*

*"Home Alone in Europe." *The Economist,* March 20, 1997.

*Jackson, Tim. "Live Better by Consuming Less? Is There a 'Double Dividend' in Sustainable Consumption?" *Journal of Industrial Ecology,* 9, 1–2. Winter–Spring 2005.

*Judt, Tony. "The New World Order." *The New York Review of Books,* July 14, 2005.

*Kaiser Family Foundation Issue Brief. "The Role of Media in Childhood Obesity" (February, 2004). *www.kff.org/entmedia/upload/The-Role-Of-Media-in-Childhood-Obesity.pdf.*

*Kersting, Karen. "Driving Teen Egos—and Buying—Through 'Branding.'" *Monitor on Psychology,* 35, no. 6 (2004). *www.apa.org/monitor/jun04/consumetoc.html.*

*KOMO Staff and News Services. "Teens' Blood Vessels Show Fats' Effects." *San Francisco Chronicle,* September 22, 2005.

Lamb, Gregory M. "We Swim in an Ocean of Media." *Christian Science Monitor,* September 2005. *www.csmonitor.com/2005/0928/p13s01-lihc.html.*

*Lay, William, and Derek Rutherford. *Families as a Cause of Alcohol Problems.* Eurocare, 1996–2005. *www.eurocare.org/projects/familyreport/english/famen_p15.html.*

*"Litter." *Prague Post Endowment Fund,* 4, no. 9. February 19, 2003.

*Massing, Michael. "The End of News?" *The New York Review of Books.* December 1, 2005

*Maranjian, Selena. "Living on Borrowed Dimes." *The Motley Fool,* March 4, 2004. *www.fool.com/news/commentary/2004/commentary040304sm.htm.*

*McMahon, Darrin M. "The Quest for Happiness." *Wilson Quarterly,* Winter 2005.

*Meyers, David G. "Our Becoming Much Better Off Over the Last Four Decades Has Not Been Accompanied by One Iota of Increased Subjective Well-Being." *American Psychologist,* 55, no. 1 (2000).

*Miller, Chaz. "Profiles in Garbage," *Waste Age,* April 1, 2003 and September 1, 2003. *www.csun.edu/~vceed002/BFI/waste_stats.html.*

*Morris, Betsy. "Big Spenders: As a Favored Pastime, Shopping Ranks High with Most Americans." *Wall Street Journal,* July 30, 1987.

*Nafee, Wael. "Cultural Imperialism: The Deadliest Export." *Muslim Students for Universal Justice,* July 18, 2005. *www.msuj.org/aritcle.php?id=29.*

*National Institute of Mental Health. "The Numbers Count: Mental Disorders in America." 2001. *www.nimh.nih.gov/publicat/numbers.cfm.*

*OBGYN Headline News. "Ten Years Later, Greater Access to Treatment Did Not Increase Cost of Depression." January, 2004. *www.obgyn.net/newsheadlines/headline_medical_news-Depression-20040128-0.asp.*

*O'Connor, Tom. "Has There Been an Increase in Juvenile Ruthlessness?" Wesleyan College, NC: MegaLinks in Criminal Justice, 2005. *faculty.ncwc.edu/toconnor/juvjusp.htm#ESSAY.*

*O'Hair, Madalyn Murray. "Murray v. Curlett." *The American Rationalist,* 17, no 3. September/October 1962.

*"The One-Handed-Economist: Paul Krugman and the Controversial Art of Popularizing Economics." *The Economist,* November 13, 2003.

*Oregon Department of Environmental Quality. "Land Quality: Solid Waste Factoids." Portland, OR: June 18, 1999 (updated). *www.deq.state.or.us/wmc/solwaste/cwrc/edpro2.html.*

*"The Polygram Test." *The Economist,* August 13, 1998.

*Parfitt, Michael. "Powering the Future." *National Geographic,* August 2005.

*Patrick, Aaron O. "Commercials by Cellphone." *Wall Street Journal,* August 22, 2005, sec. B1.

*Pinter, Harold. "Art, Truth and Politics." Prerecorded Nobel Lecture, Stockholm, Sweden, December 7, 2005. *www.commondreams.org/views05/1208-28.htm.*

*Reynolds, Paul. "US Campaign Begins to Get Dirty." *BBC News,* February 18, 2004. *news.bbc.co.uk/2/hi/americas/3493277.stm.*

*Risen, James. "The Struggle for Iraq: The Treatment of Prisoners; G.I.'s Are Accused of Abusing Iraqi Captives." *New York Times,* April 29, 2004, sec. A.

*Ryan, Alan. "The Magic of 'I'." *The New York Review of Books,* April 28, 2005.

*Saffer, Henry, and Dhaval Dave. *Alcohol Advertising and Alcohol Consumption by Adolescents.* Working Paper 9676. Cambridge, MA: National Bureau of Economic Research, May 2003.

Said, Carolyn. BIGresearch (NRF survey). "Stores Banking on Black Friday: When Do We Start Holiday Shopping?" (Graph) *San Francisco Chronicle,* November 25, 2005.

*Samuelson, Robert J. "The Kyoto Delusion." *Washington Post,* June 21, 2005, sec. A.

*Saunders, Debra. "Blair Takes Heat for Global-Warming Remarks." *San Francisco Chronicle,* October 2, 2005, sec. C5.

*Searle, John R. "Consciousness: What We Still Don't Know." *The New York Review of Books,* January 13, 2005.

*Skogrand, Linda M., et al. "The Effects of Debt on Newlyweds and Implications for Education." *Journal of Extension,* 43, no. 3, article no. 3RIB7, June 2005. *www.joe.org/joe/2005june/rb7.shtml.*

*Smith, Kristin. "Census Bureau Says 7 Million Grade-School Children Home Alone." *United States Department of Commerce News.* Washington, D.C.: Economic and Statistics Administration and Bureau of the Census, October 31, 2000.

Strasser, Susan. "Making Consumption Conspicuous: Transgressive Topics Go Mainstream." *Technology and Culture,* 43 (October, 2002): 755–770.

*Stetser, Brad, and Nouriel Roubini. "How Scary Is the Deficit? Our Money, Our Debt, Our Problem." *Foreign Affairs,* July/August 2005.

*Stutzer, Alois. "The Role of Income Aspirations in Individual Happiness." *Journal of Economic Behavior and Organization,* 54, no. 1, May 2004.

*Taylor, Betsy. "Consumption: It is Time for Economists and Scientists to Talk." *Journal of Industrial Ecology,* 9, issues 1–2, Winter–Spring 2005.

*Tucker, Robert W., and David C. Hendrickson. "The Sources of American Legitimacy." *Foreign Affairs*, November/December, 2004.

*Uchida, Norasakkunkit, and Kitayama Uchida. "Cultural Constructions of Happiness: Theory and Empirical Evidence." *Journal of Happiness Studies*, 5, no. 3, special issue, 2004.

*United States Coast Guard. *Polluting Incident Compendium: Cumulative Data and Graphics for Oil Spills 1973–2001. www.uscg.mil/hq/g-m/nmc/response/stats/Summary.htm.*

United States Environmental Protection Agency. *Global-Warming: Climate. yosemite.epa.gov/oar/globalwarming.nsf/content/climate.html.*

*Vittachi, Anuradha. "What Really Matters: A Possible Route- Beyond the Lies, Towards Global Survival." *New Internationalist*, 235, September 1992. *www.newint.org/issue235/what.htm.*

*Warner, Jessica. "Edward R. Murrow at the Movies—Just When We Need Him Most, Some Say." *San Francisco Chronicle*, October 8, 2005, sec. E1.

*Winerman, Lea. "Maxed Out: Why Do Some Succumb and Others Steer Clear?" *Monitor on Psychology*, 35, no. 6 (2004). *www.apa.org/monitor/jun04/consumetoc.html.*

Wiser, Bill. "That Hole in Your Soul." *Bruderhof Communities,* September, 2005. *www.bruderhof.com/articles/Hole-in-Your-Soul.htm.*

Movies

*Affluenza. Produced by John de Graaf and Vivia Boe. KCTS-Seattle/Oregon Public Broadcasting; Bullfrog Films, 1997.

*Auntie Mame. Produced and directed by Morton Da Costa, written by Mike Myers. Warner Brothers Studios, 1958.

*Charlie and the Chocolate Factory. Directed by Tim Burton, written by John August. Warner Bros, 2005.

*Cinema Paradiso. Produced by Franco Cristaldi and Giovanna Romagnoli, directed and written by Guiseppe Tornatore. Cristaldifilm, Les Films Ariane, RAI, and TFI Films Productions, 1989.

*Citizen Kane. Produced and directed by Orson Welles, written by Herman J. Mankiewicz and Orson Welles. RKO Pictures, 1941.

*A Clockwork Orange. Produced by Si Litvinoff and Max L. Raab, directed by Stanley Kubrick, written by Anthony Burgess and Stanley Kubrick. Warner Brothers Studios, 1971.

*Clueless. Produced by Robert Lawrence and Scott Rudin, directed and written by Amy Heckerling. Paramount Films, 1995.

David Copperfield. Produced by David O. Selznick, directed by George Cukor, written by Hugh Walpole and Howard Esterbrook. Warner Brothers Studios, 1935.

Death of a Salesman. Produced by Stanley Kramer, directed by Laszlo Benedek, written by Arthur Miller and Stanley Roberts. Stanley Kramer Productions, 1985.

Fight Club. Produced by Arnon Milchan, directed by David Fincher, written by Chuck Palahniuk and Jim Uhls. Twentieth Century Fox, 1999.

Finding Neverland. Produced by Richard Gladstein and Nellie Bellflower, directed by Marc Forster, written by David Magee. Miramax Films, 2004.

Gone with the Wind. Produced by David O. Selznick, directed by Victor Fleming, written by Sidney Howard. MGM, 1939.

Good Night, and Good Luck. Produced and directed by George Clooney; written by George Clooney and David Strathairn. Warner Independent Pictures, 2005.

Key Largo. Produced by Jerry Wald, directed by John Huston, written by Richard Brooks and John Huston. Warner Brothers Studios, 1948.

The Maltese Falcon. Produced by Hal B. Wallace and Henry Blanke, written and directed by John Huston. Warner Brothers, 1941.

The Music Man. Produced and directed by Morton Da Costa, written by Meredith Willson and Franklin Lacey. Warner Brothers, 1962.

A Night at the Opera, Produced and directed by Sam Wood; written by James Kevin McGuiness, George S. Kaufman, and Morrie Ryskind. MGM Studios, 1935.

Oliver Twist. Produced and directed by Roman Polanski, written by Ronald Harwood. Sony Pictures, 2005.

On the Waterfront. Produced by Sam Spiegel, directed by Elia Kazan, written by Malcolm Johnson and Budd Schulberg. Columbia Pictures, 1954.

Syriana. Produced by George Clooney, Ben Cosgrove, Jeff Skoll, and Steven Soderbergh; directed by Steven Gaghan; written by Robert Baer and Stephen Gaghan. Warner Brothers Studios, 2005.

Wall Street. Produced by Edward Pressman, A. Kitman Ho, and Michael Flynn; directed by Oliver Stone and Gordon Lonsdale; written by Stanley Weiser and Oliver Stone. 20th Century Fox, 1987.

The Wild One. Produced by Stanley Kramer, directed by Lazlo Benedek, written by John Paxton, from the novel by Frank Rooney. Stanley Kramer Productions. 1953.

The Wizard of Oz. Produced by Mervyn LeRoy; directed by Victor Fleming; written by Noel Langley, Florence Ryerson, and Edgar Allan Woolf. MGM Studios, 1939.

About the Authors

HARRISON SHEPPARD served in the Antitrust Division of the U.S. Department of Justice in Washington, D.C. during the Johnson and Nixon administrations. He was legal advisor to Federal Trade Commissioner Philip Elman and held a variety of executive attorney positions with the FTC until 1989, when he began private law practice in San Francisco, founding his own law and public relations firm in 1991. His essays and opinion editorials, widely published throughout the U.S., criticize the adversary model of legal education and practice and promote a problem-solving, peacemaking model. A lifetime philhellene with a classical education, his writings include essays on the enduring influence of ancient Greek thought on contemporary civilization.

ALEX ARIS, born in Athens, Greece, is the pen name of a successful entrepreneur in real estate ownership and management in the San Francisco Bay Area. His concern for the preservation of family values and for his children's future, and his many civic interests and activities at the local, state, and international level have led him to contribute to this, the first published book of Aristotle & Alexander Press, as its co-author. He is also a lifetime philhellene who deeply believes that the universal wisdom of ancient Greek thought is highly relevant to successfully addressing twenty-first century social, economic, political, ecological, and international problems caused by excessive materialism and wasteful use of energy and raw materials.

Index

Nafee, Wael, 47, 230–33, 238, 241
National Academy of Sciences, 175, 181, 236
National Bureau of Economic Research (NBER), 42
National Center for Education Statistics, 37
National Geographic, oil addiction dangers, 179
National Institute of Mental Health, 131
Natural Law, 189
Naylor, Thomas H., 12
NBER. *See* National Bureau of Economic Research
needs and wants,
 and children, 119-120
 in eco-humanism, 182, 232
 and happiness, 259-262, 274-5
 harmonization, xv, 88
Nelles, Wayne, 47
The New American Militarism (Bacevich), 292
Newsweek, materialism, 230
Newton, Isaac, 291
"The New World Order" (Judt), 290
New Yorker magazine, happiness, 102
New York Review of Books
 campaigning, 211
 community, 136
 consciousness, 100
 individuality, 102
 journalism, 214
 world faith in America, 290
New York Times
 Abu Ghraib, 251
 advertising and children, 40–41
 China, 49, 163
 Kaczynski manifesto, 299
Nichomachean Ethics (Aristotle), 103, 145
A Night at the Opera (motion picture), 28–29, 50
nihilism, 75–76
9/11, 47–48, 229, 257
1984 (Orwell), 201
Nixon, Richard (1913–1994), 199–200, 204, 207
Nobel Prize for Literature speech (2005), 229

No Gifts from Chance (Bernstock), 97–98
Noiret, Philippe, 216
nonrenewable energy sources
 fossil fuel limits, 178–80
 National Academy of Sciences, 181
Norasakkunkit, Vinai, 103
Norton, Edward, 254
"No TV Week," 235

obesity, 53
 children, 38–40, 51, 111
obsolescence, planned, 112–13, 136
O'Connor, Tom, 137
O'Hair, Madalyn Murray, 99–100
oil/gas dependency, 153, 154, 161, 279–80, 281, 283
"Oil Powering the Future," 180
Oliver Twist (Dickens, novel/motion picture), 84, 101, 241
"1000 Headlines," 52
On the Waterfront (motion picture), 109
oracle at Delphi, xiv, 108
orthopedic problems, 39
Orwell, George, 201
Oswald, Andrew, 296–97
"Our Brains Don't Work Like Computers," 100

Pakistan, personal savings rate, 26
Pan metron ariston (Greek: Balance in all things is best), xiv, 298
The Paradox of Choice (Schwartz), 92, 103
Park, Jae-Jin, 213
Pascal, Blaise (1623–1662), 59, 64, 67, 79
PATRIOT Act, 227, 250
Patten, Chris, 294, 300
PCE (personal consumer expenditures), 307, 308
 and GDP (gross domestic product), 25–26, 49, 117, 308
"Peak Oil" (Campbell), 179, 192
Pensées (Pascal), 59, 79
personal consumer expenditures. *See* PCE (personal consumer expenditures)
Peter Pan (Barrie, play/animation/